Mike Williams

THE HISTORY AND
ARCHAEOLOGY OF
PORTS

To my mother-in-law and in memory of my father-in-law:
Ethel and Edgar Kirk.

THE HISTORY AND ARCHAEOLOGY OF

PORTS

Gordon Jackson

WORLD'S WORK LTD

The Legal Quay, London, where all customable goods had to be landed (the heaviest by treadmill cranes), and where confusion reigned for centuries. Boitard's engraving was an attack on the hypocrisy of importing luxuries from France during the Seven Years' War, and on the fops who encouraged it. Here, the negro servant boy is almost overcome by the sight of fashionable French visitors, and the little London lad by the smell of French cheeses.

N.B. Mention or illustration in this book
of any port, harbour or maritime structure
does not imply any right of access,
nor that it is safe to visit it.

Designed by Victor Shreeve

Maps by Reginald and Marjorie Piggott

Index by Indexing Specialists of Hove

Copyright © 1983 by Gordon Jackson

Published by World's Work Limited
The Windmill Press, Kingswood, Tadworth, Surrey

Printed in Great Britain by BAS Printers Limited
Over Wallop, Stockbridge, Hampshire

ISBN 0 437 07539 7

GREAT BRITAIN from FRANCE.

Anti-Gallicans, and the generous promoters of the British Arts & Manufactories,
and truly devoted humble Servant, L. P. Boitard

g under a weighty Chest of **Birth-Night Cloaths**. Behind, several emaciated high liv'd Epicures, familiarly receiving a
with Hunger. A Lady of Distinction, offering the tuition of her Son & Daughter to a cringing **French Abbé**, his weeping
ified well-bred Spouse, readily complying. The English Chaplain regretting his lost Labours. Another Woman of Quality
Honour & Delight of England. On the front ground, a Cask overset: the Contents, **French Cheeses**, from Normandy bein
t-Goût: A Chest well cramm'd with Tippets, Muffs, Ribands, Flowers for the Hair, & other such **Material Bagatelles**.
dly washes, Pomatums, l'Eau d'Hongrie, l'Eau de Luce, l'Eau de Carme, &c. &c. &c. near French Wines and Brandies.
ers, Tutoresses for Boarding-schools, disguis'd Jesuits, Quacks, Valet de Chambres, &c. &c. &c.

arch 7, 1757, by John Bowles and Son, at the Black Horse in Cornhill, London. — Price Six pence.

CONTENTS

LIST OF ILLUSTRATIONS

Many of the early illustrations are from the beautiful series of colour engravings prepared by William Daniells for R. Ayton's *Voyage Round Great Britain* (8 volumes, 1814f.), and from other contemporary engravings. Photographs are by the author, except where acknowledged.

PREFACE

Despite the importance of trade to the British economy, relatively little has been written about the development of the ports through which it passes, either in general or in particular. This book attempts to redress the balance a little by tracing the relationship between the growth of trade, ports and port facilities in Britain from the early days to the recent revolution in transport and handling methods that has wrought havoc in the port system.

Few things in the world of modern redundant industry are quite so vast, solid and impressive as docks and their related works. They look, for the most part, as if they have always been there and always will be, and the idea of closing down or removing such monuments of civil engineering as London's Royal Docks was mind boggling to those brought up to regard them as an integral part of the nation's economic system. This concept of the permanence of physical structures was reinforced during the great post-war trade boom, which lasted long enough to create an illusion of equal permanence in the composition of trade, in the operation of individual ports, and in the structure of the port system as a whole.

Against such a background the collapse of the traditional port system in the last twenty years came as a great shock far beyond the ports themselves. It should not have done so: there is no such thing as permanence in trading relationships. For centuries the direction and composition of trade has changed periodically and often dramatically, and individual ports have risen or fallen in consequence. Again, transport systems, though they might appear to have a certain permanence, have nevertheless been in a state of almost continuous evolution for the best part of two centuries. Few ports have been able to cater for expanding or changing trade without creating and altering facilities, and the history of ports is therefore one of regular and frequent change in physical environment, wealth and relative standing. The theme

of constant readjustment between ports, transport and trade has only become a matter of concern recently because 'change and construct' has in general been overtaken by 'change and decay'. But it is a theme which all port operators must constantly bear in mind. If it does nothing else this book will have served a hopefully useful service by stressing the fragile nature of the prosperity of ports, and the economic waste involved in the competitive development of facilities.

When I first began working on ports, in the 1950s, it was largely a matter of the *history* of individual places and their existing facilities. Most ports had altered little since 1914: they still had the harbours, docks and machinery working or at least standing idle. Things have changed drastically in the last few years. Some ports have virtually ceased to trade and are now decaying. In others the introduction of modern handling methods has concentrated activity and devalued most of the old facilities. Many of them are now swept away, and in consequence the work has taken on an element of 'industrial archaeology' that would have been almost meaningless for the larger ports in the 1950s. I have tried to indicate where things have changed dramatically, and where the most interesting survivals of early port facilities are to be found, although it is still not necessary to adopt scientific archaeology to reconstruct either the history or topography of ports.

This attempt to record industrial remains is fraught with difficulty. When I began work it could be fairly assumed that the principal post-1800 works either survived or had long ago been completely obliterated by later works. However, the momentum of destruction has increased considerably in the last few years, and I must beg the indulgence of readers if remains are no longer as I have described them in the text. My most recent visit to Hull, for instance, revealed that Victoria Dock has been filled in since my previous visit, while Humber Dock has been dredged and fitted with a pair of the latest cylindrical lock gates; in Bristol a housing estate is currently under construction on the site of the Merchants' Dock; in Glasgow a major new exhibition centre is soon to be built over the site of Queen's Dock. There may be other similar cases of which I am unaware.

Some of the very recent changes in the ports are, in fact, more encouraging than one could have hoped in the late 1970s. In several places where harbours and town centres were mixed up, old port buildings are now being refurbished rather than replaced by modern mediocrity. Hull has redevelopment going on around Humber Dock; some of London's Thames-side warehouses are becoming middle class housing; and the centre of Bristol is being rapidly transformed as old warehouses are refurbished alongside new buildings constructed to look like—or blend with—traditional dock-side buildings. In several places interest has arisen in maritime or dock museums, ranging from the boat museum at Gloucester to the more ambitious Mersey Maritime Museum at Liverpool. There is even talk, in the aftermath of the Toxteth riots, of doing something about Albert Dock.

Although I have tried to analyse the reasons for the rise and fall of individual ports, and offer some account of the inter-dependence of particular trade flows and port facilities, this study can claim to be no more than a pioneer survey of the history of the British ports and an impression rather than a scientific study of the most significant physical remains. I have not attempted the impossible task of providing a complete chronological survey of the port system as a whole, or detailing every work in specific ports. Moreover, while I have attempted to set individual ports into the broad national picture, I have been forced to ignore local personalities, motivations and initiatives, though these were by no means unimportant in the creation of facilities required for British trade or in creating the trade—or the ships—which demanded the facilities. Partly this is a matter of space, but more importantly it reflects the paucity of modern secondary sources. Fortunately there are a number of valuable local studies (such as those by Beckett, Brown, Buchan, Hyde, Jackson, Lenman, Pudney, Riddell and Wren), but there is no adequate economic history of any port for the whole of the modern period. For the ports in general I have made extensive use of Customs records and Engineers' Reports, and I have also relied heavily on the work of others, from the eighteenth century onwards. In particular I have gained a great deal from the pioneering work of D. Swann on eighteenth-century and A. G. Kenwood on nineteenth-century port investment; from J. Bird, whose survey of the major ports is an inspiration to all subsequent scholars; and from discussions with many friends over a long period of time, especially R. S. Craig, P. N. Davies, and the late Francis Hyde and Ralph Davis.

Since the information used in this book comes from a wide variety of sources, some entirely reliable but some old and some dubious, it is likely that there are mistakes in local detail which will be revealed by further study. I can only apologise in advance, and hope that my account of the way in which trades changed and ports responded to change will remain reasonably accurate.

I am especially indebted to my colleague J. R. Hume, whose vast knowledge of industrial archaeology has been a great help to me. He also took many of the photographs for me, and I am grateful to him and to my son Nicholas Jackson for processing those photographs taken by myself. My wife and family, as always, deserve my warmest gratitude for their forbearance during the writing of this book, and the willingness—or at least tolerance—with which they made numerous excursions to docks and harbours.

GORDON JACKSON University of Strathclyde, 1983

CHAPTER ONE

The Rise of Ports
c. 1450–1660

THE WOOL TRADE AND THE GROWTH OF PORTS

For many centuries Britain's economy and culture have been influenced or sustained by the waters dividing her from the Continent or the ships linking her to it. It was perfectly natural. The first peoples to arrive soon discovered the goods which they—like colonists the world over—could exchange for luxuries left behind. Nor did their successors forget their homelands. The Vikings maintained contact with Scandinavia over many generations through Grimsby, the town of the mythical hero Grim; and the Normans kept even closer links with their homeland through the places that became leading ports along the south-east coast.

It was not only foreign countries that were contacted for their timber, cloth or wine, in exchange for wool, cloth or herrings. Communications within the country were sufficiently bad for as much heavy traffic as possible to be carried by river and sea. Fortunately there were few places too far from navigable water for this to be impracticable and, apart from what might be called 'local' trade, most places tended to look outward towards the nearest port rather than inwards towards the land.

Thus, as men began to extend their horizons, as population grew and produced surpluses of some goods and shortages of others, trade began to flow wherever water sites were suitable. Unfortunately the beaches which caused so much trouble to Julius Caesar and his army were no longer suitable for serious trade, though it was always possible to trans-ship goods into boats and land them on the open beaches if the weather was good and the need great. It was an operation for the summer months, preferably in small bays where the lie of the land gave a modicum of shelter. Protective piers were required before vessels could ride at anchor with any degree of assurance, and though they were to be found, here and there, in the late

Middle Ages, they were overwhelmingly the product of eighteenth and nineteenth century engineering.

In practice it was unimportant that open beaches could not handle much trade, since they were never required to do so. Trade was generated in places linked to the sea by navigable waterways, and there was no more natural place for a port to spring up than at the mouth of a river. The richest ports were those on the rivers flowing through the largest areas of good agricultural land, serving the densest populations and encouraging nascent industry. They were also the leading towns, controlling the economy and their surrounding regions as effectively as their churches, symbols of wealth as much as of piety, dominated the landscape. Nothing can so effectively convey the commanding position of these medieval trading centres as the sight of Boston Stump on the banks of the Witham. London, Bristol, York, Lincoln and Norwich are the best examples of such influential places in the early Middle Ages, but others, including Gloucester, Nottingham, Gainsborough and Selby, enjoyed prosperity as trans-shipment centres. So long as very small craft were used, rivers could be navigated for considerable distances even before improvements began in the late seventeenth century.

In general the position of a port was a compromise: far enough from the river mouth for safety but near enough for convenience. It was not good for ships to travel too far inland, for while the vision of sails passing through cornfields is an unforgettable sight, the hazards of navigating narrow rivers with ocean-going vessels were numerous and frequently disastrous. Too much depended on the rise and fall of tides and the shifting of mud banks.

There was nothing complicated about these early ports. In the bays ships simply threw out their anchor and landed goods by boat on the open beach, as they did in Hastings, for instance, till the nineteenth century. In the rivers they lay alongside the bank and were loaded and unloaded via

Beached ships: this was the most primitive of all methods of dealing with ships, though suitable only for shelving sandy beaches. Liverpool c. 1900.

Beached ships: Liverpool foreshore, 1797. Engraving of painting by S. F. Serres.

River ports sprang up because of the shelter they offered, though there were often problems when the water was low. Here a vessel is 'docked' in the mud at Faversham, a tiny port that never developed.

the gangway, rising and falling with the tide and grounding twice a day in the process. Indeed, the earliest use of the word 'dock' was to describe the hollows in the mud in which they lay. Unfortunately, while 'docked' ships made no difference to the mud, constant traffic rapidly broke down the banks. Most ports reinforced them with wooden quays, though there is no way of knowing when or where such refinements were first introduced.

Since ports were initially convenient sites rather than collections of expensive works, there was little to stop their proliferation along the coast wherever rights to trade could be wrested from the feudal superiors who still controlled the economy as tightly as the polity of the country. Ports struggled to grow in a context of confusion. At home they faced the occasional depredations of those superiors as they sought to establish their independent borough status. At sea they faced the greater depredations of enemies who were not always foreign. The ships of Poole spent a hundred years—off and on—fighting the French,[1] while the ships of Yarmouth had a geat deal more to fear during the reign of Edward I from the Cinque Ports; and the ships of Grimsby were not averse to fighting each other.[2]

Nevertheless, medieval legal records and local propaganda may exaggerate the unwholesome side of life. A measure of peace was to be found within the country even while barons were fighting each other for the throne, and international trade not only survived the Hundred Years' War but actually prospered in the fourteenth and fifteenth centuries.

International co-operation was necessary if the whole of Europe was to enjoy the specialised products of its regions, and great mart towns grew up in the Low Countries on the rivers affording access deep into the Continent. Britain's contributions were chiefly wool, fish, leather, tin and lead, and for these items the early galleys came from Venice, and the later Hanseatic ships from Hamburg. Wool especially was sought after for shipment to the Low Countries where ingenious spinsters and weavers could make a more valuable product than could the English themselves. It was only a matter of time before the English learned this mysterious art, though they still could not finish the cloth to perfection.

The growth of these various trades was important in the development of ports. Although corn-stuffs were the basis of agriculture, sheep were kept for wool over a large range of hills and dales in Scotland and Wales, and from Yorkshire to the south-west, and when rough undyed cloth

began to be made for export it was a true village industry scattered with abandon around the West Country, East Anglia, Kent, Yorkshire and over into Wales. The important point is that wool and cloth that were so widely produced were equally widely shipped. Any suitable haven from Hull round to Gloucester could attract ships and make money in the fifteenth century, and some of them became extraordinarily rich by the standards of the time.

These rising ports soon attracted the attention of the Crown. Taxing trade has always been an easy way of raising revenue, and technically ports were not places at all, but stretches of coastline divided up for fiscal purposes. In practice, business centred on the harbour towns, which did everything possible to confine it to their borough limits for the simple reason that they, no less than the Crown, drew revenue from trade. Thus a port was not a place where a ship might *conveniently* load or unload, but a place where it might *legally* do so in the presence of the King's 'Customer'—the collector of Royal Customs. Such a place was eventually designated the 'head port', and other havens within the limits were 'member ports' where deputy officers resided, or 'creeks' where no officer resided and where trade was illegal except under specific licence or 'sufferance'.

In a country lacking close supervision the opportunities for ignoring the law were great and, despite attempts to restrict 'staple' trades to specific places, and periodic Acts making it a felony to trade elsewhere, the leading historian of the Customs Service has described the system in the sixteenth century as 'very near chaos'.[3] In order to clarify the situation once and for all, the Crown listed, in 1558, the ports where legal trade could take place and, furthermore, defined the exact locations—the 'Legal Quays'—where all goods must be landed and loaded (1 Elizabeth I, c.11).

To these ports, with minor adjustments after 1662, fell the task of coping with the major trade expansion of the Commercial and Industrial Revolutions for which they had not, as a group, been designed.

2. THE DECLINE OF THE OUTPORTS

Substantial shifts in trade and in the comparative usefulness of ports had in fact already begun long before 1558. Some ports could no longer answer the modest demands made of them; the wool trade on which many of them had depended had died away by the 1520s and would never revive; and the cloth trade which took its place was gradually lost to the 'outports' (the generic term for all the ports outside London).

There was little that could be done about the physical decay of long-established ports. Some had never had adequate harbours. Others, lying on slow-moving rivers, found the flush of water inadequate to scour silt deposited by the river or sand brought in by the tide. Yet others did not have the depth of water to allow trading throughout the year. So long as trade was largely seasonal, matching the great fairs of the Continent or the product of harvest and fishery, this was not a great disadvantage. But once regular trade became desirable, certain ports proved inadequate. Chester, the leading medieval port of the north-west coast, found itself in this predicament. 'Shipping at this port', it was said in 1607, 'is so decayed that there are not belonging to it any barks but some few of very small burden, which only traffic for Ireland, and the merchants cannot freight any ship beyond the seas to arrive in this port but at extra-ordinary rates by reason of the danger of the river. . . .'[4]

Other ports were faced with practical difficulties of a more pressing nature: as coastal erosion overtook them they fell into the sea, like Ravensrod on the Yorkshire coast, about which little is known, and Dunwich, the most famous of all, in Suffolk. The latter suffered inundations of its harbour in the fourteenth and fifteenth centuries, was useless by 1600, and thereafter fell street by street at every overpowering storm until by 1740 nothing remained of what had once been a rich city with, it is said, fifty parish churches and religious foundations.

Equally disastrous was the withdrawal of the sea, again chiefly on the storm-swept east coast. Defoe graphically described the troubles besetting Orford, in Suffolk:[5]

> Orford was once a good town, but is decayed, and as it stands on the land side of the river, the sea daily throws up more land to it, and falls off itself from it, as if it was resolved to disown the place, and that it should be a sea port no longer.

Wisbech in the Isle of Ely was more fortunate in having a most remarkable career. Starting in the Middle Ages on the river Ouse, some four miles from the sea, it ended up in the late fifteenth century on the river Nene some eleven miles from the sea. Such apparently wayward behaviour was the consequence of drainage work in the Fens, including the diversion of the Ouse and the cutting of a new channel for the Nene, which had originally been a tributary of the Ouse.

Until the eighteenth century ports were more or less powerless to halt the movement of the coastline or the accumulation of silt. Although they might indulge in major digging operations to remove mud and sand or cut new channels and divert rivers, as they did at King's Lynn and Grimsby, there was little they could do to prevent troubles returning. That is one reason why ports precariously balanced between success and failure were usually doomed to the latter. But the truth is that ports had far more to contend with than shifting sand: equally devastating was shifting trade, and many ports with adequate harbours, and some with superlative ones, had failed by the end of the Middle Ages to realise their early promise. Southampton,

York, a great river port serving the north of England, but already decaying by the late fifteenth century.

sometime centre of the Italian trade, is, perhaps, the best example; and a close runner-up is the great Welsh non-port, Milford Haven. Both remained legal ports, but neither regained its former status until quite recent times when the advantages of their water sites for modern shipping eventually outweighed the disadvantages of their land situation.

Other ports lost their trade because their geographical location ceased to be advantageous for its conduct. The up-river ports were particularly affected in this regard, as industrial and agricultural changes in the surrounding countryside encouraged the movement of the trading site down-river. Bristol was near enough the sea to survive, but Norwich gave place to Yarmouth, Lincoln to Boston, and York to Hull. The movement of trade, ships and—in some cases—merchants and mariners to the coast did not pass unnoticed or unlamented. York, the last to go (though to be fair it had a considerable river trade down to modern times), was still bemoaning its fate as late as the sixteen-sixties: 'The shoes of our predecessors', the City Fathers told a local historian,[6]

> are too big for our feet, and the ornaments which they had will not serve now to cover our nakedness, nor will their wealth feed us, who are not able to tell you what we are, unless it be this, that we are poor and miserable. ... Trade is decayed, the river become unnavigable by reason of shelves. Leeds is nearer the manufacturers, and Hull more commodious for the vending of them; so York is, in each respect, furthest from the profit.

3. THE CLOTH TRADE AND THE DOMINANCE OF LONDON

The chief reason for the relative decay of many older places was not so much the prosperity of local rivals as the all-embracing success of London, incomparably the best harbour in the south-east, and ideally situated for political and trading links with the Continent. The merchants of York and Bristol were once as proud as the merchants of London, but by the middle of the fifteenth century there were many disgruntled outport men to advise youngsters in search of fortune that London was the only place to go. A little later and they would be suggesting that London merchants were using their nearness to the centre of power to prejudice the law in their favour, to the detriment of the outports.

Views of this sort hinged on the question of monopoly. In the troubled times of the Middle Ages merchants sought safety in numbers. The Company of Merchant Adventurers banded together for strength, for competitive advantage, and for ease in finding suppliers and customers in a disordered world. Kings were equally anxious to regulate trade, and laid down from time to time what goods could or could not be exported, and the ports to which they must be taken. This 'staple' system restricted trade to narrowly defined channels, and the Merchant Adventurers, theoretically resident in any part of the country, were increasingly Londoners doing their best to exclude others. In 1478 the merchants of York, Hull and other northern ports complained that they were no longer permitted to elect one of the two governors of the Company, and that obstacles were placed in their way in the mart towns of the Low Countries. A century later (*c.* 1575) the aggrieved merchants of Hull petitioned for the removal of 'certain causes of the decay of the traffic in Kingston-upon-Hull'.[7] They cited the 'false making' of northern cloth, which 'so overthroweth the merchants' that they were 'not able to set the navy on work, as they have done in times past', and blamed the London monopoly:

> by means of the said Companies (the Government whereof is ruled only in the City of London) all the whole trade of merchandise is in a manner brought to the City of London; whereby all the wealthy chapmen and the best clothiers are drawn to London, and other ports hath in a manner no traffic, but falleth to decay. ...

The decline of the western ports was similarly attributed by local men to London's aggressiveness: 'as it is true that many western towns are decayed, as Bristol and such like, so [it] is not to be forgotten whether London hath not engrossed all their trades, not so much for wines but even for the Welsh friezes that come over the Severn not far from Bristol.'[8] Nor were the south-eastern ports in a healthy state. Their use by London merchants had long ago ceased, and their decay was matched only by the sense of despair emanating from them. Some interested parties saw their salvation in making Kent an entrepôt for the exportation of Newcastle coal, while others looked to the imposition of a second 'fish' day to sustain a fishing fleet that would in turn revive the ports. But the truth is that while the northern and western ports might eventually revive, the south-eastern ports had truly had their day.

The malaise of the outports reflects more than their loss of the cloth trade to London. England as a whole had, during the fifteenth century, been losing her grip on trade with three traditional areas of outport interest. The Baltic trade had gradually been lost to the Dutch, and the east coast ports had suffered in consequence. The Mediterranean and Iberian trades had diminished, to the discomfort of the south-western ports. And the sea fishery had been lost to the French, the Flemings and the Dutch, to the cost of almost all the ports. Complaints about London engrossing the cloth, lead and other trades were, if anything, less indignant than assertions that the country's own waters had been invaded by foreigners. 'The port towns', wrote Burghley,

> were heretofore accustomed to occupy their people in fishing, as in Iceland, Norway, Shetland . . . and all along the coasts of England, . . . all which trades are at this time almost wholly possessed, even sometimes within a kenning of our shores, by strangers that seek politically to maintain their mariners by such trades as be directly profitable to themselves, and only hurtful to their neighbours. . . . England is besieged and deprived round about by strangers of the substance of the sea fishing . . .[9]

This first edition of the 'cod war', finally lost to the Dutch in the seventeenth century, exposed the inadequacy of both market and mercantile enterprise in England. The old involvement with deep sea fishing on any substantial scale died with the Reformation, and those places which might have been great centres for an international trade in fish were rapidly reduced in number. Interestingly enough, Sir Walter Ralegh was of the opinion that one of the major obstacles facing the fisheries trade—even that with Newfoundland—was the inadequacy of the south coast harbours, and in 1601 he spoke in Parliament in favour of a tax to support Dover harbour, on the grounds that without the tax the harbour would decay, and without the harbour the Newfoundland trade would be lost.[10]

London alone cannot, therefore, be blamed for the fact that certain trades carried on from the outports were in decline. It was her good fortune that the rising trade in woollen cloth was one for which she was ideally situated. The importance of the Merchant Adventurers Company in presenting a strong front amid the constant friction and troubles in Europe undoubtedly helped in the cloth trade, and it is quite true that the richest members of the Company resided in London. But they did not route their trade through London for the sheer delight of ruining the outports from which many of them had themselves come.

London was chosen because it offered the shortest sea crossing to the Low Countries where (especially after the 'Magnus Intercursus' of 1496) the cloth was finished and sold. London's distance from production areas was less important because cloth could bear the cost of expensive pack-horse carriage.

Moreover, the fact that much of late medieval trade was in the hands of foreign merchants may well have helped to fix it in London. The truth of the matter is that many of the outports, even when engaged in the wool or cloth trades, had few prosperous merchants or large ships of their own. Many were like Hull had been before she threw off the tutelage of York: trans-shipment centres for merchants who did not really 'belong'. To shift the export trade to London did not damage it unduly. At the beginning of the modern period the outports had almost certainly reached their nadir as contributors to the national economy.

London rose to prominence in the cloth trade in company with Antwerp, and it follows that her domination of trade would last only so long as practically the whole of the nation's trade was passed through such a narrow channel and involved so slight a range of goods. In fact the cloth trade was already past its peak by the middle of the sixteenth century, and the sacking of Antwerp during the wars of independence in the Low Countries, and the removal of English merchants to Emden and Hamburg, placed the final seal on a movement of trade away from that area which had been gathering momentum for half a century. Insofar as the Antwerp region had finished English cloth before sending it into Germany, the hardship or havoc caused by the religious and dynastic upheavals was serious indeed. But the other side of the coin—the concentration at home on the perfection of the finishing processes, the manufacture of new types of cloth, and the beginning of trading ventures on a wider geographical basis—could, in the long run, do nothing but good for both trade and ports.

For the time being, however, stagnation was the order of the day. By the middle of the sixteenth century the European economy as a whole was suffering from the effects of war, government financial manipulations and consequent austerity; and the cloth trade especially was in crisis. Falling prices cut back trade, and revival was prevented by the spread of cloth manufacture on the Continent based on plentiful supplies of good Spanish wool. The old English cloth trade was dying, and it would be a full century

Daniells' view of the Port of London: the river from the Tower to London Bridge, where ships lay in the stream and delivered or received goods by lighter. The Legal Quay and Custom House is in the centre of the picture: the treadmill crane can be seen behind the masts of ships.

before overseas trade began to revive under new influences. In such circumstances it would appear to matter little if harbours were silting up or ports falling into the sea. With London handling what was left of the the cloth trade, the rest of the ports would appear to have become redundant.

Nothing, in the long run, could have been further from the truth, and it is important to stress certain aspects of the development of London and their influence on the remaining ports. The concentration there of the cloth trade, with its attendant warehousing and shipping, encouraged the growth of the city's port function, but at the same time exerted a considerable influence on its population, which was required to grow to cater for this trade. London also had the Court, and as the Tudor monarchs exerted their power the nobles and their retinues repaired to the city, at least for part of the year. Although there cannot be any great assurance about the accuracy of estimates, it is nevertheless thought that the city's population at the beginning of the sixteenth century must have been something of the order of fifty thousand, while by the beginning of the seventeenth century it had advanced to two hundred thousand. Such a concentration of people, including the richest in the land, called for ever-increasing supplies of building materials, fuel and foodstuffs, and while at first these may have been drawn in from the sur-

rounding area, it was not long before corn was coming from East Anglia and the south coast, cheese from Cheshire, butter from Yorkshire, cattle from Wales and Scotland, and coal from Newcastle. The overwhelming preponderance of London in the cloth trade should not be allowed to obscure the role of the outports—or at least some of them—as suppliers of provisions and raw materials to London and, to a lesser degree, as distributors of Continental goods imported through London and then sent coastwise. Admittedly trade of this sort was hardly in the same money-making category as the cloth trade, being conducted more by inland contacts than by great merchant houses in the ports; but at least it meant that places no longer frequented by foreign-going shipping might still have plenty of shipping involved in the coastal trade. Looked at from the other direction, the continued existence of the coastal trade enabled London to grow to an extent that would otherwise—presumably—have been physically impossible.

The growth of London had been a consequence, at least in part, of the changes in overseas trade, and those outports which had for so long seen their own decay in the capital's control of the Low Countries' trade might with some justice have looked forward to the decay of London's trade following the collapse of Antwerp. It was not to be. The growth of London had given her such a large part of the national market for imported goods that the outports would have the greatest difficulty re-establishing any sort of position in that area, and the outports had no specially productive hinterlands on which to base a recovery of their export trade. That some of them did eventually recover was owing to changes in trade that occurred largely during the late-sixteenth and seventeenth centuries when the decline of the cloth trade outlined above was at last offset by other trades which were to lead England—and eventually Britain—to a far more exalted station among trading nations.

4. THE COMMERCIAL REVOLUTION

The internecine quarrels of the western Europeans in the sixteenth and seventeenth centuries might give the impression—at least in the old school of textbooks—that, in their endeavours to create the national state and revive or preserve the true religion, they cared for little outside their own narrow band of territory beyond repelling the Turks and murdering the Mexicans. Such an impression would be unfortunate, for while the Europeans were certainly concerned with what was going on at home, this period saw an unprecedented amount of initiative, enterprise and enthusiasm directed towards the exploration of the outside world.

During the fifteenth and early sixteenth centuries the peoples along the European coastline had perfected developments which enabled them to discover and exploit the New World. The first ocean-going ships enabled men to sail in any seas and almost any conditions. The cannon, and its adaptation to broadside use, relieved adventurers from any untoward fear of unknown peoples. The compass and the new study of navigation—principally by the Portuguese—at last gave mariners the freedom of the oceans.

These and other factors led to the discovery of America in the 1490s and its partial occupation in the early sixteenth century. It was an exercise in conquest rather than commerce. The Spanish and Portuguese took great wealth from America, but for Western Europeans as a whole this was a century of reconnaissance during which the foundations were slowly being laid upon which a great commercial edifice would be erected. For the time being, so far as England was concerned, efforts were concentrated on opening trade with regions that were nearer to hand.

One of England's principal contributions to international exploration was the search for the North East Passage to China, which failed to find China but opened up the northern route to Russia. The Muscovy Company was founded in the 1570s to exploit trade in that direction, hoping against hope that an easy way would be found into western Russia that bypassed the Hanse-dominated Baltic. There was even, for a time, a grand speculation that a route would be found down to the Middle East, thus bypassing that other troublesome area, the Turkish-dominated Mediterranean.

Besides land-based trade, the Muscovy Company also discovered whales in the waters around Spitsbergen. There then began one of the great tragedies of English trading history as the Muscovy Company fought men from Hull, Yarmouth and other places in the courts and on the high seas in an attempt to impose the sort of monopoly that Londoners had come to expect as of right. The monopoly failed, but not before the stupidity of the English had permitted the Dutch to capture the European oil market. By comparison, the rest of the northern trade was unimportant, and the major advance in trade with Russia occurred in the more direct route through the Baltic.

The decline of the Antwerp connexion had left English merchants with the alternatives of winding up their business or pressing it with increasing vigour into those regions to which English cloth had been taken hitherto by the Hanseatics or the Italians. Direct trade was by no means easy, firstly because of the need to acquire ships suitable for the longer voyages involved, and secondly because areas eager for English goods were firmly controlled by bodies hostile to English traders. Attempts to gain direct access to German markets were thwarted for a considerable period by the restrictive practices of the Hanse towns, which could also obstruct English attempts to secure the Baltic timber, tar and flax which were essential for the building of a mercantile marine.

However, the Hanse towns themselves were upset by the schisms in Germany, and their continued success in England was threatened by the hostility of the Crown for some time before their London factory—the Steelyard— was finally closed down in 1598. In the eastern Baltic they were faced by the resolute action of English merchants who in 1579 combined together as the Eastland Company and established their factory at Elbing, outside Hanse influence. In the west, English merchants deserting Antwerp had already set up their mart in Emden, also outside Hanse control. So important was English cloth to the Hanseatics that they eventually bowed to the inevitable, and English merchants were accepted in the Hanse towns, establishing their principal marts at Hamburg in the west and Danzig in the east by the end of the century.

The long-term importance of the penetration of the Baltic can hardly be exaggerated. Eastern Europe was economically backward, a vast expanse of rural estates, with few towns and little industry. It became, in effect, a source of raw materials and a consumer of finished goods for the more advanced areas, resembling, in this regard, the colonial empires that were established in the New World. The exchange of cloth for raw materials was an inestimable gain for those countries of the west that were short of timber and short of land for growing vast quantities of textile fibres and grain. It was also a gain for their shipping 'industry', since the tonnage required to carry valuable bales of cloth was nothing compared with that required for cheap bulky goods.

There was, moreover, a decided gain for the outports. The central mart system used for the periodic disposal of large quantities of high-value cloths—in effect a sort of auction system—was not appropriate for the developing market in raw materials. Instead, individual merchants had to search out their own supplies at ports along the Baltic coastline, and in inland areas, and arrange for shipment direct to England. Moreover, just as low-value bulky goods could not bear the costs of unnecessary assembly at a Baltic mart, so, also, they could not bear the cost of distribution through London unless it was to the capital's own local or immediately adjacent market.

Thus the way was opened for the eastern outports to come back into the main flow of the nation's trade. London enjoyed no geographical advantage as she had done in the Low Countries' trade, and the Eastland Company had no monopoly of the sort enjoyed by the Adventurers. Newcastle, Hull, Lynn and Yarmouth were able to send their locally manufactured cloths direct to Hamburg and Danzig, and while the merchants of Hull were still attributing their troubles to the merchants of London, some at least of the latter were reversing the argument and asserting that difficulties they were meeting in Danzig sprang from the

The Hanse Warehouse, King's Lynn, (left) used between 1428 and 1751 as the local centre of the Hanseatic League.

The London hythes were creeks or inlets where mud docks could be made and so effectively lengthen the river frontage. This engraving of Billingsgate dates from 1736, but few changes took place along the waterfront in many centuries.

fact that ships arriving before them from the outports had spoiled the market for cloth.[11] They would have done better, perhaps, to have recognised more clearly that while the merchants from the capital and the outports were haggling over a ship or two, Englishmen in general were failing to press their trade to anything like the same extent as the Dutch who, more than any other people, gained from the decline of the Hanseatics.

The second and far greater benefit accruing to the English from the troubles of the Low Countries was the revival of direct trade with the Mediterranean in the last quarter of the sixteenth century. Wars between Christians and Turks in the 1570s ruined the Venetians and persuaded the Turks of the wisdom of admitting English merchants with their plentiful supplies of tin, a vital ingredient of bronze cannons. In 1573 the English established their western base at Leghorn in north-western Italy, and in 1581 the Levant Company was formed to create a series of factories in Turkish territory. By the end of the century English ships were ranging the Mediterranean and linking up, in Smyrna in the Levant, with the routes across Asia Minor to the Near East. As a major consumer of light woollens, lead, tin and fish, and as a source of dried fruits, wines, luxuries and raw cotton, the Mediterranean trade was destined to be the most important contributor to the revival of English trade as a whole during the seventeenth century.

Perhaps because it was so much more valuable than the Baltic and Muscovy trades, the Mediterranean trade was more closely associated with London, and the Levant Company was dominated by Londoners to a greater extent than were the northern companies. London was still the centre of cloth exportation, on which the Mediterranean trade was heavily dependent, and indisputably the chief consumer of imported luxuries. But other places were drawn in, if only indirectly through the coastal trade. Exported tin came from the western ports, lead from the Severn and the Humber, and cloth from most places (though perhaps most commonly by land). The fish which went in increasing quantities to ease a growing food shortage in the Mediterranean lands came either from the Yarmouth herring fishery or the West Country cod fishery.

The cod fishery was, in fact, one of the few benefits England gained from the transatlantic trade. Having lost by a hair's breadth the discovery of America (Columbus having first approached the English king with his wild scheme for exploration), Bristol merchants were quick to despatch John Cabot on his venture in 1497. His discovery of the cod banks of Newfoundland led to a flourishing trade in the south-western ports, but did not satisfy those who lusted after the products of Central America. William Hawkins was trading from Plymouth to Brazil in the 1530s and by the middle of the century the Portuguese had been followed to the coast of Guinea in search of the slaves which might now be sold to the Spaniards in America. In practice, the direct trade with Africa, for gold, ivory, gum and (from Morocco) sugar, was probably more valuable than the general transatlantic trade.

It was soon felt in the south-western ports that the Spaniards' reluctance to admit English merchants to the Indies would make it more profitable to fight than to trade with them. Matters came to a head in 1567 when Hawkins' third slave fleet was attacked in San Juan D'Ulloa by Spanish battleships. Sir John Hawkins and his cousin Francis Drake who led the fleet barely escaped with their lives. Spain was never forgiven, and the English turned to illegal trade—'interloping'—where it was practicable and to privateering where it was not. The exploits of Drake and a host of lesser men on the Spanish Main were no doubt highly profitable, but it should be remembered that there was a price to pay. While the harbours of the south-west concentrated on fighting the Spaniards, a stop was put to their traditional connexion with the Iberian peninsula, and, privateering apart, the ports of this region reached the nadir of their fortunes during the last quarter of the sixteenth century.

The most important gains to the south-west were surely intangible ones. The 'Sea Dogs' tradition tends to convey the impression that the English were masters of oceanic affairs, with first-rate ships and crews, by comparison with which the Spaniards were incompetent landlubbers in crazy ships which turned turtle at the drop of a cannon-ball. Nothing could be further from the truth. The Portuguese and Spanish had great experience and a combined mercantile marine which at the time of the Armada is estimated to have been around 250,000 tons, some four times as large as that of England.[12] Portugal had the Far Eastern trade, Spain the western empire. England had virtually nothing but the promise of success off the Newfoundland

coast and the unhappy Virginia Plantation established by Walter Ralegh in the 1580s. It was privateering which provided the experience in navigation needed by English captains, and showed them that persistent interloping could wear down the Spanish claim to exclusive trade with the *whole* of America. When peace was agreed at the Treaty of London in 1604 it was finally recognised by the English that the Spanish had a right to exclude their ships from territory effectively occupied, and by the Spanish that the English had a right to trade or settle in those areas which were not occupied.

The Anglo-Spanish treaty of 1604 opened the way for the settlement of colonies which were to transform English trade. In 1606 the Virginia Company was formed to revive the plantation of that name and introduced tobacco from the Spanish Indies. In the Indies themselves other adventurers settled in St. Kitts and Barbados, where sugar was introduced in 1610 from Portuguese Brazil. And in the far north the best known of all emigrants, the 'Pilgrim Fathers', settled in New England. Unlike the plantations to the south, the New England settlements produced nothing worth trading to England, but they made admirable homes for people tired, for one reason or another, of life in Europe. Consequently they grew in number and population: Massachusetts was followed by Maine, New Hampshire, Connecticut and Rhode Island. A valuable market for English manufactures was already developing, with imports paid for in fish, corn and timber exported to the West Indian colonies, which also grew in number and economic strength during the seventeenth century, chiefly because of the introduction of slave labour.

The trade with New England, Virginia and the West Indies would eventually encourage the growth of the western ports, but in the meantime the balance was again redressed in favour of London by the major innovation of the early seventeenth century: the East India Company. Founded in 1601 to take part in the Far Eastern spice trade, its ships and servants were eventually forced out by the Dutch (who had themselves seized the spice trade from its Portuguese founders) and compelled to retire to India, where their factory at Surat soon became an excellent source of cottons, muslins, saltpetre and dyestuffs. Such things were in high demand in Europe, and shared the immense potential of sugar and tobacco. England had thus acquired, almost accidentally, three separate trades which had the power of raising English ports to the position lately occupied by Antwerp. In the case of the Eastern trade, however, London alone benefited, since the terms of the monopoly restricted shipping outside the Atlantic to the East India Company and the port of London.

The situation at the start of the seventeenth century was, therefore, generally cloudy with bright spots on the horizon. The old woollen cloth trade had lost its dynamism. Trade in general throughout Europe was stagnant and would remain so for another half century. The new trades with America, the West Indies and the East Indies awaited development as soon as general economic conditions became favourable. But the crucial issue was whether the English ports would be able to keep and foster these trades, or would lose them to more enterprising merchants abroad. The right to send settlers to America had been won by fighting the Spaniards; the right to exclusive trade with them was won by fighting the Dutch.

The Dutch were the principal traders of the seventeenth century. They had gained most from the decline of the Hanse and of Antwerp. Holland was centrally placed for the interchange of goods between the Baltic and southern Europe. Her ships were also to be found in great numbers in the North Sea herring fishery, the Spitsbergen whale fishery and the Far Eastern spice trade. Over the years she had built up a vast resource of mercantile expertise and—largely through her intimate connexion with the Spanish, her old masters—the largest store of liquid assets in Europe. She could finance trade beyond the wildest dreams of most countries, while her ingenious shipping interest also had evolved a new kind of ship to carry large sections of it.

The *fluit* was the first 'modern' ship designed specifically for carrying cargo. By contrast with the heavily armed, fast-sailing, long-distance vessels which the English were still building, the *fluit* was lighter (and therefore cheaper) in construction, and equipped with a simplified sail pattern which required a smaller crew. 'Few merchant ships among the Hollanders', wrote a pamphleteer in favour of England's adopting the *fluit*, 'were ships of much defence, unless those going to India; and so they were neither at so great a charge of guns in building them, nor did carry a proportion of men or victuals (in setting them out) near, or answerable to English shipping of the same burthen.'[13] So good were the ships—or so clever their operators—that they inhibited the growth of an English marine: a large proportion of ships entering London were Dutch, and they formed the majority at Newcastle, Hull, Ipswich, Lynn and Yarmouth in some years before 1651.

The Irish trade, too, was in the holds of Dutch shipping.[14]

There was, therefore, every reason for doubting Englands ability to introduce her own shipping—and so accumulate mercantile capital—in the European trades, and even better reason for supposing that Dutch merchants would capture the trade between Europe and the English colonies. During the English Civil War they were indeed active in the West Indies, and it was actually Dutch merchants who encouraged the cultivation of sugar in the English colonies. They did not reap their reward.

It was ironic that the Puritan Republic which emerged triumphant from the Civil War should almost immediately have found itself in conflict with the other major Puritan power. It had little choice. The re-establishment of government authority in the West Indies and attempts to build a navy to protect trade with the infant colonies were a direct threat to Holland, and were intended to be so: only by political action, it was thought, could English merchants make headway against the overwhelming superiority of the Dutch.

It was not a novel concept. Exclusive rights to trade had been the foundation of Hanse power, and the exercise of such by Spain had been the provocation leading to the depredations of the West Country privateers. The new government, following the advice of the merchants who had staunchly supported their cause, accepted that prosperous trade required the elimination of the 'middleman' foreigner and the binding of colonial trade to English ports by legal constraints.

To this end the Navigation Act of 1651 imposed various restrictions on trade: no goods from the plantations or East Indies could be imported save in English ships with predominantly English crews; no European goods could be imported save in English ships or those of the exporting country; no European goods could be imported in foreign ships save from the port of usual first shipment; no fish or train oil could be imported or exported in foreign ships; and no foreign ships could take part in the coastal trade.

The 1651 Act was more a declaration of intent than an effective support for English trade: England did not have the ships to carry her own trade. However, during the Anglo-Dutch War of 1652–4 she set about getting them, and it is variously estimated that something between 1,000 and 1,700 were seized from the Dutch.[15] To the surprise of many in Europe, the English were not driven from the seas. The Commonwealth navy acquitted itself well during the set-piece battles of the war, and added some two hundred ships to its strength thereafter to threaten Dutch shipping should they resist the Navigation Act. With a multitude of troubles facing it—including yet another war with Spain between 1655 and 1660—it would be too much to claim that the Commonwealth had established the 'Old Colonial System', but it had made a very good start (and the war with Spain brought it another four hundred ships seized from that country).

The Restoration of Charles II destroyed the Commonwealth, but the King was as anxious as the Protector to maintain the 1651 Act, which was replaced in 1660 by one going still further in encouraging English trade and shipping. In order to stimulate the buildup of native shipping in the Mediterranean and Baltic trades, 'alien dues' were imposed on any goods from Spain, Portugal, Turkey or Russia, and on certain goods such as naval stores and fruit from any country carried in foreign ships. And in order that English ports might benefit from the sale of plantation products, goods such as tobacco, sugar, dyestuffs and cotton could be shipped only to England.

Nevertheless, a country whose maritime heroes made their name evading the colonial monopoly of the Spanish might be expected to realise that there was little chance of resisting a full-scale onslaught by Dutch ships and traders, despite the fact that the 1660 Act required the removal of all foreign merchants from English colonies. The Dutch, it should be noted, had their own colony of New Netherlands—with its strategic port of New Amsterdam—immediately adjacent to the New England colonies, and were quite capable of surreptitious trading. They had to be moved, and the second Anglo-Dutch War of 1664–7 was the excuse. Bearing in mind the growing English interest in slaves, it is understandable that the war was provoked by English attacks on the Dutch slaving stations on the Guinea coast, but the immediate cause of the war was of no significance: 'What matters this or that reason', asked the Duke of Albemarle. 'What we want is more of the trade that the Dutch now have.'[16] New Amsterdam was promptly occupied by an expeditionary force under the king's brother, and renamed New York in his honour, while on the high seas a number of relatively indecisive naval battles confirmed England's position as a naval power. The Dutch were forced not only to surrender New Netherlands, which became the centre for English trade along the American coastline, but also to recognise England's right to enforce the Navigation Laws. Their 'third party' status as the carriers of English trade was des-

troyed, and the way was opened for English merchants to push their way into European trades in which the Dutch had hitherto predominated.

The great boom in the late seventeenth century was not achieved solely by Act of Parliament or benefit of war. A necessary contribution was also made by the growing popularity of 'new' English goods and the greater degree of initiative and enterprise exhibited by English merchants. The expanding production of 'New Draperies' provided the lighter mixed cloths—the worsteds—that were eagerly sought after in western Europe and especially the Mediterranean, while the great efforts put into building up the meagre economies of Virginia, Maryland and the West Indian colonies produced a rapid expansion of re-exportable goods which made the Navigation Laws worth while. The importation of tobacco rose from 7 million pounds in 1662–3 to 22 millions in 1699–1701, while the importation of sugar rose from 148,000 cwt in 1663–9 to 371,000 in 1699–1701;[17] and in both cases—and with other re-exportable goods—rising production was followed by drastic price reductions which opened up a vast market which further encouraged major investment in colonial and East Indian trade. By 1699–1701 the value of 'colonial imports' was 32 per cent of total imports, though in terms of shipping the colonies supplied only 18·4 per cent.

The post-Restoration boom came to an end around 1689, and the country had to wait till the 1740s before a similar growth rate was achieved; but the object of Restoration statesmen 'to turn the course of a trade' had been achieved.[18] English merchants and ships had secured their national trade from foreign domination, and effectively turned its orientation away from a dangerous and inhibiting concentration on the Low Countries. While it would be easy to exaggerate the extent of English commerce compared with Dutch in 1700, it is nevertheless true that it was now virtually world-wide, poised for expansion in both west and east.

5. THE REVIVAL OF THE OUTPORTS

English commerce was also increasingly spread around the English ports. 'London led at first in freeing itself from the Dutch yoke', wrote the historian of the Navigation Laws, 'but by 1715 the outports were even more successful in that regard . . . the English, who had formerly been retail purchasers at the Dutch emporium, had now become wholesalers who supplied the entrepôt. The Navigation

Laws must receive much credit for bringing about the change.'[19]

The likely results of the changes for the English ports have already been touched on. London's paramount position was not in doubt. She was, and would remain, by far the most important port, with the largest market, the richest merchants and the greatest stock of shipping. But the great advantage of the short distance to the major trading centre was passing into history. Trade with the Mediterranean remained fairly strongly in London hands, though the south-western ports began to revive their interest. By contrast the Baltic trade was increasingly channelled through the eastern ports having the easiest access to the centre of the country. The natural advantages which London possessed for importing dried fruit for distribution to the Midlands did not apply to flax or timber: it was easier to bring them in through Hull and distribute them along the inland navigations. Hull gained also as the woollen industry, for so long concentrated in the south-west and east of the country, converged on the West Riding of Yorkshire; as the linen industry grew around Leeds; and as metal working developed in the south of Yorkshire and along the upper reaches of the Trent. To the north the development of the coalfield which eased the growth of London also brought massive changes to the local ports of Newcastle and Sunderland: coal shipped from Newcastle grew from around 140,000 tons per annum in the late 1590s to 560,000 tons a century later.[20]

With both coal and the sorts of raw materials now coming from the Baltic, volume was of infinitely greater importance than value, compared with cloth, with the result that the overall volume of trade passing through the northern ports grew very much faster than might otherwise have been the case. At the same time, the longer distances involved in trade required a greater fleet to carry it. Lord Burghley, when considering reasons for the decay, around 1580, of many ports involved in the southern wine trade, had pointed out that 'now the commodities which English ships were accustomed to bring thence is for the most part found in Antwerp, from which place one hoy will bring as much in one year as ten merchant ships were wont to bring from the other places in two years.'[21] Now the situation went into reverse, and there is little wonder that Charles Davenant, writing in 1695, thought that 'the north and west of late years have had a greater proportion of foreign trade than the home counties.'[22] It was, perhaps, just as well that alternative outlets to London were emerging, for the stoppages caused by plague in the capital proved very serious on a number of occasions, and, in fact, may well have encouraged some merchants to bypass London where possible.[23]

While the growth of the northern ports—despite the coal trade—was relatively neglected by later writers, the growth of the western ports has always attracted attention. Exeter, like Hull, had retained a measure of its early trade because of its convenient situation for Portuguese traffic, and was still one of the major outports in the seventeenth century. But it was Bristol that surpassed all expectations by rising from a lengthy decline. Her merchants had managed to hang on just long enough to hazard their capital across the Atlantic, and their success was phenomenal. Despite London's interest in New England, Virginia and the West Indies, Bristol forged ahead in the fish trade with Newfoundland and was able in consequence to build up a trade with the fish-eating south of Europe; her old interest in the Portuguese trade and its sugar supplies encouraged her early entry into the West Indian sugar trade; and her direct involvement in sugar plantations there encouraged her entry into the slave trade towards the end of the seventeenth century. Add to this a growing interest in tobacco and Bristol had the makings of an entrepôt to rival London in the re-export trade, at least with southern Europe and the Mediterranean. However, what Bristol could not achieve was the same sort of monopoly position on the west coast as London enjoyed on the east. Plymouth, Dartmouth, Falmouth, Poole and other places also took their share of the transatlantic trade, if only in fish.

The rise of Liverpool was not, like the rise of Bristol, a revival of past glories. Liverpool had no past. Though an ancient (and rotten) borough, she did not even have that humblest of distinctions, a parish church. Chester was the trading centre of the north-west, and might well have remained so but for two unfortunate factors: the river Dee, as noted above, was becoming impassable; and industrial development was taking place in an area of the hinterland more easily reached by the Mersey than the Dee. The opening up of the rock salt mines at Northwich on the river Weaver provided, in the 1670s, the foundation for trade with many areas of the world where salt did not occur naturally. Coal was also to be had in the hinterland, though not yet easily transported. But the most important development was in the manufacture of lightweight cloth of wool or linen with, eventually, a mixture of cotton. Light cloths and salt, in particular, were suitable for colonial trade and, in the years following the Restoration, they were exchanged for both tobacco and sugar, part of which was distributed in Lancashire and part in Ireland.

At the same time, in order to service the plantations with more than the provisions picked up in southern Ireland, Liverpool entered the slave trade which had been a Bristol preserve. The point at issue, however, is not that Liverpool was soon rivalling Bristol, but that both of them would in the long run threaten London's early dominance of colonial trade. Freight rates to the western ports were appreciably lower than to London during the French wars because of the threat of capture in the Channel, and though London maintained a majority share of the imported sugar, she was unable to drive the western ports out of the tobacco trade, for which they made fine entrepôts.

The importation trades were, of course, attracted to London by her vast local market, but the exportation trades to the colonies gained from the developing hinterlands of the western ports, and the ability of Liverpool merchants to export provisions, metal goods and Manchester cottons was repaid by the ease with which they were able to attract return cargoes to their port which might otherwise have gone to London.

There was one further development worth noting: the Irish trade. Contact between the two islands had been growing stronger during the sixteenth and seventeenth centuries and, despite the troubles at the end of the century, the imposition of firm English rule encouraged a measure of economic development in Ireland. In particular Ireland was able to provide foodstuffs and linen yarn, and in return took large quantities of salt, coal, cloth and tobacco. The western ports were incomparably well placed to serve these trades, and not only Bristol and Liverpool but also Whitehaven and other smaller northern ports were to benefit. Thus, quite apart from any share in the European or colonial trades, the western ports received a tremendous boost to their mercantile expertise and their shipowning skills from their quasi-monopoly links with Ireland.[24]

The extent to which certain outports were able to overcome the influence of London while others succumbed to overwhelming pressures was a matter which drew the attention of Defoe as late as 1724, and was used by him to explain, for example, the unhappy state in which he found Ipswich:

But the neighbourhood of London, which sucks the vitals of trade in this island to itself, is the chief reason

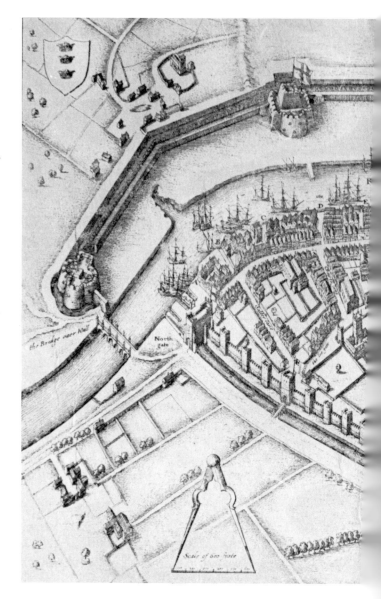

Hull in 1640, showing the shipping congregating in the Haven and the merchant warehouses at right angles to the Haven along High Street.

of any decay of business in this place; and I shall in the course of these observations, hint at it, where many good sea-ports and large towns, tho' farther off than Ipswich, and well fitted for commerce, are yet swallowed up by the immense indraft of trade to the city of London; and more decayed beyond all comparison, than Ipswich is supposed to be; as Southampton, Weymouth, Dartmouth, and several others which I shall speak to in their order: And if it be otherwise at this time, with some other towns, which are lately increased in trade

Hull (and to a lesser extent Yarmouth and the other eastern ports), while the rise of the transatlantic and Irish trades encouraged Bristol, Liverpool and Whitehaven. Moreover, the extent to which new trades involved bulky goods encouraged the development of a mercantile marine in these 'new' ports which was greater than would have been required for the same value of cloth in the older London-Antwerp trade. The increasing distances involved in overseas trade further encouraged the growth of provincial as well as London shipping. In this respect the expansion of the outports was quite rapid after 1660, and by 1700, while still offering no significant challenge to London's supremacy, they were well on the way to becoming 'major' ports.

However, the growth of the outports was not simply a result of mechanical changes. People also were involved. For generations the most lively members of the provincial trading communities had, from all accounts, migrated to London to take advantage of the lucrative but unexciting trade with the Low Countries. Within the protective organisation of the Merchant Adventurers they had little need to initiate new trades or adventure far from the traditional market of goods, and 'a predominating characteristic of English trade in the first half of the seventeenth century was specialisation by area rather than specialisation by commodities.'[26] While it would be nonsense to exaggerate the point and deny any sense of adventure or inspiration to London merchants, there does seem to be some justification for pointing to a growing awareness of new opportunities in the outports. Admittedly it was Londoners who pushed the East Indian trade, but the men of Hull and Yarmouth were soon deeply involved in the Baltic trades, and the western ports were pioneers in the transatlantic trades. It was all a matter of connexion, that personal contact between English merchant and foreign supplier or customer which had been dominated by London people, but which was open for readjustment once new trading areas were involved. 'The Dutch master us in trade,' it was argued before the Lords' Committee on the Decay of Trade in 1669; 'We always begin young men here; there it holds from generation to generation.'[27] It was an argument frequently heard. Of Hull it was said, somewhat earlier, that 'every merchant (be his adventure never so small) doth for the most part send over [to the Baltic] an inexperienced youth, unfit for merchandising', while the agents of the West Country merchants were described as 'young men of small experience'.[28]

Inexperience does not last for ever, and it may have been

and navigation, wealth, and people, while their neighbours decay, it is because they have some particular trade or accident to trade, which is a kind of nostrum to them, inseparable to the place, and which fixes there by nature of the thing; as the herring fishery to Yarmouth; the coal trade to Newcastle; the Leeds clothing trade, the export of butter and lead, and the great corn trade for Holland, is to Hull; the Virginia and West India trade at Liverpool, the Irish trade at Bristol, and the like.[25]

So far it has been implied that the growth of the outports was largely a matter of their geographical position: the rise of the northern European trade encouraged Newcastle and to the advantage rather than the disadvantage of the outports that at a crucial period in the reshaping of trade they had a goodly number of young men willing to push trade in unknown places beyond the experience of their elders and betters in London. Hull factors were already well established in the Baltic by 1700, while the rapid rise of Bristol, Liverpool and eventually (after the Union of 1707) Glasgow in the tobacco trade was owing to the more adventurous and forceful methods employed by the agents of those places in attacking the market among American tobacco producers.[29] We might point also to the pioneering ventures of the western ports in the Newfoundland trade, of the eastern ports in the herring trade, and so on. By 1700 there was a new spirit in the air, and it was moving in the outports as well as the capital.

There was another factor which may have worked in favour of growing trade through the outports. When England acted through the Navigation Laws to exclude Dutch shipping from her trade she had, in fact, little ship-

ping of her own and, apparently, no significant ship-building industry. Much of the traditional trade of the past had been carried in Hanse and later in Dutch ships and in consequence London had no control over shipping to match her predominance in trade. As noted above, many of the ships required to service the protected trade after 1651 were, in fact, seized as prizes from the Dutch, Spanish and French during the wars that followed, and it has been estimated that their total was anything from 3,700 to 4,400 vessels.[30] Enterprising merchants in the outports were therefore able to acquire and operate ships without having to compete directly with a massive existing stock of ships in London which might have inhibited their freedom of action. Since the new trades in which the outports were interested required a large volume of shipping space, the growth of the total English tonnage from around 67,000 tons in 1582 to 340,000 in 1686 was not entirely concentrated in London. By the latter date some 190,000 tons, or 56 per cent of the total, was owned in the outports and presumably operated from them.[31] However, it must be stressed that London was still overwhelmingly the largest shipowning port, and that most other places around the turn of the century owned a very small tonnage of shipping by later standards, as can be seen from the figures published by Professor Davis:

Shipping owned in the Leading English Ports, 1582 and 1702

	(000 tons)	
	1582	1702
Newcastle	6·8	11·0
Sunderland	nil	3·9
Whitby	nil	8·3
Hull	2·5	7·6
Lynn	1·7	5·7
Yarmouth	6·8	9·9
Aldeburgh	2·8	1·8
Ipswich	3·0	11·2
London	12·3	140·0
Southampton	2·9	3·8
Exeter	1·0	7·1
Bristol	2·3	17·3
Liverpool	0·4	8·6
Whitehaven	nil	7·2

Source: R Davis, *The Rise of the English Shipping Industry*, p. 35.

Outport prosperity. Substantial houses began to appear in the late seventeenth century as trade revived. This property in King's Lynn is called Greenland House, once the headquarters of a whaling company.

6. SCOTLAND

What of Scotland? Much of the discussion of the evolution of English trade also applies north of the border. The difficulty of inland communications had encouraged the creation of a large number of small ports, and a tradition of mixing farming and fishing meant that even more places were involved in a minor way with the sea. The smaller places were the sheltered spots on exposed coasts; the larger ones were those standing on the major estuaries. Even more than in England, the large towns were natural ports. They alone appeared capable of supporting a significant population, and much of their trade tended to be in goods produced by or consumed by their own people or in the adjacent countryside.

From early times the east coast had kept up communications with northern Europe and the wine countries of the south, the leading ports gaining from their position opposite Europe. Scotsmen were in the van of the push into the Baltic which overcame the Hanseatics, and Scottish factors were to be found from Scandinavia to Danzig. They established the same sort of agencies in Holland as did the English, though they concentrated on Veere rather than Rotterdam. They had their factors in France, principally in Bordeaux. What they did not do was follow the English into the more exotic of their adventures, to the Arctic, America, the West Indies and the East. Even Muscovy and the Levant remained closed to them.

It was not that Scottish merchants lacked enterprise. They were held back by the poverty of the economy they served, and by the shortage of exportable commodities (apart from herring). The Union of 1707 offered to Scottish ports the same advantages that the transatlantic trades had bestowed on the western outports in England, namely a chance to exploit a wider market and seek new imports. In particular it offered goods such as tobacco that could be sold in Europe, thus creating an entrepôt trade that was not dependent on the low level of domestic consumption. Hitherto the western Scottish ports had been principally involved in trade with Ireland, and there were far fewer of them than on the east coast.

As in England, the trend in the sixteenth and seventeenth centuries had been for foreign trade to concentrate in the larger ports on the estuaries of Tay, Forth and Clyde. Inverness, Aberdeen, Montrose and Dunbar (and such unlikely places as Crail) had their share of European commerce, but the bulk of east coast traffic went through Dundee, Perth, Kirkcaldy, Leith and Bo'ness. In the west, Glasgow and Greenock were the only significant ports. Thus, at the start of the eighteenth century, Scottish trade was even more concentrated on a few ports than was English trade, and the potential for growth was such that the situation would be intensified as transatlantic trade favoured the Clyde ports.[32] The vast majority of Scottish ports were unbelievably tiny, and would remain so.

Many of the simplest forms of harbours survive in Scotland to give some indication of what English harbours must often have been like in the early period of their history. Here Staxigoe, in Caithness, consists of no more than two small walls.

Portsoy, Banffshire. The Inner Harbour, built in 1692, illustrates the way in which buildings in the richer Scottish ports huddled together for protection from the sea and wind.

CHAPTER TWO

Harbour Developments and Port Improvement 1660–1840

1. THE DIMENSIONS OF TRADE

The expansion and reorientation of trade in the decades following the Restoration marked the beginning of a long period of growth which placed unprecedented strains on ports which had been stagnant for generations. Ancient facilities which had coped in the past were overloaded: quays were too small, cranage or other handling systems inadequate, and harbour room insufficient for the number of ships. Water depth was less of a problem, but it, too, would become a matter of concern in many places as ships increased in size in certain trades towards the end of the eighteenth century.

Above all it was the simple increase in the bulk of trade which created problems in ports. Although there is no way of accurately discovering its real volume, a very rough indication is to be found in Customs valuations, which were based on fixed prices and therefore offer an approximate index of the volume of imports, exports and re-exports. From these figures (Graph on page 33) it is apparent that the volume of trade grew fairly steadily until the last two decades of the century, when upsets caused by the American Revolution were followed by the very substantial growth associated with the Industrial Revolution.

This increasing volume of trade can also be expressed in terms of shipping clearing outwards, for which figures of a sort exist for single years at seven year intervals. While they cannot be used with the same confidence as average figures (which eliminate the wilder and unrepresentative fluctuations), they nevertheless show roughly the same trend as the trade figures. But it is important to note that these indicators refer to the increase in *total national activity*. To appreciate the effects on the individual ports it is necessary to emphasise the great and growing disparities

between them. On the eve of the Industrial Revolution, in 1772, some sixteen English ports, or 22 per cent of those listed in the Reports of the Inspector General of Customs, owned no ships engaged in overseas trade, and a further twenty-eight, or 38 per cent of the total, owned less than 500 tons. At the other end of the scale ten ports between them owned 287,000 tons, or 88 per cent of all the country's foreign-going shipping.[1]

Admittedly foreign trade is only part of the story, and many ports might be expected to be more involved in coastal shipping. However, an analysis of the total tonnage (including both coasters and fishing vessels) owned by the various ports reveals the top eleven having 74 per cent of the entire shipping of England and Wales, and thirty-seven at the bottom of the list each owing less than 2,000 tons and two—Poulton and Scilly—owning none at all. There are good grounds for arguing that ownership of vessels is a less reliable guide to the standing of ports than is the tonnage of vessels entering and clearing them, but the truth of the matter is that an analysis of the latter figures makes little difference to the arguments advanced here: that many of the smaller ports enjoyed no appreciable share of the nation's trade, which was channelled overwhelmingly through a dozen or so larger ones.

The growing disparity between ports was connected in no small measure with the specialisation of regional trade discussed in the last chapter. London remained predominant in the south-east, stifling the foreign trade of the surrounding places, but encouraging them to send her cornstuffs and other provisions. None of them was able to make headway because none had a sufficiently bustling and extensive hinterland on which a major trade might be founded. By contrast, the growing industrial areas of central and northern England and Scotland encouraged the ports north of the Wash and Dee and on the Clyde and Forth.

There was, however, a very significant difference between the two areas of the country so far as the distribution of ports was concerned. In the south of England, where ports were easily built for a small traffic and where they had been greatly encouraged in the distant past, there were very many of them. But in the north of England, where population and economic activity had in the past been comparatively sparse, few ports had opened before the onset of Customs regulations discouraged their spreading. Nor were many new ports encouraged by the expansion of economic activity. So closely related were industrial development and internal water communications that importation of raw materials and exportation of manufactured goods or materials were concentrated on the handful of ports which commanded the major estuaries. The same was roughly true of Scotland. Many small places around the coast owed their existence to fishing rather than trade, and the few large ports commanded the bulk of the country's trade.

By 1789–91, when the Industrial Revolution boom was well under way, the north-eastern and north-western ports between them handled 40 per cent of the tonnage entering and 51 per cent of the tonnage leaving England and Wales, while London accounted for a further 37 per cent and 27 per cent respectively. The shares of the remaining regions were very low. Similarly, while large ports were to be found in all regions of the country, the largest were overwhelmingly in the north, leaving London and Bristol as the major trading centres and Dover as the principal packet port south of the line from Dee to Humber.

The same pattern was true of Scotland. Out of 30–34 Scottish ports, Port Glasgow and Greenock on the Clyde and Leith and Bo'ness on the Forth accounted for 46 per cent of tonnage entering and 57 per cent of tonnage clearing in the years 1776–1780, and in 1790 those same ports owned 46 per cent of all the Scottish tonnage. The only other significant places were Aberdeen, Alloa, Dundee, Kirkcaldy and Montrose, which between them owned a further 29 per cent. By 1789–91 things had changed slightly with the growth of western ports such as Ayr, Irvine and Portpatrick that were involved in the Irish trade (especially in coal), and the four major ports entered and cleared only 43 and 47 per cent respectively of the Scottish totals.[2]

Shipping Entering and Clearing English and Welsh Ports in the Foreign Trade, by Region, 1789–91

a) Regional Aggregates and Percentage of Total Tonnage

		ENTERING		CLEARING	
	No. of Ports	tonnage (000)	% of Total	tonnage (000)	% of Total
London	1	527	37·0	391	26·6
North-west	6	302	21·1	484	32·9
North-east	8	266	18·7	269	18·3
East Anglia	13	52	3·6	62	4·2
South-east	5	72	5·0	55	3·7
South	10	61	4·3	33	2·2
South-west	19	135	9·5	114	7·8
Wales	8	11	0·8	62	4·2

b) Average Tonnage Entering and Clearing Major and Minor Ports

Region	ENTERING		CLEARING	
	MAJOR PORTS	MINOR PORTS	MAJOR PORTS	MINOR PORTS
London	526,509	—	391,357	—
North-west	74,474	1,834	120,753	290
North-east	81,068	4,561	84,060	3,403
East Anglia	16,651	1,744	25,420	1,013
South-east	31,739	2,853	27,072	330
South	16,445	1,710	9,119	852
South-west	32,732	2,304	22,199	2,634
Wales	0	1,421	31,755	4,394

Calculated from Tables in PRO CUSTOMS 17/11-13

Despite this vast range in the tonnage of shipping frequenting the various ports, there were clearly defined patterns of development into which most, if not all, of them fell during the eighteenth century. There were those in which improvements were unnecessary; those where the provision of piers or the cutting of channels was enough; and those where increasing trade could be accommodated only by the construction of wet docks. The ports might also be further subdivided into those where improvements flowed naturally from pre-existing levels of trade, and those which were deliberately created *ab initio* to serve the needs of local landowners, industrialists or speculators. The last sort were most commonly to be found as 'artificial' harbours created outside the traditional port towns.

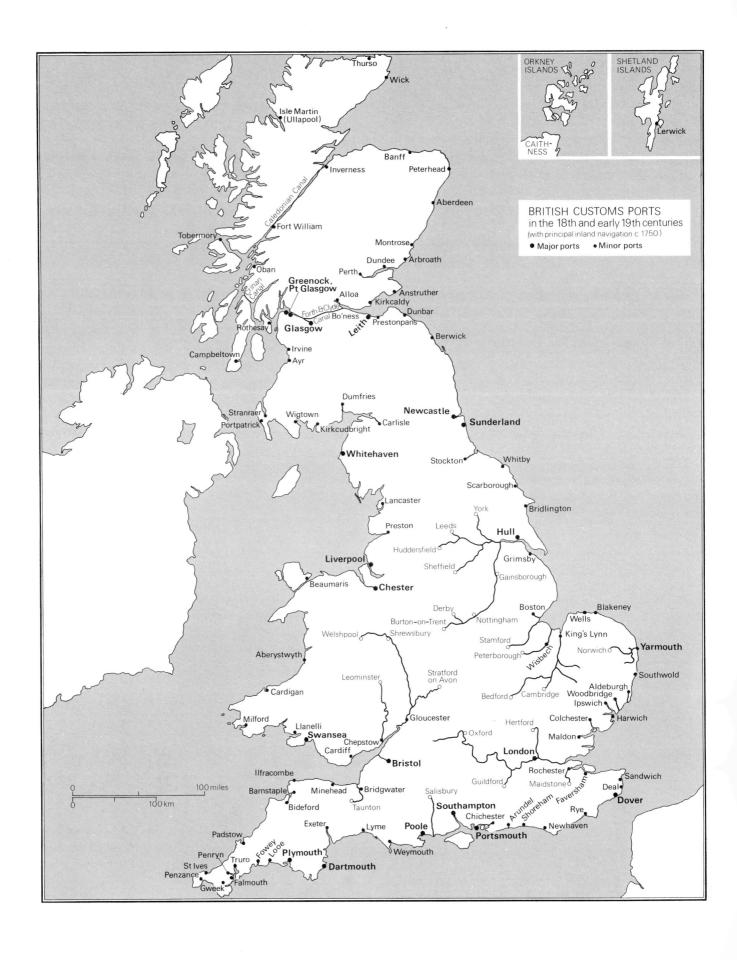

ORKNEY ISLANDS

SHETLAND ISLANDS

CAITH-NESS

Lerwick

BRITISH CUSTOMS PORTS
in the 18th and early 19th centuries
(with principal inland navigation c. 1750)
● Major ports   • Minor ports

Thurso
Wick
Isle Martin
(Ullapool)
Banff
Inverness
Peterhead
Aberdeen
Tobermory
Fort William
Montrose
Oban
Dundee
Arbroath
Perth
**Greenock,
Pt Glasgow**
Alloa
Anstruther
Caledonian Canal
Kirkcaldy
Crinan Canal
Forth & Clyde
Canal Bo'ness
Dunbar
Rothesay
Glasgow
Leith
Prestonpans
Irvine
Berwick
Campbeltown
Ayr
Dumfries
Stranraer
Wigtown
Newcastle
Portpatrick
Kirkcudbright
Carlisle
Sunderland
Whitehaven
Stockton
Whitby
Scarborough
Lancaster
Bridlington
York
Preston
Leeds
Hull
Huddersfield
Grimsby
Liverpool
Sheffield
Gainsborough
Beaumaris
Chester
Boston
Blakeney
Derby
Wells
Aberystwyth
Burton-on-Trent
Nottingham
King's Lynn
Shrewsbury
Yarmouth
Welshpool
Stamford
Norwich
Peterborough
Wisbech
Southwold
Cardigan
Leominster
Stratford
on Avon
Aldeburgh
Woodbridge
Bedford
Cambridge
Ipswich
Milford
Llanelli
Gloucester
Colchester
Harwich
Swansea
Hertford
Maldon
Chepstow
Oxford
Cardiff
London
Bristol
Rochester
Sandwich
Ilfracombe
Guildford
Maidstone
Deal
Barnstaple
Minehead
Bridgwater
Salisbury
Faversham
Dover
Bideford
Taunton
Southampton
Shoreham
Rye
Exeter
Lyme
Chichester
Arundel
Newhaven
Padstow
Poole
Penryn
Fowey
Weymouth
Portsmouth
Truro
Looe
St Ives
Plymouth
Penzance
Falmouth
Dartmouth
Gweek

100 miles
100 km

2. THE UNIMPROVED HARBOURS

The first group of ports—those undergoing no significant improvement—fall fairly easily into three broad categories. There were decayed or decaying places such as Blakeney and Rye, where the level of trade was insufficient to finance even necessary physical improvements. More common were the prosperous small places with limited agricultural hinterlands which were expanding too slowly to cause congestion in reasonably adequate harbours. Moreover, ports such as Wisbech which were involved chiefly in coastal trade were able to build up a large aggregate tonnage without straining their facilities because of the relatively rapid turn-round of coasters. Other small ports—especially those owning little of their own shipping—were not subject to the same congestion as the larger ports because, on the whole, ships did not lay up in them. They were visited for specific purposes, and often only at certain seasons of the year, following the harvest or during the fishery.

In marked constrast stood those fortunate major ports serving rapidly developing, or very substantial, hinterlands, yet possessing natural harbours able to accommodate the changes of the seventeenth century and the immense growth of the eighteenth century with only minor adjustments, chiefly to their quays and handling equipment. Lynn, Yarmouth, Portsmouth, Southampton, Poole and Dartmouth all managed to receive and despatch more than 10,000 tons of shipping per annum in the late eighteenth century without significant changes, while Newcastle built up a very large foreign trade and an immense coastal trade without extending her harbour. Its historian, Guthrie, sometime Secretary of the Tyne Improvement Commissioners, thought the Tyne had been more than adequate till the middle of the nineteenth century: 'the capabilities of the river in its unimproved state—a "Natural Dock", as it was called—were great for the class of vessels then in use'.[3] Some of the tonnage accredited to Newcastle actually passed through coal shipment places such as Blyth and Seaton which were within the port of Newcastle but not classified as separate ports for Customs purposes, but it seems unlikely that this would alter the position very much. Certainly it was possible for all the major ports except Liverpool to manage without improvements during the Commercial Revolution, and only towards the end of the eighteenth century did dock-building become essential. Or perhaps, as we shall see, it would be more accurate to say that towards the end of the century the major ports were able to put off dock-building no longer.

3. THE RIVER PORTS

Many places, both large and small, were not in a position to defer improvement: either they modified their facilities or they failed as ports. Those situated many miles from the mouths of navigable rivers were among the first to react to expanding trade, since their deficiencies appeared more catastrophic than those of ports nearer the sea. Accumulations of silt and excessive meanders would assuredly strangle them, while any increase in the number or size of ships would create more problems by weakening river banks and demanding wider or deeper navigation channels.

Fortunately the need to do something substantial to the rivers coincided with two encouraging factors, one consequential and the other quite fortuitous. An increase in the number of ships provided the money; and the awareness of the possibilities of cutting and embanking, learned from the drainage of the Fens earlier in the seventeenth century, prepared the way for the necessary 'engineering'. How the engineers were trained, and to what extent they were qualified in the seventeenth century is, unfortunately, far from clear.[4]

At least four ports—Exeter, Chester, Colchester and

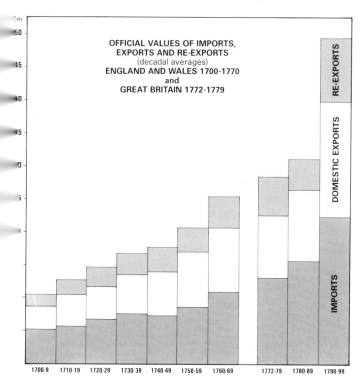

OFFICIAL VALUES OF IMPORTS, EXPORTS AND RE-EXPORTS (decadal averages) ENGLAND AND WALES 1700-1770 and GREAT BRITAIN 1772-1779

Grimsby—endeavoured to improve their prospects by making cuts during the period 1695–1705 (at roughly the same time as a number of rivers were also being improved). Exeter was probably the first of them. Neighbouring Dartmouth and Plymouth had good port facilities, but were cut off from the industrial districts of the West Country by Dartmoor, while Exeter, which had excellent communications with the hinterland, had poor communications with the sea. The Exe had long been navigable only as far as Topsham, some three or four miles down river, and as early as the 1560s a new cut had bypassed the worst of the river. This cut was extended in the 1670s and considerably improved in the 1690s at a cost of around £20,000, to enable ships of 150 tons—large for that time—to reach Exeter. The situation at Chester was similar. With extensive silting threatening to close the Dee, an Act of 1700 empowered the Corporation of Chester to appoint Commissioners to improve it, though little is known about their work. At Colchester an Act of 1698 enabled that town's Corporation to improve the river Colne from Colchester to the sea at Wivenhoe. And between 1697 and 1703 the Corporation of Grimsby (so decayed that it no longer appeared in Customs' lists of ports) attempted to cleanse and improve their silted haven by diverting through it the river Freshney, which had long ago deserted it for another exit to the sea north of the town.

None of these schemes was totally successful, and it is clear that there was a limit to the extent to which cutting and cleansing could re-establish ports which were 'too far' from the sea in places given to excessive silting. At Grimsby, for instance, the Freshney soon broke through to its preferred route to the sea, though the major problem here was inadequate finance to indulge in effective works, and it was almost a century before repairs were effected. Colchester also had problems derived from heavy silting and poor finance. When Defoe visited the place in the 1720s he found that only 'hoys and small barks' could reach the hithe—the landing stage—in the town, and that larger vessels were handled at Wivenhoe.[5] By 1750 the Colne was 'much choked up' and the lock 'in decaying condition'.[6]

At Chester the river Dee also fell into decay within a few years, but there was a world of difference between Chester, a small major port, and Colchester or Grimsby. Formidable financial resources were assembled (to the dismay of Liverpool, which petitioned in Parliament against a Dee improvement Bill in 1733), and eventually the works were handed over to a Company of Proprietors with a capital of £52,000.[7] Nathaniel Kinderley, who organised the company, was also the engineer who, between 1733 and c. 1737, planned and executed a new cut, almost ten miles long, between Chester and Flint Castle.

Needless to say, there was controversy among engineers almost from the start as to the efficiency of this cut (and similar works). One side argued that impounded water would be adequate for scouring the cut and its entrance, while the other side argued that such a narrow cut would forego the scouring action of tidal water.[8] Whichever side was theoretically correct, the fact remains that the new cut was not a long-term solution to Chester's problem, and ships increasingly made use of down-river trans-shipment places such as Connah's Quay, and again the old problem of Custom's definition arises. Some at least of the trade 'of Chester' was in fact coal exported from the north Wales coast to Ireland.

Compared with the works at Grimsby, Colchester and Chester, the improvement to the Exe served its town well for the whole of the eighteenth century. Nevertheless a considerable volume of trade continued to be carried by barge or land between the city and Topsham and, though no new work was necessary in the eighteenth century, it was thought advisable in the early nineteenth century to deepen, straighten and lengthen the canal by two and a half miles, in order to admit larger vessels to the city quay. At the same time a small basin was constructed opposite the quay where ships could float and discharge their cargoes, and wharves and warehouses were erected. Together the works cost over £113,000, which is some indication of the city's will to survive as a port, and also of its relative success in the recent past.[9]

Apart from the ports mentioned above, there was only one place of any note where extensive river work was feasible in the eighteenth century, namely Boston, where access to the Wash via the river Witham was beginning to cause concern by the middle of the century. Improvements were undertaken in the late 1760s with the erection of a 'Grand Sluice' on the Witham, which deepened the river for inland navigation and also scoured below the town, where the river was adequate for large vessels until the late nineteenth century, when a dock became necessary.[10]

With the completion of these works it is reasonably true to say that all river ports either possessed good natural rivers, had improved imperfect rivers, or were not worth bothering about in view of current technical skills. It was not until the early nineteenth century that increasing trade

Boston: riverside warehouses of the early nineteenth century. The stone ground floor of that on the left above dates from the Middle Ages, probably early C13th. Left, a fine warehouse of c. 1810, with Boston Stump in the background.

cast doubt on the adequacy of river channels at four notable ports: Stockton, Ipswich, Lowestoft and Lynn.

Stockton was a rapidly growing provision and coal port which was well placed on the Tees until the pressure of trade led to the creation of the Tees Navigation Company in 1808. Two cuts were made to straighten and deepen the river, and jetties were built to fix some of the sandbanks, with the result that the tonnage of vessels using the port almost doubled between 1804 and 1814.[11] But for Stockton the improvements came too late: within two decades she was overtaken by a new port—Middlesbrough—created nearer the sea. By contrast a longer-term success resulted from the improvement of the river Orwell below Ipswich in the years following 1806, when the inefficient—or incompetent—Corporation of Ipswich had the control of the navigation taken out of its hands in favour of a body of commissioners drawn from the users of the port. Not only was the cutting and dredging a success: by the late 1830s the port was already beginning a most important new venture which brought it into the ranks of dock-building ports.[12]

King's Lynn also suffered from heavy silting obstructing navigation in the couple of miles of river leading down to the Wash. However, the solution in this case, recommended by John Rennie, was to remove meanders in the river Ouse immediately above Lynn in order to bring a greater force of water past the port. After many delays the Eau Brink Cut was completed in 1821, its vast cost—around half a million pounds—reflecting both the strength

of the commercial community and the benefit accruing to local agriculture through better land drainage. The cut was successful, and it was not until 1852/3 that the river below Lynn was straightened by the Norfolk Estuary Cut.[13]

Long-term prosperity eluded most of the river ports described above. Some of them had poor inland communications, and most of them had a continuing battle with sand or silt which in the end they lost. Even in the eighteenth century several had difficulty in keeping open their newly dredged channels, and shortage of money ruined them as effectively as superfluous silt. In the long run neither meandering nor straight cut rivers were adequate for extensive shipping unless they were of immense dimensions and expensively maintained. However, failure did not immediately follow the silting of the Exe or Dee, for the simple reason that in the eighteenth century the profits on trade were able to encompass the trans-shipment of goods from ship to barge or barge to ship. It did not matter unduly if goods travelled from Exeter to Topsham by barge, since land carriage would have been much more expensive. Eventually excessive handling charges would inhibit such trans-shipment and encourage merchants to bypass the inland ports in favour of more direct communication between down-river ports and the hinterland. But for the time being, at least, the up-river ports were able to hold their own, as can be seen from the relative success of Wisbech which, though the furthest of all river ports from the sea, was ahead of more than forty ports in the number of coasters (388) she received in 1791.

4. THE PIER PORTS

The problems of up-river ports were probably less than those of many ports on the open coastline. Silt worked insidiously but could be removed, whereas the pressure of wind and wave, and the overwhelming ferocity of storms, constantly threatened the very existence of exposed ports which did not take energetic measures to protect themselves and their shipping. 'Artificial' ports could be created, where some specific and pressing need arose, by building piers. The commonest approach was to use a pier to form a harbour in the sharpest curve of a cove or small bay, where surrounding hills would add shelter; but it was also possible, as a last resort, to form a harbour by pushing out two piers from a straight beach. In both cases there were natural limits to size, and it is not surprising that the majority of these ports were located in the sheltered coves of the Cornish coast, beneath the chalk cliffs of the south-east, along the wild hills of the north-east coast, and in Scotland. These were the areas where the terrain precluded the erection of other, more satisfactory facilities, but where, for various reasons, ports had to be made in the seventeenth and eighteenth centuries.

St. Ives was a typical example of the larger cove or bay ports. Standing on the sheltered western shore of St. Ives bay, it was difficult of access by land and concerned chiefly with fishing and the exportation of locally mined tin and copper. Imports were almost entirely provisions and equipment for the local community, brought coastwise. The port itself lay in a smaller bay within the bay, and was protected by 'Battery Point', a large promontory from which a single pier was projected southwards, long before the 1760s when an old decayed pier was replaced, at a cost of around £10,000, by another designed by Smeaton. However, St. Ives found, as did most similarly situated places, that piers built out into the sea to protect shipping are themselves subject to immense forces, and Smeaton's work required constant and expensive attention. Moreover, again typically, the waves driving into the bay from the north-west which were barred from shipping by the pier nevertheless caused trouble for the rest of the port's history by bringing sand across the harbour mouth. Cove or bay ports, almost by definition, had no fresh water flowing through them to flush out the harbour, and the buildup of beach within them was a common problem. (Dover, a notable exception, nevertheless had an inadequte flow of water for scouring purposes.) On the other hand the pier did at least mean that ships could anchor and load and unload in deeper

Pier harbours in Scotland: (from top) Scullomie, Sutherland, making use of natural rock line. Ham, Caithness, built of flagstone for the coastal shipment of flagstones. Ollaberry, Shetland: a simple stone pier with protecting wall. Keiss, Caithness, with inner harbour and outer stilling basin; incoming waves spend themselves on the sloping beach and do not enter the inner harbour.

water than might otherwise have been available: the alternative was loading on the open beach or at an unprotected quay if the water happened to be deep enough, neither of which courses was very satisfactory.

Pier ports, nestling against the picturesque backdrop of surrounding cliffs, are generally so small and compact as to be fully comprehended at a glance in a way that is quite impossible in the major commercial ports. But the ease with which their basic functions can be grasped is an indication that they were never likely to succeed on any grand scale. On the water side they were usually small, tidal and difficult to maintain. On the land side they suffered from difficult communications with restricted hinterlands whose small populations generated little general commerce. Fish and minerals were their usual trade. In fact many of the smaller cove ports do not appear as ports on the Customs' lists.

Some pier ports, such as Ilfracombe, Mevagissey or Torquay were built by local landowners for purely local purposes, and on the whole 'back-carriage' was so poor in the south-west as to encourage many tiny places along the coast. They enjoyed a modicum of success only when their *raison d'être* was the sea rather than inland connexions, or where there was some very special reason for their creation. Thus they performed well as fishing harbours when the catch was sold out of the port. Many of the south-western harbours, such as St. Ives, Penzance and Polkerris, all with piers built or rebuilt in the 1750s or 1760s, and Trevaunance with an ancient pier rebuilt in the 1790s, owed as much to the pilchard, herring or mackerel as to anything else. Brixham, built specifically for the fishery in the early nineteenth century, was one of the leading fishing ports (sending its expertise round the coast when the fishing industry grew up in the northern ports in the mid-nineteenth century), and, intent on maintaining that position, petitioned vigorously against the building of a pier-harbour in neighbouring Torquay for fear that it might make a better fishing port. The pier harbours of Ramsgate in the south-east, and Scarborough and Bridlington in the north-east also became important fishing places, though that was not why they were built.

On the broad sweep of the east coast of Scotland, almost the only alternative to landing fish or provisions on the open beach was provided by diminutive piers in small—and not very frequent—natural bays, or by simple pier harbours. Several of the more important Scottish fishing harbours were subsidised by the Scottish Fisheries Board in

the eighteenth century, though many of the poorer fishing communities (that is those without natural harbours and access to good markets) were too poor even to erect simple piers for protection, and had to make do with the meagre shelter provided by natural features alone.[14]

Although 'artificial' harbours might be built for general local needs or for the fishery, the most successful were those built for mineral shipment. Certain types of mineral exploitation, especially of tin and copper deposits, took place in the geological formations which were likely to be associated with rocky coastlines, as in Cornwall. In other words, there was a symbiotic relationship between mines and adjacent harbours such as Portreath built in the 1760s, Hayle (by the Cornish Copper Company) in the 1780s, and—for export of china clay—Charlestown in the 1790s and Pentewan in the 1820s. Porthleven, hewn out of granite between 1811 and 1825 under the supervision of Thomas Telford, performed a triple function as mineral port, service port for Helston, and speculative harbour of refuge.[15]

Fortunately, the hills and precipitous roads down to water level that would have hampered normal port operations worked in favour of mineral shipment, since gravity feed was the best and cheapest means of loading ships. (Ports on flat coastlines had eventually to devise complicated mechanisms for raising minerals before they could be loaded on board ship.) However, while gravity offers a positive advantage to cove ports, what must drop down will not so easily go up: such ports could never match their export facilities with corresponding import facilities. In fact the relatively primitive nature of their hinterlands made few demands upon them in this regard.

Cornwall was undoubtedly the area with the most spectacular cove ports, but it was not the only region with minerals adjacent to a coastline lacking good natural harbours. Parts of the Northumberland and Cumberland coalfields were similarly placed, and Cullercoats, Blyth, Seaton and Seaham on the east, and Maryport, Harrington and Whitehaven on the west were developed as pier ports to serve them. On the east coast there were, of course, the major natural harbours of Tyne, Wear and Tees, but there were also long stretches north and south of them which encouraged the building of new ports. Cullercoats, for instance, was built specifically to serve the Whitley colliery in the 1670s, and declined with the colliery and was in ruins by the 1770s. Seaton was constructed at almost the same time by the Delavel family of coal-owners, who built two piers around the mouth of the Seaton burn, on which a sluice was built to provide water for flushing the harbour. It was not a success, partly because of the shallowness of the entrance and the damage to the piers, and in the 1750s a completely new entrance, 800 feet long, 30 feet wide and 52 feet deep, was cut through solid rock. A new pier and breakwaters were built for protection from the rough seas, but the most important feature was the provision of gates at both ends of the new entrance, making it the earliest 'dock' on the east coast, capable of floating fifteen to twenty 300 ton vessels.[16]

Despite the colossal work involved in the excavation of Seaton Sluice, the most substantial new harbour for the coalfield was that at Seaham, built by Lord Londonderry for his local mines in the 1830s. Unlike most pier ports it was not a simple harbour enclosed by two piers, but a series of interconnecting docks placed at the foot of steep cliffs from which coal was fed by gravity to waiting ships. Because it was so late in construction, and so well built and maintained (at least until recently), Seaham remains a most impressive place, all the more so because of its isolation and because it is incongruously surrounded by agriculture rather than by the remains of industry or mining.

If, however, ports are to be classified by incongruity, surely the most curious on the east coast must be Port Mulgrave, to the north of Whitby. Built in the seventeenth century for the local alum mines, it consisted of a sheltered pier fed by cable buckets from the cliff top. No road was built, and since the paths have decayed the ruined pier cannot now be reached safely from the road.

None of these artificial harbours can compare in importance with Whitehaven. About the port itself there was nothing particularly remarkable apart from its size. 'The inner harbour', Sir John Rennie wrote,[17]

> is formed at the head of the bay, and consists of a number of artificial piers constructed from time to time as the case required, without regard to scientific arrangement as to the design or construction; but as these works were completed previous to Smeaton's Report, 8th April 1768, when this branch of Civil Engineering was but little understood, this need not be a matter of surprise.

The harbour was, in fact, begun as a simple pier harbour in the late seventeenth century by the local colliery owner, Lowther, and the collieries and the port (handed over to a Trust in 1708) grew together. The 'Old Quay' and 'Old Tongue' taken over by the Trust were extended northwards by the 'New Tongue', the 'Bulwark' and the 'North Wall', but all of them, whether used for shipping coal or iron ore, or receiving colonial tobacco in return, were dry at low water. An attempt to gain access to deeper water led to the building of the 'New Quay' early in the eighteenth century, but it was not completely successful, and it certainly did not cure the main problem, the sanding up of the harbour. Recommendations by Smeaton and John Rennie (the latter in 1814) suggesting the lengthening of the piers out beyond the low water mark were rejected because of the heavy cost, though suggestions by Huddart that the harbour entrance should be narrowed by splaying the Old Quay and North Pier were taken up around 1804, 'by which means it was calculated that the waves would be deflected and dispersed.'[18] They were not. Eventually the nineteenth century port was created to the design of Sir John Rennie in the years following 1822, when the piers were extended out to sea.

As a result of these various extensions of quay space, Whitehaven was able to handle one of the largest tonnages of vessels in the country, with 2,153 ships of 224,934 tons clearing for Ireland in 1790,[19] with a few others—though not many—going elsewhere, chiefly to America, and around 25,000 tons going coastwise. It must, however, be noted that this large tonnage was handled not because of the extent of the harbour room or quay length alone, but because of highly efficient equipment, which will be discussed below (p. 100).

The Lowthers (who became earls of Lonsdale) were the leading Cumberland coal-owners, but there were others struggling to assert themselves and seeking to build ports in order to open up their mines. The Curwen family had waggonways linking their mines to Harrington and Workington in the eighteenth century, while others shipped ironstone, lime and fireclay, chiefly to Scotland. However, neither port enjoyed much improvement in the eighteenth or early nineteenth centuries, not least because of the hostility of Sir James Lowther, who, though he employed Smeaton to report on possible improvements to his property in the harbour at Workington,[20] appears to have opposed improvements which would have benefited rival coal-owners. More substantial work than the wooden piers at Workington was, however, undertaken by the Senhouse family at Maryport, where a small harbour, again for shipping coals to Ireland, was created by building huge wooden breakwaters at the mouth of the river Eden which, according to Ayton when he visited the place around 1814, 'show by various gaps and fractures the power of the body that they have to withstand.'[21]

5. HARBOURS OF REFUGE

A second group of ports relying heavily on piers were the harbours of refuge, serving a purpose that was determined by their situation on the coast rather than their relationship to a hinterland. Exceptionally stormy or dangerous coasts where shipping was at risk did not always enjoy the benefit of good natural harbours into which ships might run for shelter, and the only relief, as ships grew in number and in size, and ventured to sea in winter as well as summer, was to be gained by building artificial harbours. There was, from time to time, pressure for harbours of refuge in the south-west, but there were, in reality, plenty of safe anchorages in that part of the country, and nothing was done beyond the speculative creation of Porthleven *c.* 1811–1825 by the Porthleven Harbour Company, at least

The flourishing fishing port of Eyemouth bases its security on a large stone pier and a diverted river. Girvan harbour (below), once a minor railway port, now reduced to receiving fishing boats at the quay and yachts at the wooden pier within its river mouth: most of the 15 acres of harbour are unused.

Lights were a vital ingredient of port life: the octagonal tower at Harwich, replacing an earlier light in the 1820s and itself replaced in the 1870s.

partially as a harbour of refuge. The chief demand for refuge was on the long run down the exposed east coast, which was devoid of good natural harbours between the Tees and the Wash; and the vessels chiefly at risk were the colliers bound for London.

The concentrated nature of this east coast trade provided a solution to the worst problem facing harbours of refuge, which was not so much violence of the seas as the shortage of funds. Those created for the coal trade could be paid for by that trade simply by levying a tax at the limited number of shipping places, and this was done. In 1701 an Act of Parliament granted duties on all coal leaving the northern ports for the maintenance of piers at Whitby (which differed from the ports discussed above insofar as it was a river port rather than a cove port) and as a result two ancient piers were largely rebuilt. Further Acts in 1735 and 1750 provided funds for their improvement, and later Acts supported other works which made Whitby one of the most crowded of the eastern anchorages whenever impending storms made it wise to run for cover.

Two further harbours built for the coal trade were at Scarborough and Bridlington, where typical cove ports were constructed. Bridlington was probably the first of the three ports to receive duties on coal as a result of a Privy Council grant, which was followed by an Act in 1697 creating a Harbour Commission to rebuild the piers, which at this stage were still made of wood and subject to regular and extensive damage. Not until the end of the eighteenth century, when both north and south piers had been greatly lengthened to make a bigger harbour, was an attempt made to case part of the north pier with stone.

Scarborough was improved by a tax on coal following an Act of 1732. Before that date there was only one pier maintained by the town itself, but once the coal duties were available a programme of building, rebuilding and extension began and continued for the rest of the century. The Scarborough Harbour Commission appointed by an Act of 1752 to maintain the works built a third pier in the 1760s, but they were still adding to the piers at the end of the Napoleonic Wars, a reflection, perhaps, of the value of the coal duties rather than the tonnage of shipping sheltering in the three Yorkshire ports.

The second area where there was no natural harbour of refuge was the Downs, and this was a particularly serious matter as the growth of London's long-distance overseas trade and south-western coastal trade involved an increasing number of ships anchoring on the Downs waiting to enter the Thames. In 1774, as pressure mounted from London merchants, the House of Commons took the unusual step of instituting an enquiry into the whole business, and four years later a formidable pressure group led by the Lord Mayor of London expressed itself in favour of building a new port at Ramsgate, roughly where vessels losing their anchors or slipping their cables during storms would be brought by the flood tide and prevailing winds.[22] In marked contrast to the cove ports, where piers were used to extend and sharpen the curve of a natural bay, Ramsgate was to consist entirely of water enclosed by two vast piers pushed out into the sea. Commenced in 1749 by the Ramsgate Harbour Trust, it was a bold venture which, in the event, was more easily conceived in general terms than executed in particular.

Without going into intricate detail (which may be obtained from Smeaton's *Reports* and, with perceptive comments, in Sir John Rennie's *Theory . . . of . . . Harbours*), it is worth considering some of the features of Ramsgate for their general implications. Firstly, it was not designed and executed by a civil engineer, but evolved out of the advice of many engineers, some of whom were competent and some less so. The east and west piers, for instance, were begun to two different designs employing completely different materials and, even when wood was abandoned in favour of stone, there was no agreement or consistency about the method of laying foundations. Moreover, the *detail* of construction was the concern not of the early engineers but of the contractors, masons and carpenters, while the role of the resident engineer—who was quite capable of ignoring the advice of the consulting engineer—has yet to be explored for this crucial period in the emergence of civil engineering as a profession. It would not be unfair to suggest that in 1750 there was nobody who fully understood the problems involved in large scale construction on difficult sites, and the consequences were disastrous and expensive. 'As they', wrote Sir John Rennie of the piers[23]

had been constructed when the science of Civil Engineering had made but comparatively little progress in Great Britain, they were not finished in that substantial and durable manner which is so essential in all maritime works: it was not therefore to be expected that they could withstand the test of ages much less the violent storms of the ocean, without continual heavy repairs, in addition to the expense of keeping the harbour clear of mud and silt.

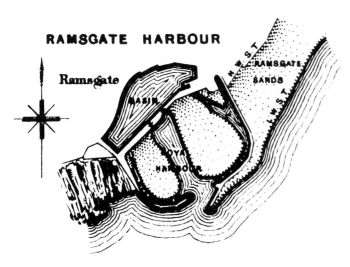

Ramsgate harbour of refuge: two massive piers pushed out to sea with great difficulty and little effect.

Quite apart from the damage which lengthy piers were liable to sustain, there were two major problems associated with this kind of site. The first was silt. 'Harbours which have no land or backwater cannot naturally keep open for a long course of years', Smeaton wrote in his *Report* of 1774.[24]

> For, in proportion as the work of the piers has advanced, the space being inclosed, and the water rendered more quiet, and in that respect more fit for the purposes of a harbour, in much about the same proportion has the silting taken place, and must continue to increase till the area of the harbour becomes dry land, and, instead of a receptacle for ships, exhibits a field of corn.

Smeaton calculated that current dredging methods could remove one-tenth of an inch of silt per week from the harbour, whereas it accumulated at the rate of one-fifth of an inch! His solution to the problem was the creation of an inner harbour with lock gates and sluices which could hold back water from high tides and release it at low tides to provide a carefully directed scour, so effective in fact that initially they undermined their own foundations. Eventually this inner harbour, achieved by building a cross wall, was able to act as a twelve-acre floating harbour, though this was not, of course, its purpose.

The second problem was what Smeaton called the 'agitation and inquietude which in general rendered it more eligible for vessels of burden . . . to subject themselves to . . . the risk of riding it out in the Downs, than come into the harbour till they had received some actual damage.'[25] In other words, the harbour was so big, and its wide mouth

so exposed, that the sea was almost as rough inside as it was outside. It was not until 1790 that the 'advanced pier' suggested by Smeaton to protect and narrow the entrance at last made Ramsgate a really useful harbour of refuge. It had taken forty years, and was accomplished at such a huge cost that the merchants who had advocated it—or their successors—were soon doubting whether the returns were worthwhile. With constant repairs to the piers, adjustments to the cross wall and sluices, endless dredging, a silly mistake in constructing the dry dock, and the reconstruction of the entrance, the harbour had cost £1·5 million when the chairman of the Trust gave evidence to the Select Committee on Foreign Trade in 1822, and Sir John Rennie thought it had cost a further £0·5 million by 1850 and though by deducting the various charges he reduced the total to £1·29 million the fact remains that Ramsgate was the most expensive exercise in port building in the eighteenth century outside London.

Whether or not Ramsgate harbour was worth such an expenditure is not easily determined. Rennie produced average figures showing an impressive number of vessels taking refuge there:[26]

1780–9	1,723	1820–9	13,268
1790–9	4,993	1830–9	14,344
1800–9	6,954	1840–9	14,149
1810–19	11,371		

Assuming these would have been lost without the harbour, many thousands of lives and tens of millions of pounds were saved, and the passing toll of 3d. per ton would seem amply justified as an insurance against loss. But it could equally be argued that a smaller and cheaper harbour would have done as well, and would have been ready sooner and so saved an equally large number of ships that were lost during the lengthy period in which Ramsgate was unserviceable.

Compared with Ramsgate's meagre commercial activity, Dover, always the busiest of the cove ports, was hugely successful. The crossing thence to France was the shortest possible, and consequently much favoured both by passengers and mail packets. Pier ports were ideal for this sort of traffic, depending as it did on the very fast turn-round of a limited number of relatively small vessels requiring little in the way of warehousing, handling equipment or quay space, and Dover was able initially to capture this trade because of the shelter afforded by the Western Heights. At least as early as 1495 a pier had been built, and Henry VIII contributed a substantial sum of money to build a second one. Inevitably beach drift began to block the harbour, and at the end of the sixteenth century the river Dour (which entered the bay to the east of the harbour) was diverted between the piers and pent up, in what became known as the Pent, to facilitate flushing. The problem was still only partially solved, and a century later an effort was made to concentrate the flushing by building a cross wall between the piers and penning up water with gates in what may well have been the first floating harbour in Britain. Nevertheless, when Defoe visited Dover in 1724, only a decade after the cross wall had been constructed, he found 'an ill repaired, dangerous, and good for little harbour and pier, very chargeable and little worth.'[27]

Improvements were eventually made, including gates at the landward end of the Pent which allowed small vessels to float there and provided more water for scouring purposes, but it must be stressed that the chief factor encouraging the development of shipping at Dover was not the quality of the harbour but the nature of the shipping itself. As noted above, the operation of packet boats, to which Dover's trade was almost entirely confined, did not demand magnificent facilities, and Dover enjoyed at an early date the same high ratio of tonnage to facilities that eluded the major commercial ports until the introduction of railways and steam shipping. (It was not until the middle of the nineteenth century that the vast modern harbour at Dover was built, partly as a harbour of refuge to replace Ramsgate, and partly for the convenience of the Royal Navy.)

6. THE TRAINING OF RIVERS

Compared with the many places where the pier made the port, there were a few where activity was basically in the natural mouth of the river which had to be 'trained' in order to improve its navigability. Here again the problem was silt, or rather the inability of the river to force its way through banks of mud, sand or shingle without moving over time or splitting into a delta system which was useless for shipping. Yarmouth is an excellent example of an undoubtedly important port, engaged particularly in the provision and fish trades, which fought a constant battle in early times against the southward drift of shingle which tended to push the mouth of the Yare with it. After digging

(over a period of almost three centuries) no fewer than seven new entrances to the Yare, the inhabitants, directed by a Dutch engineer, began the erection of two wooden piers which were completed around 1613 and effectively stabilised the haven entrance through to modern times.[28] 'Should this pier decay', wrote Greenville Collins in the 1690s, 'it would be the ruin of the herring fishery; notwithstanding the badness of the haven, yet such is the industry of the people of that place, that they have about 500 sail of ships belonging thereto.'[29]

A far more important port of this sort was Sunderland which, because of its coal shipments, was potentially one of the leading ports. Nevertheless, despite a huge trade, larger vessels took their loading in the roads, from flat-bottomed keels, and this expensive method of shipping continued until the beginning of the nineteenth century.[30] The problem is all too apparent from the plan of the harbour mouth in 1719, which shows a bifurcated stream losing its impetus among many sandbanks. The answer to this problem—a narrowing of the river to secure a more effective scour—was appreciated, but there was, in truth, no real understanding of the methods to be adopted to accomplish the desired end. The creation in 1717 of an agency for improvement—the River Wear Commission—was a step in the right direction, but the South Pier which they commenced in 1723 to direct the full force of the current against the sand bars was only partially successful because the northern channel—the Stell—was still open. In 1748 Charles Labelye (who built Westminster Bridge) reported in favour of building another pier to provide a stable entrance, and then directing all the river water through one channel, but he admitted that same degree of ignorance regarding tidal flows round piers that we have already noted concerning Ramsgate: 'After all,' he wrote, 'as no man can foresee all the consequences that may attend the erecting of a north pier, if it should happen to occasion visibly (which I hope it will not) a greater obstruction to navigation than it removes, it must be unbuilt and taken up.'[31] Understandably the Commissioners were not enthusiastic, and though they began the closure of the Stell channel, and altered the South Pier on many occasions, it was 1788 (after experiments with framework weighted with stones) before work on the North Pier began. It was more or less finished by the end of the century, but both piers were subject to subsequent alterations from time to time in order to improve their effects on the sands and waves.

CHAPTER THREE

The Emergence of Dock Systems 1690–1840

1. CONGESTION IN PORTS AND THE PROVISION OF LAYING-UP BASINS

Piers built in the seventeenth and eighteenth centuries enabled many ports to play a valuable role in the growth of their immediate hinterlands, but of the dozens of places improved in this way only Whitehaven, Sunderland and Dover made any significant contribution to the volume of trade during the Industrial Revolution, and then only because of the very specialised nature of the traffic they handled. The major commercial ports were river ports, and remained so. For them, docks alone could serve the needs of expanding trade.

The first, and for a long time the most serious, difficulty facing the major ports was not the provision of accommodation for ships while loading or unloading, but their disposition between voyages. Ships in many trades were laid up for the winter, and others were subject to seasonal demand. Lengthy stays in port were commonplace, and light ships—as empty ships were called—were an embarrassment in many places by the mid-eighteenth century. In the haven at Hull, for instance, ships lay several deep along the quays, and those on the outside were unloaded over those on the inside. Congestion such as this hampered the free movement of vessels, and caused endless damage to spars and rigging. Occasionally, it was said at Hull, small ships found themselves suspended between larger ones as the tide went out and the vessels grounded.

The damage sustained by regular grounding, though unavoidable during short stays in many ports, encouraged vessels to seek out sheltered and deeper water ports for wintering. One of the reasons why Whitby and Scarborough became considerable ship-owning places was that they were able to give adequate shelter to colliers in the winter. Other harbours were more commonly used by light

ships than by loaded ones. 'In the winter time', Defoe observed when he visited Ipswich,

> those great collier ships ... are always laid up: that is to say, the coal trade abates at London, the citizens are generally furnished, their stores taken in, and the demand is over; so that the great ships, the northern seas and coast being also dangerous, the nights long, and the voyage hazardous, go to sea no more, but lie by, the ships are unrigged, the sails, etc., carried ashore, the topmasts struck, and they ride moored in the river, under the advantages and security of sound ground, and a high woody shore, where they lie as safe as in a wet dock.[1]

This more attractive alternative—that ships might remain permanently afloat during their 'laying up'—had been available for no more than a quarter of a century. The first wet dock for commercial vessels—the Howland Great Wet Dock at Rotherhithe on the Thames—was built between 1697 and 1700 by the Bedford estate to enhance the value of property acquired through a marriage with the Howland heiress, and by 1703 there was a complete range of services for shipping, including the wet dock (with facilities for erecting masts) and two dry docks. Despite the importance of ship-repair facilities, it was the ten-acre dock which attracted most attention from commentators, artists and, eventually, historians. Unfortunately little is known about it, and there is even doubt about its designers (as there is for many of the early harbour and dock works). Traditionally the work is ascribed to George Sorocold, assisted by Thomas Steers,[2] but Professor Swann, in his pioneering investigation of dock engineers, has suggested that it should in fact be attributed to John Wells, of the famous Rotherhithe shipbuilding firm of that name (which eventually acquired the dock in 1763).[3]

As for its ancestry, there were two possible lines. The

first was the pound lock, originating on the Continent in the fifteenth century and introduced to a number of English rivers to impound and deepen their water in the sixteenth century. It was a very similar idea to the later floating harbour, and engineers writing in the nineteenth century were inclined to see the lock on the Exeter canal (*c.* 1564) as the forerunner of the eighteenth century docks.[4] The second ancestor was the dry dock, originally for large vessels which could not easily be hauled out of the water, and which was basically a pound lock in reverse.

In fact the earliest known wet dock was not the Howland, but a one-and-a-half acre dock constructed around 1660 at Blackwall for fitting out, repairing and sheltering the large East Indiamen built there. It was later absorbed into the Brunswick fitting out dock (see below, p. 55).[5] However, as the Blackwall dock was of limited size, for

the use of the shipyard rather than for receiving light ships generally, the Howland Dock can justly claim to have been the first 'dock' in Britain. But it must be emphasised that it was not a *commercial* dock in the modern sense. There were no quays at which goods might be handled, and no Customs business was transacted; it was, as indicated above, simply a place for laying up light ships, and so relieving congestion in the commercial area of the river.

The Howland Dock was not speedily and generally copied, on the Thames or elsewhere, because docks were not generally needed in the early years of the century. The Thames was not overcrowded, and it is possible that the Howland Dock did not offer very much in the way of additional benefits compared with, say, the harbour at Ipswich. Certainly there is no evidence that Howland Dock itself was congested, and in 1725 it was leased by the South

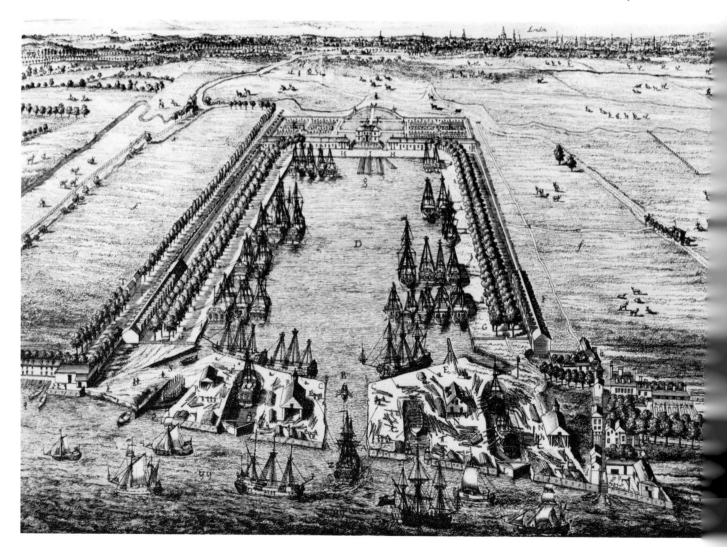

Sea Company as a base for its whaling operations.[6] Other whaling firms used it after the South Sea Company withdrew, so much so that it became known as Greenland Dock, and that name was retained for the modern dock that replaced it.

The only port known to have followed London's example was Bristol, where the laying up of ships between seasons was also a matter of some inconvenience. Around 1710 a private company led by Joshua Franklyn constructed a small dock at Sea Mills on the Avon, roughly half way between Bristol and the Severn. It was no more successful than Howland Dock, and was similarly turned over to whalers for a time. It appears to have been abandoned around 1760 (though pieces of the wall still remain), at approximately the same time that another such dock, later called Merchants' Dock, was constructed on the Avon just

over three-quarters of a mile from the commercial centre of the port, and immediately to the north of the later entrance to the Floating Harbour at Rownham.[7]

Howland Dock—and presumably Sea Mills Dock— would never have been built so easily by merchants for existing or potential *trade*, and it is doubtful if it would have been built for idle *shipping* before the situation on the river became intolerable. In other words, it was more easily built as a landowner's speculation than a merchant's investment. Getting a decision in favour of communal action when expenditure was involved, and dock duties would be required, was never easy: merchants who had enjoyed 'free' facilities for generations were not eager to construct 'unfree' facilities for the sake of newcomers in the absence of whom, it was assumed, the new facilities would not be required. But there was more to it than a reluctance

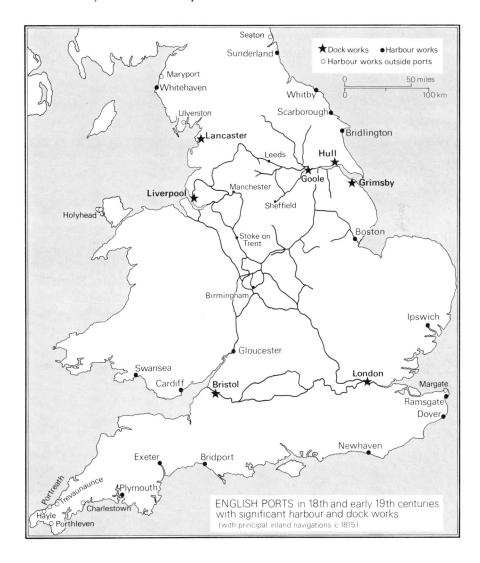

ENGLISH PORTS in 18th and early 19th centuries with significant harbour and dock works
(with principal inland navigations c.1815)

Howland Great Wet Dock (left), a laying-up basin and fitting-out dock eventually associated with the whaling trade.

to pay duties to enter a dock when the river was free. Any-thing which tended to shift the centre of gravity of the commercial area upset vested interests with prime trading sites, established warehouses, and all the evolved conven-ience of an interlocking mercantile community.

Moreover, even if it was agreed that some geographical movement was desirable, there was still the problem of deciding when a dock was necessary; and merchants were sufficiently pessimistic—or realistic—to expect that booms would never last. Throughout the eighteenth and nine-teenth centuries they always built to accommodate *existing* rather than *future* trade.

2. COMMERCIAL DOCKS

a) Liverpool Takes the Initiative

Bearing these factors in mind, it is not surprising that Liverpool alone thought in terms of commercial wet docks in the first three-quarters of the eighteenth century. For Liverpool was unique in having the incentive and oppor-tunity without the drawbacks which hampered develop-ment in Hull, London and Bristol. The growth of her trade with Ireland and the beginning of the transatlantic trade—especially, in the early days, in salt—was obvious, but the chief influence was its size relative to the town's poor water site. Although standing on the Mersey, Liverpool was not a river port in the same sense as were Newcastle, Hull, London and Bristol, with their narrower rivers and shel-tered quays. Much of Liverpool's business was done on the gentle gradient of the Mersey foreshore, where ships lay aground at low water and where there was no system of quays or handling equipment. 'Here', wrote Defoe in retrospect, 'was no mole or haven to bring in their ships and lay them up (as the seamen call it) for the winter; nor any key for the delivering their goods, as at Bristol, Bide-ford, Newcastle, Hull, and other sea ports.'[8] Contempor-ary documents do in fact make mention of a quay in the seventeenth century, and the Corporation ordered it to be repaired in 1669,[9] but it was clearly insubstantial and inadequate; indeed, the town was still losing land to the river.[10] Moreover, the narrow neck of the Mersey estuary caused grave problems. Collins warned his readers of the inadequacy of the port for shipping in the 1690s: 'The ships lie aground before the town of Liverpool; 'tis bad riding afloat before the town by reason of the strong tides

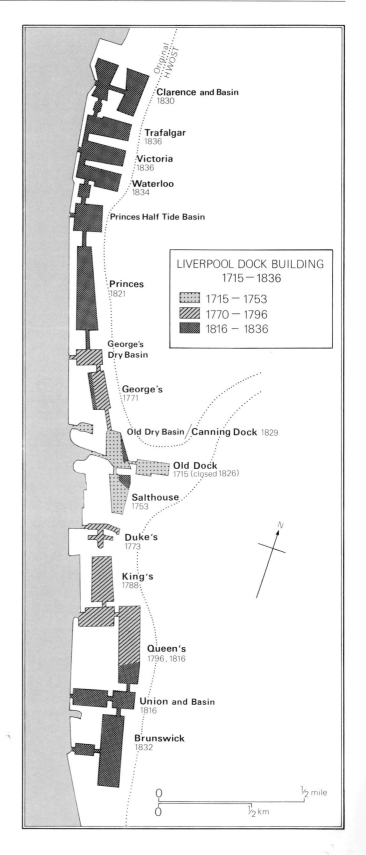

that run there.'[11] Ships laying up were expected to use the Pool—'out of the way'—but otherwise it was unfit for use.[12] In the middle of the seventeenth century the town's principal landowner, Moore, had advised his son that 'if ever the Pool be cut and become navigable, . . . there being no other place in Liverpool the like for cellars and warehouses, . . . the shipping must be all along those closes [part of Moore's property] and the trade will be all in them for the whole town.'[13]

Nothing came immediately from Moore's hopes for his estate, but there could be no doubt about the danger of the roads and inadequacy of the quays. Following the London example, there could also be little doubt as to the solution. In 1708, with increasing pressure of trade, the Corporation instructed its members of parliament to find an engineer to construct a 'dock'. In consequence George Sorocold proposed to create an artificial harbour of some four acres by canalising part of the stream—the Mosslake—flowing into the Pool, but the plan was abandoned at his death. His successor, Thomas Steers, resident engineer of the Howland Dock, proposed instead to move nearer the Mersey and construct a dock after the Howland pattern. A great deal has been made of the fact that this dock was on a 'water encroaching site', but this is not really an appropriate way of looking at the work. The dock was certainly formed by building a sea wall with gates, but it was done by impounding part of the Pool rather than by pushing walls out into the fast moving currents of the Mersey as happened in the case of later docks.

This site in the Pool had many advantages. It avoided part of the excavation which would have been necessary for a dock or canal further inland, and the site itself cost nothing. The dumping of assorted materials to reclaim the remainder of the Pool (completed around 1720) was not particularly difficult, and the cost was recovered from the value of the 'new' land adjacent to the dock. The net result was that a dock of around four acres' water space, with a pair of gates, was opened in 1715 for a sum variously estimated at between £15,000 and £30,000. If we add another £20,000 for warehouses and ancillary works around the dock estate, it would not be far wrong to suggest that the town had spent approximately £50,000 on improvements.[14]

Liverpool's ability to spend so much is a sign not that her merchants were richer than any others, but that they answered an obviously pressing need with an equally obvious organisation: the work was undertaken by the

Corporation, borrowing money against a more or less guaranteed return. But having recognised the need, the Corporation also avoided difficulties which might otherwise have arisen by building in a place which was unlikely to upset vested interests. In this respect Liverpool was singularly fortunate: the Pool belonged to nobody, the Corporation owned the adjacent ground, and nobody among the merchants was likely to gain or suffer overmuch by the decision to build there. Perhaps in this regard Liverpool actually gained from being a relatively new port compared with Hull, London and Bristol, where long established commercial areas militated against the reorganisation inherent in the construction of a commercial dock. Almost by accident, and aided by the favourable geography of the place, Liverpool was able to overcome her problems not by building a dock for light ships that was completely separate from her commercial haven with its Legal Quays (as happened at London and Bristol and was threatened at Hull), but by combining the two in the first commercial dock in Britain.

It would, however, be a mistake to argue that Liverpool's trade grew in the eighteenth century *because* she developed a dock system. No doubt some trade was attracted by good facilities, but it would be truer to say that the docks were created because trade was growing. It should also be emphasised that the first dock, novel as it was, did not bestow on Liverpool facilities which were automatically better than facilities elsewhere. The modern assumption that docks are an indispensable part of ports (which is not universally true even today) cannot be applied in any sensible fashion to the eighteenth century. Liverpool's dock was the answer to Liverpool's need, and the

Custom House, Liverpool: a splendid example of the elegant classical Custom Houses built around the country during the trade expansion of the late eighteenth and early nineteenth centuries.

fact that Newcastle or Hull did not immediately follow suit is more a reflection of their superior havens than of Liverpool's superior wisdom or engineering skills.

Liverpool's spectacular growth in the eighteenth century as she began to benefit from the economic expansion of the colonies did not, therefore, take place in immediate response to the opening of the first dock. There was no noticeable rise in the tonnage of vessels entering and leaving the port until the late 1730s, and at that point the major flaw in the arrangements at Liverpool became apparent: since she had only a dock, and no haven or adequate tidal basin, there was nowhere for ships to lie before entering or after leaving the dock except in the narrow channel or 'gut' leading from the river to the gates. There was a need, it was said in 1737, for 'a convenient pier to be erected in the open harbour . . . for the safety of all ships when ready to sail from the port, to lie till a fair wind happens, which very often are prevented when in the wet dock by other ships lying at the entrance and are all pressing to get out before them.'[15] An Act in the following year authorised the enlarging of the gut to form a four-acre 'dry dock' (so-called locally because it was dry at low water) to solve this problem. However, while this was completed by 1743 it took a further ten years to complete the second dock—South Dock, later altered and renamed Salthouse Dock—to the south of it, largely because of insecure foundations and the current in what (compared with the Old Dock) was a true water-encroaching site beyond the old shore line into the Mersey.

Thus by the middle of the century Liverpool had constructed two docks and a tidal basin and, since there was no alternative way of catering for shipping, was committed to the development of a whole system of docks once trade began to expand rapidly in the second half of the century. North Dock (later altered and called George's Dock) was completed in 1771 to the design of Henry Berry, who had succeeded Steers as chief docks engineer at Liverpool, and the very important Duke's Dock, which accommodated barges from the Bridgewater Canal, was opened two years later to the plan of James Brindley. Neither of them was a spectacular work. North Dock followed the pattern of the first two docks by covering only three acres with water; and Duke's Dock (which was not built as a normal commercial dock for foreign trade) was less than half that size. It was not until after the American war that Liverpool at last embarked on the building of relatively large docks. Old Dock was already of limited value when the seven-and-

three-quarter acre King's Dock was completed in 1788 by Henry Berry and the six-and-a-half acre Queen's Dock was completed in 1796 to the design of Thomas Morris, who had designed the minor dock at Glasson (see below, p. 64).[16]

b) Hull Dock Company

Although Liverpool pioneered the commercial dock, it was Hull which produced the first large dock and, moreover, turned to private enterprise to do it. Congestion in that port increased noticeably in the first half of the century, and a Howland-type dock was planned to relieve the pressure on the traditional landing places in the Haven. 'The harbour', it was said in January 1756, 'is sufficient for the loading and delivering of ships provided the light ships be removed to some convenient place or places.'[17] Such a place was found on the Humber foreshore, and plans of the latest Liverpool dock were obtained as a guide to the construction of a dock there, but the outbreak of the Seven Years' War removed the necessary sense of urgency. It did not return until 1766, and by then a dock specifically

Hull's first dock 1778/9, with ships lying alongside as they had done in the river. Some cargoes were handled over intervening vessels to the quays and others, perhaps most, went over-side into barges.

for light ships was an anachronism for a major port, where the chief future difficulty was likely to be finding space for loaded rather than light ships.

Local vested interests did not see the matter quite in this light, and interest turned away from a commercial dock in favour of another attempt to build a dock for light ships outside the trading area. What tipped the balance in favour of a commercial dock was not a flash of enterprising vision on the part of local merchants, but unashamed blackmail by the Customs authorities. In an age not given to over-much interference in economic activities by government agencies, the Customs occasionally imposed their will on recalcitrant subjects in order to promote the public good in the broadest sense. In this case they spurred on local discussion by threatening to make a port elsewhere on the Humber if Hull did not quickly create adequate accommodation for trade (Gainsborough was a possible place, since most sea-going vessels could reach it at that time), and when the merchants stuck to a dock for light ships only, further pressure was applied to ensure that the Legal Quay should be transferred to it. A carrot was also held out, in the form of a subsidy of £15,000 and a free

grant of all the Crown land covered by the ancient fortifications still surrounding the town, which would provide more than enough land for the dock and so circumvent some of the obstacles associated with the siting of a dock within an existing mercantile community.[18]

It was natural enough that Hull should remove some of the uncertainty in dock building by reliance on Liverpool's precedents, and Henry Berry, the Liverpool docks engineer who was the only man in Britain with experience in this sphere, was engaged to design the Hull dock. This he did, by courtesy of Liverpool Corporation, but for a number of reasons Hull did not follow the Liverpool system and, in fact, the four major ports evolved four entirely different approaches to their problems, as we shall see in the remainder of this chapter.

The chief difference between Hull and Liverpool was not, therefore, in the actual design and construction of the dock, though its size — at nine acres — was obviously greater than anything previously constructed in Liverpool. (Not until 1821 did Liverpool's ninth dock exceed the size of Hull's first.) The difference was in its position. Whereas Liverpool had adopted a water frontage site for its docks, Hull (and London after it) adopted inland sites. In the case of Hull this was chiefly because of the gift of Crown land which, though it surrounded the town, was contiguous to the old commercial centre only to the north of the town. (The inadequacy of Humberside foundations, which became apparent when Albert Dock was built, may not have been known in the eighteenth century, and it would seem unwise to lay too much stress on this very obvious difference between Liverpool and Hull, where the longest wooden piles failed to find rock or other secure foundations.) Unfortunately, any vessel seeking to enter the dock to the north of the town had to pass through the Haven, which was already crowded with vessels using the quays there (which remained as sufferance quays when the Legal Quay was removed to the dock). By the end of the century it was argued — though one never knows how seriously — that ship could sail from St Petersburgh to Hull roads in less time than she took to get from the roads to the dock.

The second difference — and one which had far reaching consequences — was in the method of financing, and therefore of organising, the dock. Almost all harbour and dock work was done by public bodies which had emerged in the past as an integral part of the mercantile community. They paid for their works by levying dues which had been accepted from time immemorial as the just payment

for facilities commonly enjoyed. But building large harbour works and docks created a new order of magnitude
in costs as well as benefits. Most of the expensive harbours
were paid for out of passing tolls in return for shelter. But
dock works had to be paid for by the local community
actually using them and that, in effect, meant that they
had initially been organised and administered by the same
body—the local Corporation—which had controlled the
ports since the Middle Ages. This was the case at Liverpool, where it was automatically accepted that the Corporation should build the necessary dock and its successors.
It was certainly also fully accepted that this would be the
case in Hull when proposals for a dock were first mooted,
and during all the negotiations between the Town and the
Board of Customs leading to the Act of 1774. However,
with no ceremony and no recorded reason, those principally involved in the negotiations suddenly deviated from
this well-trodden path and produced the first dock
company in Britain.

Bearing in mind the phenomenal early financial success
of Hull Dock Company, the first thought might be that
the leading merchants had decided to divert a considerable
income from the Corporation to themselves as shareholders, as the Corporation of Edinburgh later tried to do
with Leith (below, p. 54). But there is no reason to suspect
that those who became shareholders were less altruistic or
public spirited than their fellows, and equally there are no
grounds for believing that they expected a huge profit or,
indeed, any profit at all. The simple truth is that the Corporation of Hull had a limited income which was required
for a variety of good purposes, and any struggle to borrow
funds for dock-building by public bodies appeared needless now that the canal system had introduced and
seemingly perfected the device of the public utility company. If such a company could be formed to build the dock,
the Corporation could busy itself with the overall supervision of the town's affairs while retaining certain powers
(which turned out to be less real than had been expected)
within the company which, for its first twenty years was
regarded universally as one of the town's three Corpor-
ations—the Bench of Aldermen, Trinity House, and the
Dock Company.

The success of Hull Dock Company set a precedent,
alternative to the experience of Liverpool, for Bristol and
London to follow; but there was an unexpected drawback
which was revealed as soon as expanding trade overtook
the facilities of both haven and dock at Hull. No provision

*Humber Dock, Hull, showing tying-up post for vessels awaiting their turn
at the quays and also the 'open' nature of Hull's 'town docks'.*

had been made for the building of subsequent docks. At
Liverpool it was automatically assumed that the Corporation would carry on building docks out of accumulated
funds and mortgaged duties, but Hull Dock Company
could argue with justice that it was incorporated to build
the first dock and was thereafter entitled to enjoy the revenue from it. Unfortunately, since nobody had expected a
rapid increase in trade that would require further docks, the
Company had been created as *the* Dock Company of
Kingston-upon-Hull, with a sole and absolute right to levy
dues on all vessels entering the port whether or not they
entered the dock (since they all benefited from the relief
brought by the dock to the port as a whole). A further
dock would therefore cost the company a great deal without
producing a proportional increase in income, and inevitably any enthusiasm for improvement was inhibited by
the desire to maximise short-term profit. If to these
considerations of private profit we add a lively debate over
the correct siting of further docks, it will be readily appreciated that many erstwhile supporters soon viewed the Hull
Dock Company as a recipe for disaster. Since there was
no way of compelling the Company to build, and since
Parliament was unlikely to countenance the subversion of
private property, it was, perhaps, inevitable that the
necessary compromise should involve public subvention
of the Company which, in the end, provided only forty
per cent of the cost of the first two docks out of calls on
shareholders.

It was, therefore, with the greatest difficulty that Hull
acquired her second dock which, with delays caused by
war, was not opened until 1809. Its position was finally

settled by the desirability of using as much as possible of the land granted by the Crown along the old walls, and the necessity of providing an entrance independent of the Haven. In consequence the economic importance of the latter appeared to be further diminished. However, as at Liverpool, the docks were not yet surrounded by warehouses. Merchants still, for the most part, used their own, transporting goods from open dockside to riverside warehouses by lighter where possible and across the town by sleds where necessary. Moreover, Hull more than any other port relied on inland water transport, and while goods for export were likely to be warehoused pending shipment, imported goods were likely to be trans-shipped into lighters and floated up-river without ever being landed on the quayside. Unsawn timber was commonly thrown over the side into the docks and helped to cause even greater congestion before it was loaded into barges, made up into rafts for floating up-river, or hauled out for sawing in one of the many timber yards associated with this trade.

The seven-acre Humber Dock was not itself particularly noteworthy: by 1800 any engineering problems there might have been in the construction of docks had been solved chiefly through the use of waterproof mortar perfected by Smeaton and lighter stone and brick walls introduced by John Rennie. But it is worth pausing to emphasise the significance of the Humber lock. Henry Berry appears to have designed the first Hull dock and lock on the basis of his experience at Liverpool, where the foreshore rested on a bed of sandstone some eighteen feet below the first dock sill. But unfortunately Hull enjoyed no such underlying strata, and within five years of its opening some six hundred feet of dock wall (which was 24 ft high and 10 ft thick at the bottom and 4 ft 6 in at the top) had 'yielded forward' by as much as 3 ft 10 in; parts of it had fallen down and had to be rebuilt. The lock was already in a dangerous condition, with the walls sinking and the floor rising, a movement which would ultimately cause the

The remains of Rennie's important lock, with 'hollow walls', at Grimsby; now part of Alexandra Dock.

underlying semi-wet mud to burst through the floor and ruin the whole lock. If some method could not be found of building a secure lock on insecure foundations, Hull's future would be bleak indeed, and other ports with similar problems would never have been constructed.

c) The Grimsby Sea Lock

It was not at Hull, but at neighbouring Grimsby that this problem was first solved. In 1796 a group of local landowners had endeavoured to revive that port and improve their urban and agricultural estates in north Lincolnshire by forming the Grimsby Haven Company to build a huge floating harbour which, they naively believed, would attract trade from a congested Hull.[19] But from the start things went wrong. The plans drawn up by Jonathan Pickernell of Whitby did not take full account of poor foundations, and their execution—and alteration—by local amateurs who fancied themselves as engineers was disastrous. The mud walls of the dock collapsed, the stone walls of the lock sank, and the wooden floor of the lock was blown up by the pressure of the underlying mud. Eventually John Rennie was called in to save the day, and did so with a number of useful innovations.

Firstly he floated the entire lock on a huge timber raft anchored by piles which were similar to, but more substantial than, those in the first Hull lock planned by Berry. It was protected from the seeping water by an apron of sheet piling at both ends, and the upthrust of mud was effectively countered by resting the raft on an inverted arch of brick which could absorb the upward pressure in the same way that a normal arch sustains downward pressure.

Secondly he reduced the weight of the brick and stone walls (which were subsequently referred to as 'hollow' walls) and anchored them on the landward side in order to prevent them from toeing in and crashing through the timber floor of the lock. As an added precaution against water undermining the lock from the side, he built wing walls, or, rather, the local engineers did, and initially showed their scant regard for Rennie by insisting that his lighter walls were inadequate. It was not until their heavier version fell down that in Grimsby, at least, the importance of the engineer was acknowledged. 'I beg and entreat if the Subscribers have any regard to the stability and success of the work,' Rennie wrote to one of the leaders of the Haven Company, 'that they will let their engineering knowledge be displayed on other parts of the work.'[20] The work was, indeed, completed under a resident engineer of Rennie's choice, and the fifteen-acre floating harbour or dock was opened on the last day of 1800.

The new Grimsby Haven was conceived as an attack on the mercantile prosperity of Hull, but Grimsby had nothing to offer, apart from its dock, which could attract goods entering or leaving the hinterland already admirably served by Hull. The Haven was a miserable failure, and the port of Grimsby did not revive. The example of her lock, securely founded and bravely facing the open waters of the Humber estuary, was nevertheless an inspiration to Hull, and Rennie reproduced it for the new Humber dock and again, in 1814, when he rebuilt the entrance basin and lock of the first Hull dock. Hull was consequently assured of her future so far as docks were concerned, but it was some time before she again attempted to build a lock opening directly into the Humber: the six-acre third dock, opened in 1829, was constructed on the remaining walls and ditches between the first and second docks and linked to both, thus saving the expense of an independent lock and at the same time providing the west end of the first dock with an outlet alternative to the lengthy progress through the Haven.

Bristol Floating Harbour: a small ship is tied up alongside The Grove, a set of ancient mud docks before the harbour was formed. The original Bathurst Basin, 1809, enters the Floating Harbour opposite this quay.

d) Bristol Floating Harbour

The arrangements of docks at Liverpool and Hull were, given local conditions, perfectly logical, and there is no doubt that these early docks served the purpose for which they were created. But the arrangement at Grimsby had two very considerable advantages: by following the line of the old haven of the river Freshney, a considerable saving was made in excavation costs; and at the same time the old commercial centre remained at the heart of the port. In Hull and Liverpool there were practical obstacles to such a plan, but in Bristol, where there had never been any suggestion of the inadequacy of the mile-long quays, the possibility of impounding the rivers Avon or Frome (which met in the city) had been mooted from time to time since at least 1755, when the Corporation advertised for an engineer.

The merchants of Bristol were no more decisive than those of Hull, debating for almost fifty years the relative merits of Liverpool-style docks and Exeter-style impounded water while a succession of engineers produced plans and arguments doing little to quieten local fears of flooding or answer the objections of dry-dock owners who

Brunel's South Lock, Cumberland Basin, Bristol (c. 1848). The huge tidal range has revealed the semi-circular walls and the position of the single leaf, floating iron gate made necessary by the narrowness of land between this lock and its neighbour, where gate machinery would have had to be. Also exposed is the gridiron on which ships were allowed to settle for repairs. The tubular swing bridge in the foreground is another unique Brunel feature.

feared that they could not drain their docks if the river water ceased to ebb. In the end, those who wished to maintain the city-centre quays prevailed over those who wanted a wet dock at Rownham (dry-dock owners were introduced to the steam pump!), but there were still those doubting the competence of contemporary engineering to solve the physical problems. 'Your engineers', the city's Water Bailiff advised the Society of Merchants who organised the works, 'may be men of experience in erecting inland canal navigations, please to remember here is a great flow of tide and floods in the river Avon to encounter with.'[21] This was hardly fair comment on William Jessop, whose plan for the Floating Harbour was eventually chosen in 1803. Having learned his trade from Smeaton, he was in demand as a harbour consultant in the 1780s, built docks at Dublin in the 1790s, and the West India docks in London in 1800.[22]

The Floating Harbour—its name implying a natural harbour where, by human ingenuity, ships remained permanently afloat—was really very simple in conception. The danger of flooding which had cast doubt on earlier schemes was avoided by cutting a new channel for the Avon to the south of the town and then impounding some two and a half miles of the old channel (plus a quarter of a mile of the Frome) beginning just upstream of the Avon Gorge and running through the town. The water level within the Floating Harbour itself was kept up by a feeder canal from the Avon which also served as a linkage for barge traffic.

The result was a dock of huge proportions, containing something over seventy acres in all, through by their very nature floating harbours of this sort were not generally suitable for such highly concentrated usage as modern dock systems. The great advantage, as noted above, was the continued use of the existing quays on the Frome and Avon, with consequent financial and business advantages to the merchants involved. On the other hand the work at Bristol shared with contemporary work at Hull the unhappy distinction of costing greatly more than the original estimates. War inflation was an obvious excuse (the rising cost of iron railways used in the excavation work was, for instance, a cause of some concern), but the fact remains that, as at Grimsby, the engineers underestimated the cost and difficulty of excavating and preparing non-walled basins. The Cumberland entrance basin, which was necessary to avoid serious water loss in locking in and out of the Floating Harbour, had in the end to be completely lined because

the presence of freshwater springs caused the earth walls to collapse. As a result of this and similar mishaps, the final cost of the Floating Harbour was of the order of £600,000, exactly six times Jessop's original estimate and three times his revised estimate allowing for the final, more elaborate, scheme. It sounds a great deal of money, but in terms of acreage it was exceedingly cheap: the Floating Harbour worked out at roughly £8,000 per acre of water, compared with £33,000 per acre for the almost exactly contemporaneous Humber Dock at Hull.

There was another respect in which Bristol copied Grimsby rather than Liverpool: the Floating Harbour was built by a private company. Unlike the Corporation of Hull, which had at least intended to build the dock there until the very eve of the Dock Bill, the Corporation of Bristol had long since handed over part of its duty-raising function to the very influential Society of Merchants, and it was accepted almost without question that this body should organise the dock and pay for it by issuing shares to the public. If Bristol was, in the event, better served by her dock company than was Hull, this was largely a matter of chance. The Floating Harbour was sufficiently large to accommodate trade for years to come, and in any case trade did not grow at a rate which would render further works necessary. Indeed, because trade did not grow to any extent, the initial cost of the Floating Harbour had to be borne by trade which in truth hardly justified such elaborate facilities, and many people in the years following 1809 argued that the duties payable at Bristol were high enough to divert trade to any other port which had communications with those parts of the hinterland which Bristol ought to have been able to dominate. The Chamber of Commerce drew up tables from time to time showing, for example, that in the early 1820s, the total duties on ships and goods payable at Bristol were more than double those at London and Liverpool, three times those at Hull, and almost six times those at neighbouring Gloucester.[23] By the middle of the century, despite changes, duties were still almost double those at Liverpool and Hull and twenty per cent more than those at London. It was partly in an attempt to reduce the general level of charges that the Corporation of Bristol relinquished some of its own duties in the 1830s and finally took over the Dock Company in 1848.

Unfortunately for Bristol, the principal reason for the adequacy of the Floating Harbour was the general inadequacy of the port for large ships. Until the end of the Napoleonic War there was never a doubt that any ship desiring to sail up to the city could do so if it chose its tides carefully. However, as ships were made longer and deeper they had increasing difficulty navigating the river, which was particularly awkward for long ships at the point appropriately called Horseshoe Bend, and which really had too great a tidal range for easy and convenient working up and down. The question in the future would be not whether the City 'docks' should be improved, but whether they should be abandoned altogether for long-distance overseas trade. In the meantime, Jessop's Floating Harbour, with its entrance improved by Brunel's southern lock in the late 1840s, undoubtedly gave the city centre a new lease of commercial life.

e) Leith: the Dangers of City Control

Of the major Scottish ports, whose trade was also growing rapidly by the end of the eighteenth century, only one—Leith—found it necessary to build wet docks. The docks themselves were of no great importance, but the circumstances surrounding their construction are worth noting. Leith grew with Edinburgh, and by the end of the century was second only to Glasgow/Greenock in the tonnage of shipping entering from abroad and well ahead in the tonnage of coasters entering the port. The mouth of the river called the Water of Leith became completely inadequate as a harbour, but funds available for port improvement were inadequate too.[24]

The port authority was the City of Edinburgh, which followed the Liverpool lead by building its own docks. John Rennie was engaged, and the city secured authority to raise £80,000 on the security of the rates to construct a series of small (c. 10 acres) docks leading off the west side of the river. The first was finished in 1806/7 and the second in 1817, but the third was never started: the city had already run into those financial difficulties that turned Hull and London away from dock-building. Inflation and the inevitable under-estimates produced costs vastly greater than the city had expected. The two docks cost almost £300,000 by 1817, and the cost of completing the outer harbour was put at about as much again. The city did not have the money. Port towns usually enjoy their status so long as the port relieves the rates, but when it comes to charging the rates to support the port they are less happy. Edinburgh could not or would not tax its citizens to pay for the necessary outer harbour. How then should it be built?

In the context of the nineteenth century there was only one possible answer: sell the port to private enterprise, or turn it over to a trust. Since the government had already lent a considerable sum because of the port's strategic importance, and was prepared to lend more, it refused to countenance the private sale, which turned out to be somewhat corrupt in so far as the council was proposing to sell the docks to certain of its own members. In 1826 the Leith Dock Commission was therefore created, but it was another twelve years before it became financially independent of the city.

The Commission built the piers of the outer harbour, which was finished in 1829, but by then so much money had been spent that the burden of dues was turning shipping away to other ports on the Forth. However, the problem was not that the docks had been built by a city. It was that they had been built by a city which was not really a port and which had too many other commitments to leave enough money for adequate building. A further complication was the inadequacy of the shipping presenting itself in the post-war depression. Many ports in the 1820s were wondering if they had not been too generous in the provision of spectacular improvements.

f) Private Enterprise and Dock Competition in London

The most spectacular change of all was in London. It occurred relatively late in the chronology of improvement, largely because the huge water area of the Pool had served the port so well. Moreover, the customary pattern of working, in which ships anchored in mid-stream and received or discharged cargoes via lighters, placed less pressure on the Legal Quay than would have been exerted by a similar volume of shipping tying up alongside. There had, however, been no extension of the Legal Quay commensurate with trade growth, and in the eighteenth century it still measured a mere 1,419 feet (though for certain goods it was supplemented by Sufferance Wharves, which stretched for 2,890 feet on the south bank below London Bridge, and for 790 feet on the north bank below the Tower). As a result, the first serious problem for London was not competition for shipping room so much as competition for Legal Quay space. In this regard London faced difficulties similar to those in Hull, where Customs facilities no longer answered the demands made upon them. In 1762 and again in 1765 merchants petitioned for an extension of the Legal Quay, but made no headway in the face of vested interests which saw extension as a threat to the value of private property associated with Customs facilities.

Over the next thirty years the quality of service offered by the port of London declined to the point where it was intolerable. The number of coasters and foreign-going vessels had doubled since the middle of the century, and there were 10,112 of the former and 3,463 of the latter entering the port in 1791, with an aggregate tonnage of 1,558,396. Conditions of the river were aggravated by some 3,400 lighters passing back and forth between ships and quays and between the quays and warehouses in various parts of the river.

To make matters worse, the traditional mooring pattern within the port had the short-stay coasters nearest to London Bridge, the smaller North European traders off St. Katharine's church, the colliers in the Lower Pool (around Wapping), the larger foreign-going vessels and West Indiamen in Limehouse Reach, and the largest ships and East Indiamen in Blackwall Reach. It had been a sensible arrangement, allowing the coasters carrying provisions for London to come right up to the city while keeping at arm's length the larger foreign traders which took much longer to load or unload their cargoes. It ceased to be sensible with the great increase in the number of coasters constantly moving through the overseas shipping, especially since lighters carrying valuable goods had to make the same journey through the Pool, and were subject to delay, damage and loss. So doubtful was the East India Company about the movement of goods by river that all the goods from the east were landed at Blackwall and brough in armed processions to the Company's warehouse in the City.

The situation on land was, if anything, worse than on the river. The geographical concentration of the Legal Quays meant that private warehouses within a reasonable distance were totally inadequate, especially for sugar, the chief commodity (by weight) entered at the Legal Quay and requiring lengthy warehousing because the annual importation arrived during a period of only three or four months. Indeed, it was estimated in the 1790s that the entire quay and warehouse space of the port was inadequate for the convenient handling and storage of this one commodity; and there were many others. Containers were piled high on the quays for weeks on end when conditions were at their worst, to the distress of those attempting to use the quays for their intended purpose. Streets leading from quays to warehouses were reduced to a state of overcrowded confusion which attracted the engravers and was still presented as a normal part of dockside experience when Doré produced his famous views of London in 1872.

It is doubtful if any amount of statistical investigation will ever be able to adduce the real cost to merchants of the delays and extra handling charges involved in the traditional working of the port, and their inhibiting effects on

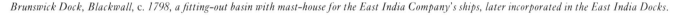

Brunswick Dock, Blackwall, c. *1798, a fitting-out basin with mast-house for the East India Company's ships, later incorporated in the East India Docks.*

price-sensitive trades. Far more concern was aroused towards the end of the century by a more obvious cost arising
from congestion, namely the criminal activity flourishing
in such conditions. It was the valuable West India trade
which bore the brunt of malpractices, and an ex-Glasgow
West India merchant and London magistrate—Patrick
Colquhoun—who revealed the huge extent of pilfering in
his *Treatise on the Police of the Metropolis*, published in
1796.

The core of the problem was, he said, 'the prevailing
practice of discharging and delivering the cargoes of ships
by a class of aquatic labourers known by the name of
lumpers': in other words the lighterage system.[25] However, the opportunities for dishonesty spread much further
than this and, in his *Treatise on the Commerce and Police
of the River Thames*, Colquhoun listed the variety of crimi-
nals who appear far less quaint and deserving of sympathy
than their fellows who later appeared in Henry Mayhew's
London. There were, he wrote,

> the 'river pirates', who were connected with the marine
> store shops; they reconnoitred by day and made their
> attacks in armed boats on dark nights, cutting adrift the
> lighters and barges, and taking out the merchandize.
> The 'night plunderers'—the watermen of the lowest
> class, who attacked unprotected lighters and made over
> the stolen goods to receivers. The 'light horsemen'—
> comprising mates of ships and revenue officers, who
> would wink at the robbery of the ship, in which coopers,
> porters, and watermen take part. The 'heavy horse-
> men'—porters and labourers, who wore an inner dress,
> called a guernsey, provided with pockets wherein to
> stow away small quantities of colonial produce, whilst
> portering about the ships and quays. Besides these orga-
> nized depredators, the wine coopers pilfered whilst
> opening and refining casks; the mudlarks picked up
> stolen bits, which others by concert threw into the mud;
> the rat catchers employed on board the ships carried
> away produce; the lightermen concealed goods whilst
> going from the ships to the quays; and the warehouse-
> men, when sugar reached the warehouses, pilfered and
> sold the stolen sugar to small dealers at public houses.[26]

Since the West India trade lost the most—sugar ships
were reckoned to lose half a ton a day—it is not surprising
that it was the West India interest which began clamouring
for change in the structure of the port. In this respect they
were not following the lead of Colquhoun, as is sometimes
thought, since he offered no answer to depredation beyond

adequate policing *of the river*: 'it only requires exertion
and perseverence'. In fact, though Colquhoun made no
reference to it, William Vaughan (a London merchant and
director of the Royal Exchange Assurance Company, who
had a professional interest in losses within the port) had,
in 1793, published his treatise *On Wet Docks, Quays, and
Warehouses for the Port of London*. It was this tract which
sparked off serious discussion, leading to the emergence
of a committee of West India merchants which in 1795
declared that the very existence of their trade demanded
more adequate provision for discharging and warehousing
valuable goods. And this, it was agreed, could only be
accomplished by building a wet dock and associated warehouses as advocated by Vaughan. Some £800,000 was
subscribed to a proposed company and a Bill was drawn
up in January 1796, only to run into the overwhelming
opposition of vested interests.

It is all too easy to refer to opposition by vested interests
while overlooking the simple fact that the West India interest was itself a vested interest. It proposed to solve the
problems of West Indian shipping, not those of the port
of London. The impression left by the writings of Vaughan
and Colquhoun is that the West India interest was the
major user of the port, whereas in reality its physical presence was in no way equal to the value of West Indian
produce. In 1790, for instance, ships arriving from the
West Indies were only nine per cent of total entries, and
West India tonnage was only fourteen per cent of total
tonnage from abroad. It was therefore an essential
prerequisite to dock-building—which normally involved
monopoly rights and legally enforceable duties—that a
thorough investigation should be made of the interests of
the port in general. (The House of Commons had already
been made aware of the unfortunate consequences of creating the Hull Dock Company without adequate thought to
the future.) The presentation of the Dock Bill, with its
counter-petition, was consequently the occasion for a
major enquiry by Select Committee into the state of the
port of London and proposals for reform.

A great deal of evidence was presented to the Committee, emphasising the points outlined above about
congestion, delays, damage and losses (together with two
that have not been discussed, namely the fire hazard under
the old system of working and the poor condition of the
Thames, which in places had lost four or five feet of depth
within living memory). It was accepted at face value, and
the Committee reported that 'the natural, fundamental and

actual resources of the Port of London', were 'incompetent to the great purpose of its extended commerce.'[27] It was, however, more difficult to assess the merits of possible solutions. Broodbank and others have listed in some detail the eight dock schemes considered by the Committee,[28] but the location and exact nature of the dock works were not the key issue. The first matters to be settled were the extent of reorganisation, and the body or bodies that should be responsible for it.

The fundamental issue was soon settled: docks, rather than extensive river works, were to be the basis for reorganisation. But were they to be part of the port, as docks were—or were in the process of becoming—in Liverpool, Bristol and Hull; or were they to be ports within the port, serving only specialised interests? The latter proposal was that of the West India interest, but it was clear from the start that neither the City nor the other merchant groups would accept it. In 1796 the City brought forward a scheme of its own to build docks on the Isle of Dogs and at Rother-hithe, covering some two hundred acres, but quite apart from the doubts about the validity of the scheme there were good enough reasons for supposing that the City Fathers were neither willing nor able to become involved in such extensive works. One thing was now certain: London would have to follow the unfortunate example of Hull and rely upon a private company to construct its dock, and in 1797 the West India interest again presented a Bill for the construction of a dock for their own purpose at Wapping, with a canal through the Isle of Dogs to Blackwall Reach where the ships traditionally anchored.

It may, perhaps, be a mistake to emphasise the exclusive nature of the proposed dock at this stage: there was nothing to stop ships from other parts of the world entering if they so wished. The question hinged on the monopoly rights which the docks needed to secure their income. In Hull, for instance, subscribers to the Dock Company invested in the knowledge that ships entering the port must pay dock dues whether or not they entered the dock. But how could ships entering the much larger port of London be charged if they chose not to enter a specific dock which was, compared with Liverpool and Hull, merely an ancillary to the port? The answer was to identify the cargo rather than the ship and compel all West India goods to be discharged within West India Dock, where the ships then paid dues.

This possibility opened the way for more than one dock company, since they would not be competing for the same ships and could each be granted a monopoly which could be roughly assessed in terms of the size of particular foreign trades. After a couple of years of hostility between the major parties, the way was cleared for a division of interests and, after minor interests such as the quay owners had been bought off, a compromise was reached. The West India interest, after reconsidering its plans, decided to move its site to the Isle of Dogs, where its dock could be entered from Blackwall Reach. The rival group, representing the North American and European traders, then formed the London Dock Company to build on the Wapping site. And the City of London agreed to build the 'City Canal' across the Isle of Dogs for the convenience of shipping using both the Wapping dock and the Pool. Bills to effect these proposals were introduced in 1799, the West India Dock Act being approved late in 1799 and the London Dock Act early in 1800. (The City Canal was authorised by sections of the West India Act.)

The first two dock companies proceeded with a speed which reflects both the essential simplicity of the design and the suitability of the subsoil. For the West India company William Jessop designed two parallel docks some 2,600 feet long: the 30-acre Import Dock to receive and warehouse incoming cargoes, and the 24-acre Export Dock to handle outgoing cargoes, hoping to eliminate the confusion and opportunity for malpractices which occurred when ships discharging and loading were intermingled, and avoiding the tendency for ships to remain alongside in the interval between unloading and loading. For the London company John Rennie designed a single 20-acre dock, the discrepancy in the extent of facilities in the two estates reflecting the speedier turn-round expected in London Dock's European trades and the financial superiority of the West Indian trades. On the other hand the London Dock was deliberately made more square than, for instance, the first Hull dock, in order to create a larger water to quay-space ratio which would facilitate both the laying up of vessels when necessary and transfer of goods between ship and lighter when desirable.

There were no engineering problems involved in building these docks. The theoretical principles were well known and the engineers were men of great experience. But above all, the gravelly clay proved to be of the right consistency to facilitate easy excavation and provide secure foundations for the dock and lock walls, a matter which was causing Rennie considerable trouble at Hull and Grimsby. There was, it is true, an unfortunate and serious

West India Docks, showing the extensive warehousing and City Canal on the left.

accident (in terms of loss of life rather than permanent damage) to the coffer dam of West India Dock, but that resulted from human error rather than failure of the foundations. The chief delaying factor was competition between the two companies for materials—especially bricks—and labour. In this respect West India Dock, which was begun first, had a considerable advantage in fixing contracts, and despite its much greater size it was opened in 1802. London Dock, which had had a much slower start because of the necessity of clearing its site of over a thousand houses, was largely finished in 1803, but the opening was delayed until January 1805 by the shortages of materials and men associated with naval operations after the breakdown of the Peace of Amiens.

If the design and engineering of the docks were nothing very novel, the dock estates marked a new departure in the physical organisation and methods of working within ports. In order to secure both goods and the Revenue, the docks were completely surrounded by massive walls (which were originally specified at thirty feet but eventually built to twenty feet), and West India Docks were further defended by a ditch six feet deep and twelve feet wide, and an area of 'no man's land' on which nothing might be built, in order to detect nefarious activity outside the walls. Armed with their monopolies in particular trades, the dock estates thus became ports within the port, with their own Legal Quays surrounded by immense warehouses owned by the dock companies, operated by their

own labour force, and patrolled by their own police force. Thus the traditional lightering of goods around the port for purposes of Customs registration and warehousing was brought to a welcome end, at least for certain trades.

This shift of emphasis from 'private' to 'public' warehousing was an important one. Warehousing had always been closely associated with riverside quays, but the building of docks at Liverpool, Lancaster (Glasson), Hull and Grimsby had broken this tradition by separating the landing areas and Legal Quays from the warehouses, which remained chiefly private property. Now the warehouse was brought back to the quayside in a move that was encouraged by the Warehousing Act of 1803. The payment of duties on imports at the point of landing had always been a burden to merchants, especially where they might be a time lapse before sale, or where goods were destined for re-exportation when a 'draw-back' of duty was allowed. Concessions in the 1730s had allowed certain goods to be warehoused under Customs lock, the owner giving bond to avoid fraud, but the system was cumbersome in operation, requiring separate locks and bonds for each parcel of goods, and prohibiting mixing and removal of part of the goods. When the 1803 Act transferred responsibility for the bond from the owner of the goods to the owner of the warehouse, the way was opened for dock-side warehouses owned by the dock company, and private warehouses lost some of their attraction.

The importance of the dock-side warehouse deserves

emphasis, not only for the security it offered, but also for the acceleration of dock-side business which it made possible. It was a fundamental principle of shipping until well into the nineteenth century that cargoes were made up of what might be described as 'man-sized' parcels. Everything, even bulk cargoes, had to be manhandled at some stage, and the object generally was to minimise horizontal movement employing men and maximise vertical movement involving cranes. The multi-storey quayside warehouse did just this, and in its final development stood at the water's edge—as merchants' warehouses had done in the old days on the Thames and most other rivers—to facilitate the unloading of vessels straight into the warehouse. Goods were then sorted on the warehouse floors rather than on the quay (thus eliminating much of the earlier congestion) and could be re-shipped as necessary or alternatively discharged from the rear of the warehouse onto the roadway.

It follows that only certain types of goods of high value in relation to volume were suitable for—or could bear the cost of—this kind of warehousing, and it was the concentration in London of specific trades which made the bonded warehouse and closed dock system possible. Indeed, in some respects the tall warehouse was essential for concentrated flows of trade through a relatively small dock space. In other words, the demand for speedy operations as well as for security made dock warehousing more necessary in London than in Hull, Liverpool or Bristol, none of which followed London's example during the first quarter of the nineteenth century. The well-known Liverpool dock warehouses were not constructed until the 1830s.

The respective Dock Acts decreed that, under penalty of forfeiture and fine, all West India produce except tobacco (which must be taken to the Customs' warehouse on the Thames) must be unloaded in West India Dock, and all tobacco, rice, wine and brandy (except when imported from the East or West Indies) must be unloaded in London Dock. Although these were among the most valuable and highly taxed items of trade there were many others, and it was only a matter of time before the dock system began to proliferate to cater for them. There were still two major branches of trade to be accommodated: the East Indian and the Northern European.

East India Dock was unusual in being created by the East India Company for its own ships engaged in its monopoly trade with the Far East, and in order to avoid frauds and theft no others were admitted. It also differed from the other docks in having no warehouses attached. The East India Company's ships had always anchored at Blackwall, and their extremely valuable cargoes were taken in quasi-military procession to the Company's ten acres of City warehouses, of which the massive fortress-like Cutler Street warehouse had been completed as recently as 1782. Now the Act confirmed the position by ordering that all East India goods should continue to be warehoused in Cutler Street, and the East India Company joined with the West India Dock Company to build the new Commercial Road linking their two docks with the City. Thus the main object of the East India Dock was the care and protection of shipping and, appropriately, it was built adjacent to the Brunswick Dock of Messrs J. and W. Wells which had been used as a fitting out dock for East Indiamen for many years. The plans of John Rennie and Ralph Walker (who had been Jessop's assistant for West India Dock) left Brunswick Dock as a fitting out basin (it was turned into a full dock in the 1860s), and made a smaller adjoining basin into the entrance basin for both docks, saving considerable time and money in the process.

The northern European trades were, on the whole, less valuable and more bulky than those for which the monopoly docks were built, and the dock system that emerged to handle them was quite different. The sort of goods involved—flax, hemp, tar and timber—were not such as to encourage smuggling or excessive pilfering, and the chief difficulty was finding for them not secure room but sufficient room. Timber in particular could not be warehoused. Quite apart from the physical problems involved, sawn wood had to be seasoned by the importer either in the open air or in partially open sheds, and large balks of unsawn timber—which greatly exceeded the man-sized parcels referred to above—were traditionally handled in the easiest way by throwing them over the side and floating them in—and out of—the dock.

Dock estates handling timber had, therefore, to be much larger than those handling other goods and, given the pattern of land-ownership and the competition likely to arise in the building of relatively inexpensive docks, no single company was able to provide sufficient accommodation for the whole of the trade.

The first minor dock for 'general' trade was created almost accidentally by the Grand Surrey Canal Company, which was incorporated in 1801 to build a canal from Rotherhithe to Epsom for the market garden trade, and which was sufficiently impressed by the building going on on the other side of the river to widen the canal entrance into a three-acre dock with a ship lock. However, the Grand Surrey Canal Basin was soon overtaken by the formation in 1807 of two pressure groups intent on making extensive provision for timber. One of them became, in 1810, the Commercial Dock Company, and the other, in 1811, the East Country Dock Company. The former achieved its purpose quickly by buying Greenland (ex-Howland) Dock and converting it into Commercial Dock in 1808, while the latter began work in the same year on East Country Dock immediately to the south of it.

The obvious rivalry for northern European trades between these three groups, which contrasts so markedly with the division of trade between the first three dock companies, made monopoly impossible when they went to Parliament, but public statements by the companies indicate that, timber apart, the Commercial Dock Company was providing storage for, and attracting, hemp, flax and tar, while the East Country Dock Company made a play for grain, salt, fruit and—unsuccessfully—coal. In fact the Commercial Dock Company soon gained ground over its rivals by buying out a further company—the Baltic Dock Company—founded in 1809 to develop timber ponds to

the north of Commercial Dock, and making one of those ponds into another dock called, rather unromantically, Dock No. III. (Dock No. II was a short-lived annexe of Commercial Dock turned into a timber yard when the docks were developed northwards.) Eventually in 1850 the Commercial Dock Company bought East Country Dock and reconstructed it as South Dock at a cost of around a quarter of a million pounds, thus leaving only two competing 'general' companies. They finally amalgamated in 1864 as the Surrey Commercial Dock Company.

The enclosed warehouse docks were, in the event, too expensive and could only be maintained adequately, with reasonable dividends paid, by drawing on monopoly income. This was no doubt fair enough while merchants valued their facilities, but the ending of the Napoleonic War was followed by a growing hostility towards the mercantile system in general and cost-raising monopolies in particular. An obviously selfish concern to reduce costs was tempered by the growing acceptance of the theory that costs could be reduced and legitimate profits still made by dock authorities if only free competition was allowed. The East India Company's monopoly over Indian trade had not been renewed by Parliament in 1813, and

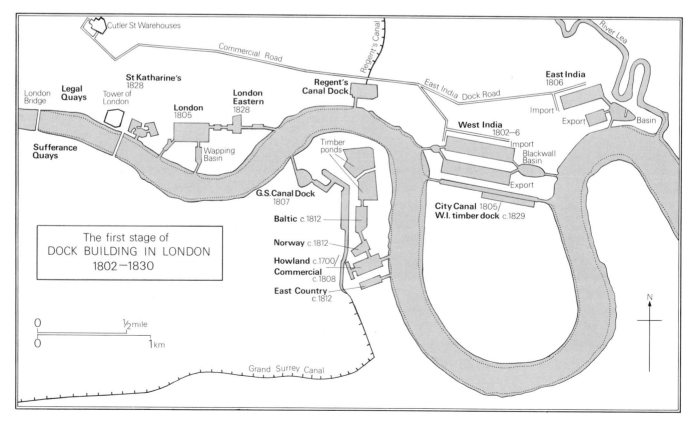

Above, Doré emphasises the labour intensive activity in London's warehousing district, which created a huge demand for men but also led to the under-employment that caused much poverty and labour unrest later in the century.

The docks made little impact on some areas of port work. Coal was still laboriously handled at Limehouse, as Doré shows, c. 1870.

when the dock companies' monopolies came up for renewal there were few who really expected them to survive. They did not. The attack was led by Thomas Tooke, who had organised the first great Free Trade agitation in Parliament in 1820. The West India Dock Company which had made good profits and had large reserves, did not even bother to defend its position; the London Dock Company tried, and failed.

The value of monopoly was raised almost immediately in practical terms because the St. Katharine's Dock Company, with Tooke as chairman, was formed in 1823 to build a new dock on the narrow site between London Dock and the Tower of London. All the London Dock Company could do was oppose the move by denying that 'any additional Docks were required by the state of the commerce of the port, by the burden of rates and charges, by want of accommodation, or by want of further competition amongst the dock companies'.[29] It petitioned Parliament to reject 'the expenditure of immense sums in the construction of supernumerary docks, to the serious detriment of commerce and shipping'. But it was no longer a popular stand, and when the St. Katharine's Company urged in their preamble that docks in future 'should be established on the principle of free competition in trade, and without any exclusive privileges and immunities', Parliament agreed and passed their Act in the teeth of the London Company's strong—though bungled—opposition.

The St. Katharine's Dock Company proceeded to construct their dock which, perhaps more than any other, conjures up the idea—incorrectly—of a 'typical' dock. Its ridiculously small and ruinously expensive site (£68,000 per acre) limited its size to no more than eight acres of water space, located in two roughly equal basins (to allow one to be cleaned while the other still functioned) with an entrance basin of no more than one and a half acres. The smallest of all the docks (except Grand Surrey Basin), it was also built in the most crowded and difficult part of the river, though Broodbank suggested that the underlying intention of the promoters was 'to cater for the warehousing business rather than for the shipping business'.[30] The dock was almost completely surrounded by monumental warehouses, flush with the quay wall and standing on iron pillars to leave open quay space beneath them while allowing direct working between warehouse and ship. The concept of direct working has impressed generations of historians with its modernity, but in practice it was less labour-saving than it appeared at the time or since. As

Broodbank pointed out, it actually demanded more man-handling of goods in many cases where the whole of a cargo was not to be unloaded or warehoused in the area immediately above the ship: there was still need for a sorting area at quay level.

St. Katharine's Dock was the magnificent culmination of the first phase of dock building in London and, as often happens in such cases, it was out of date before it was opened. The warehouses were more grand than useful, as the London Dock Company had forecast, and the inevitable rate-cutting that ensued showed not that freedom brought cheapness with profits, but that over-capacity reduced profits to a dangerously low level without bringing worth-while relief to merchants or shipowners, who still had to support more warehousing space than the port as a whole demanded of its dock system.

Indeed, the plan for St. Katharine's Dock was based on a number of misconceptions. Firstly it was assumed that the increased number of ships using the port since 1800 were using the river only until further docks and warehouses were built, whereas in fact the bulk of the additional ships were colliers, coasters and short-haul European traders of the sort that never or rarely used the docks. If they docked at all it was in the cheaper Surrey docks. Secondly, the value of bonding facilities was already diminishing as the Customs authorities extended bonding privileges to many of the cheaper and more convenient riverside wharves and warehouses. The run-down of protection starting in the 1820s drastically reduced the number of goods passing through Customs, and so eased pressure on Legal Quay space. Thirdly, it was assumed that the nearness to the heart of things that had given London Dock some advantage over West India Dock would continue to operate in the future when, as Capper put it, 'they proposed to construct a very limited dock, at a vast cost, in the immediate proximity of London Bridge, instead of an extensive dock at a small cost, on a less expensive site'.[31] But the first steam train was already running while St. Katharine's was still building, and there was an equally serious miscalculation so far as steam shipping was concerned. It would soon make up a considerable proportion of the coastal and short-haul foreign-going vessels, but St. Katharine's was no more planned with the easy working of steamers in mind than had been London Dock a quarter of a century earlier. In this, at least, it shared its disappointment with other dock authorities both in London and elsewhere.

3. THE CANAL PORTS

The contribution of canals to the rise of the major ports is indisputable: they greatly extended the hinterlands, and accelerated the growth of industries demanding imports and supplying exports. Yet few canals actually terminated in ports, largely because it was not necessary for them to duplicate the navigable waterways on which many large ports stood. Indeed, the only important canals entering a major port were the Regent's and Grand Surrey canals in London. Both companies constructed their own small docks within the port, to assist the locking of barges between the canals and the Thames, and the transfer of goods between barge and ship. Regent's Canal Dock was initially only a barge dock when opened in 1812 (eight years before the canal was completed), and though it was enlarged to take ships in the 1820s, and again in the 1830s and 1860s until it extended to some ten acres, it never really became a full trading dock and was merely a useful ancillary to the main docks. By comparison the Grand Surrey Canal Company's basin was altogether a more substantial affair and almost from its opening, in 1807, it was used for shipping and eventually became part of the extensive Surrey Commercial Docks.

The Regent's Canal and Surrey Canal Docks were part of the port of London and assisted its trade. But where canals entered a navigable river there was always the temptation to create a new port. For example, the Duke of Bridgewater's Manchester to Liverpool canal did not terminate in Liverpool but, for reasons of cost, was taken to the Mersey at Runcorn. Here a basin was constructed in 1773, another—'Old Dock'—in 1791 and a third—'Coal Basin'—in 1800; attempts were made to attract coasters by deepening the Mersey outside the 'port'; and in 1816 one visitor found the place well equipped with facilities 'more like storehouses and conveniences for a royal navy, than auxiliaries for a canal.'[32] Six years later Runcorn got her Custom House, but her ambitions were thwarted by the reluctance of masters to commit their ships to the upper reaches of the Mersey. In 1773 Bridgewater had also opened Duke's Dock in Liverpool as the 'terminus' for his canal traffic, and it was here, rather than at Runcorn, that the bulk of trans-shipment occurred.

The situation on the Humber was quite different, and the consequences for Hull were more serious than for Liverpool. Most of the canals entering the Humber made no effort whatever to bypass Hull, but the Aire & Calder Navigation, fearing rivals and hoping to tap the growing

Yorkshire coalfield, decided in 1820 to make a new cut from Knottingley to Goole in order to bypass the Ouse between Selby, which had served as the terminus of the navigation since 1778, and Goole.[33] 'The most difficult parts of the river Ouse are cut off,' the Company's engineer, George Leather, reported in 1822,[34]

> which will be a strong inducement for Ships now stopping at Hull to make for this place, and as they can navigate with a greater draft of water by several feet to this place than they can to Selby, trades will in all probability be established here which cannot be carried further up the Ouse, such as the Hamburg and Baltic trades.

To this end he adapted plans drawn up by John Rennie just before his death and constructed a three-acre Barge Dock at the end of the canal, adjacent to a two-and-three-quarter-acre Ship Dock, with warehouses at the junction of the two. Despite their small size (at full capacity they could hold around 200 barges and up to 60 small ships) the two docks could handle a large amount of tonnage by efficient and speedy working between barge and ship; and to save time and water, both docks were locked into a collecting basin (only recently destroyed) which was itself double locked—Barge Lock and Ship Lock—into the Ouse. Hull, with congestion in its Haven, and with ships, coasters, barges, lighters and floating timber all mixed up in its docks, could not match the smooth working which began in Goole in 1828.

In that year, mindful of the potential of the novel steamship trades, the Aire & Calder Navigation obtained an Act to construct Steamship Dock, with its own independent Steamship Lock, at 210×58 feet the largest in Britain. After various delays it was eventually built in the mid 1830s and opened in 1838. Here, it was said, 'the largest class of sea-going vessels can be moored in safety, and have uninterrupted means of approach alongside the different quays, sheds, and warehouses, either to take on board or discharge their cargoes.'[35] However, while coastal trade grew by leaps and bounds, to pass that of Hull in the late 1840s, foreign trade remained elusive.

A small number of places gained from their positions at the ends of canals, most notably Bowling, Grangemouth and Lowestoft. Bowling and Grangemouth were the termini of the first British ship canal: the Forth and Clyde. Both were up-river from established ports at Greenock and Leith, and there was a possibility that with their ability to handle ships between the west coast and the Continent and the east coast and Ireland they would emerge as ports

in their own right. In fact Bowling never developed, though 'Port Dundas', an inland basin where the canal ran through the suburbs of Glasgow, enjoyed an active participation in the trade between Glasgow and the east coast. Grangemouth, on the other hand, was transformed, becoming the industrial outlet for Stirlingshire (and for the important Carron Company) as well as for the west, to the detriment of Bo'ness, which previously held these trades: 'It was the arrival of the canal age in Scotland', wrote the historian of the eastern Scottish ports, 'which raised up the rival port of Grangemouth to steal away much of the glory of Bo'ness'.[36]

If Grangemouth did not become a major port in the nineteenth century it was largely because she served a hinterland which was itself relatively unimportant. The same is true of Lowestoft, created under an Act of 1827 by the Norwich and Lowestoft Navigation Company. Their object was to allow vessels from Norwich to bypass the old river route to an ailing Yarmouth with a ship canal which brought some 200 vessels of assorted sizes to the Company's Norwich quays in 1833. But despite an excellent floating harbour constructed out of Lake Lothing at no very great cost, the tonnage of shipping seeking to use Lowestoft or travel up to Norwich was severely limited and by 1835 the Company was bankrupt and the port up for sale. It was only saved—and Lowestoft confirmed as a minor port—when it was acquired in 1844 by Samuel Peto, the railway contractor. To this extent Lowestoft shares with Runcorn, Ellesmere Port, Grangemouth and Goole the general characteristics of a canal port which, having been founded for that mode of transport, attracted railway attention and, to a greater or lesser extent, was re-orientated around railway working.

All these ports were at the seaward end of canals, but two at least—Glasgow and Gloucester—came to prominence because new cuts were made between them and the sea. Glasgow had been a medieval trading place on the Clyde, but like so many ancient towns had found difficulty in maintaining her connexion with the sea. By the seventeenth century the Clyde was silting so badly that she could receive only lighters, and in 1668 the Town Council decided to build a trans-shipment port below the worst of the shoals, eighteen miles down-river where the deep channel touched the southern shore.[37]

Having failed to purchase a site in Greenock, they built a harbour slightly up-river at what became Port Glasgow, and this was made the Custom port for the Clyde. For trans-shipment alone Port Glasgow was reasonable, but her land site was poor because of towering cliffs that come to within a few hundred feet of the water, and in consequence the landowners of neighbouring Greenock began to recognise the advantages of their own burgh, with more flat land and a better water site. In 1710 they opened their own harbour (long since built over) to take advantage of the opening of colonial trade after the Union of 1707, and thereafter Greenock played an increasing part in Glasgow's trade. But it was still Glasgow's trade. The ships might stay in Greenock, but the merchants stayed in Glasgow, and that is where industrial growth later took place.

It was never terribly convenient to deal through transshipment places so far away from the centre of commercial activity and so difficult of access by land; and since industry could not easily develop around the ports, a new port, it seemed, must be made in Glasgow itself. It was not a question of impounding the river to provide access—an impossible and unnecessary task—but of deepening it by removing rock and centuries of accumulated silt. A start was made in the 1770s by dredging and by narrowing the channel to increase the scour, with the result that the low water depth at the lowest point, Dumbuck Ford, was increased from a few inches to fourteen feet. At the turn of the century further work, following reports by both Rennie and Telford, led to Glasgow being made an independent port in 1812 but, while the coastal trade grew by leaps and bounds, it was not until the 1840s that the tonnage of foreign-going vessels at Glasgow exceeded that at Greenock, and the early part of the nineteenth century witnessed the parallel growth of quays in Glasgow and a new harbour—East India Harbour—in Greenock (1809).[38]

Gloucester's potential was by no means so great as Glasgow's, but she had traditionally served the considerable trade on the river Severn in much the same way as Selby served the Ouse, Gainsborough the Trent, or Perth the Tay. The Severn below Gloucester was, however, treacherous, and ships could sail only on the spring tide. The object of the Gloucester and Berkeley Canal Company was, therefore, to cut a ship canal from Gloucester to the Severn estuary, halving the distance by water and opening Gloucester to ships of three hundred tons. After much debate and work, the canal was opened in 1827 at a cost of around half a million pounds and, though trade was slow to pick up, the new port gradually squeezed Bristol out of part at least of the trans-shipment business. 'The City of Gloucester', it was recorded in 1830, 'is becoming a regular port,

and is a steady and important depot for the shipment of goods.'[39] Eventually the basins at Gloucester covered about ten acres, but the later ones were built to cater for traffic brought there by rail rather than river. The most impressive feature of the port was the range of warehouses around the docks and straddling the entrance to the river. And the maritime nature of the port was visible in the seamen's Bethel, which still remains.

One interesting little place that tried – and failed – to turn itself into a flourishing canal port was Lancaster. With a local trade based on the river Lune and some minor interest in the West Indies, commercial ambition in the mideighteenth century led to the construction, by the Lancaster Port Commission, of St. George's Quay. However, shifting sand made for treacherous navigation on the six or seven miles of river below the town, while a bar at Scaleford blocked the passage of larger vessels. To provide for their safety in the estuary a pier was erected at Glasson, some five miles down-river, and thereafter goods were lightered between that place and Lancaster. Finally, in 1787–91 this pier was transformed into the 2.5-acre Glasson Dock, to the design of Thomas Morris, a little-known engineer who for a brief period succeeded Henry Berry at Liverpool.

More seriously, with expectations of canals encouraging mining and textile production in the hinterland, attention at Lancaster in the 1790s turned into the possibility of a ship canal bypassing the difficult sections of the Lune and bringing ocean-going vessels up to a basin in the town itself. In view of the port's minor position it was not really a practical scheme, and it was, perhaps fortunately, aborted by the ecomonic upsets of the Napoleonic War. When John Rennie visited the town it was therefore not to plan docks but to construct the aqueduct carrying the Lancaster Canal over the river Lune towards its more sensible terminus at Glasson. The latter place continued to handle the deeper draughted ships, though coasters could still tie up at St. Georges's Quay if they wished. But Glasson Dock and the canal together – like the Haven at Grimsby – were not enough to confer a much higher status on the port of Lancaster, and in the 1840s the tonnage of its registered shipping was still little more than 5,000.

HASTINGS, Sussex. The most primitive of all forms of 'harbour': a shelving beach on which ships were grounded at low tide.

BRIDPORT, Dorset (below). A dry harbour created in the 1740s by excavating a shallow basin and diverting the river Brit between two entrance piers, and extended in the 1820s.

PORTLOE, Cornwall (above). A picturesque dry harbour on a sheltered shelving beach still suitable for small fishing and pleasure craft.

GORRAN, *Cornwall (left). A typical simple harbour made by erecting a small stone pier in a natural cove.*

RAMSGATE, *Kent (right). An unusual view of Ramsgate, the most substantial pier harbour built in the eighteenth century, chiefly as a harbour of refuge for Channel traffic.*

TORQUAY, *Devon (below right). Daniells' view of Torquay in the early nineteenth century, showing the more elaborate sort of harbour created by the building of two piers, c. 1805–15, in the shelter of Torbay. The number of ships is probably an exaggeration. The harbour was built in an attempt to attract shipping from other ports in the south-west, but was not a commercial success.*

SOUTHWOLD, *Suffolk (below). The light wooden piers at Southwold were typical of early harbour works on the east coast, where stone was not easily available and foundations commonly insecure.*

MARYPORT, Cumberland (above). The eighteenth-century harbour was made of wood. Although later reconstructed and extended in stone, remains of a wooden wall of this sort can still be seen at the harbour mouth (below). Now greatly decayed, 1982.

FOLKESTONE, Kent (above). A pier harbour given added protection by a cross wall of the kind found in several ports, most notably Dover and Ardrossan. Built by the Folkestone Harbour Company for cross-Channel traffic, it was not a success before the railway.

KINGSTON-UPON-HULL. The eastern pier of the entrance basin designed by John Rennie to protect his Humber Dock from excessive silting. It did not do so, and was soon altered to its present shape. The basin became the resort of the first steamers to use the port, one of which is seen clearing, with a curious tarpaulin 'roof' to keep its cargo, or perhaps its passengers dry.

CRINAN, Argyll. This tiny dock is no longer crowded with 'puffers' servicing the west coast of Scotland from Glasgow via the Crinan Canal (1801), but the locking and sheltering of pleasure craft keep it just as busy during the summer months. It is typical of many small places that survive because their simple facilities are excellent for recreational purposes without being ruinously expensive to maintain.

CHAPTER FOUR

Expansion: New Docks and New Ports 1840–1870

1. DOCK-BUILDING IN THE MAJOR PORTS

a) The Shortcomings of 'Old' Docks

The first great phase of dock-building produced the 'city-centre' docks. They followed a fairly clearly defined pattern which was based on assumptions derived from the needs of the eighteenth century and not necessarily appropriate for the nineteenth century. The second generation of docks was therefore required partly because of expanding trade, but also because some at least of the older docks were not easily adapted to new trades and ships, or new working methods.

The first dock estates were too small for later purposes. When, as in London or Hull, houses and churches had to be pulled down and expensive land purchased, engineers had applied their ingenuity to provide the maximum area of water on the minimum area of land. Few poeple in the early nineteenth century would have regarded this as a problem because most large ports continued to operate the lighterage system, in which goods entering the dock by water also left by water, to be landed at some more convenient place than the crowded quays. The advantages of such a system during the canal age are obvious; but so, too, are the disadvantages when canals gave way to railways.

A further problem resulted from the assumption that ships using the docks would remain as they were in 1800. By later standards even a three-hundred-tonner was an inadequate model around which to construct a dock, especially since the dimensions of the locks were based on the ratio between length and beam common among sailing ships but vastly altered in the first generation of steamships.

It was not simply that the early docks were built before the 'modern' ship evolved; they were also the wrong shape for quayside working. It was commonly accepted that ships might remain in dock for weeks on end between voyages or out of season, and squarish docks, with their high water area to quay length ratio, were better suited to sheltering ships than berthing them. Not only did ships tied up in the centre of docks obstruct movement; they also occupied expensively constructed space which, if reduced to the width of a navigation channel, would allow a greater quay length for the same amount of excavation. Apparently it was Thomas Telford (or his assistant, Philip Hardwick) who first gave thought to this problem when he planned St. Katharine's Dock. Given the small extent of his perimeter, he drew within it not one dock, as precedents would suggest, but two, by the simple method of introducing internal piers. Within three years London Dock Company followed suit by constructing a large jetty into the western end of their western dock and so gaining almost a quarter of a mile of quay for the loss of only a fifth of the water space. It was a lesson soon learned, and followed elsewhere: docks should either be long and narrow (with Hull's Albert Dock as the extreme example), or provided with internal piers which gave them the appearance of having 'branches', as in most of the Liverpool and, for a time, the London docks.

While one set of factors encouraged changes in the shape of docks, others demanded even more drastic changes in the nature of dock-side facilities. It would be a mistake to suggest that the type of docks built in London in the early nineteenth century were typical early docks, for it is quite clear that they were not. Earlier docks did not have warehouses on the quayside. There was, however, a distinctive phase of dock building in which attempts were made to bring warehouses within the orbit of dock companies, whether for concern for security or desire for monopoly.

To some extent the warehouse was necessary because the vast increase in trade created bottle-necks in the internal transport system, and especially because London attracted much of the country's trade. Quayside warehouses were particularly suited for the re-export trades, for example. On the other hand there was a growing volume of trade in raw materials and manufactured goods which required neither the security nor the storage offered by the warehousing system. Those docks such as St. Katharine's in London and Albert, King's and Stanley in Liverpool which had their warehouses actually built over the quay were immensely useful for the rapid loading and unloading of small parcels of valuable goods, but almost impossible for the working of cheap bulky goods. During the Napoleonic War it had been the valuable trades which had dictated the form of docks in London, though not in the rest of the country. Thereafter, while the main outports might copy London to some extent for their own valuable trades, the new need was for open quays and timber ponds to satisfy the raw material trades. Even in London the general cry in the late 1820s was that the port was over-stocked with warehouses for the luxury trades.

b) The Influence of the Steamship

It is difficult to distinguish between the influences arising from the changing composition of trade and those consequent upon the adoption of steam power. The latter, perhaps, were more obvious to contemporaries and more appreciated by historians. Steam transport was new, physically impressive and above all fast. But it was also very expensive, and consequently was applied a good deal more rapidly to water than to land, partly because ships were less demanding of capital investment and engineering works, and partly because in the Firth of Clyde, where it was first developed commercially from 1812 onwards, it was the only possible form of decent transport in very difficult terrain. Twenty-eight steamers out of Glasgow were listed in the *Glasgow Directory, 1820* as carrying passengers and groceries to the Highlands and Islands, and their success brought others to the Thames, Ouse, Trent and Severn. But they were small shallow-draughted boats for passengers and parcels rather than freighters. They ran to timetables between river piers, and the last thing their

owners wanted was to be caught up in the press of vessels negotiating locks governed by tide tables. Furthermore they were certainly not welcomed—especially after the *Caledonia* blew up in Hull in 1816—in docks where banning ship-board fires was considered an essential precaution against the conflagration that was universally feared.

No sooner had steamers proved themselves—or, rather, improved themselves—on the river and coastal runs than their money-spinning passenger trade was threatened by the railways. They then turned increasingly to the short-haul European passenger routes and finally, in the 1840s began to displace sailing vessels in valuable short-haul freight trades. By 1850 steamers accounted for no less than 41 per cent of the foreign-going tonnage entering and 52 per cent of tonnage clearing at Hull, and for 28 and 34 per cent at London. By comparison Liverpool's steamer traffic was still a small percentage of the total, but the beginning of transatlantic steam navigation in the 1840s soon raised problems there of accommodating very large vessels.

These early steamers benefited from the freedom they enjoyed outside the docks, and many ports went to great lengths to accommodate them at special river or harbour berths and quays which they were reluctant to leave. When, for instance, the local worthies of Aberdeen, which had almost no foreign trade, thought to attract ships to the port by building a dock in the 1830s, they were opposed by the coastal steamship owners using the port. The latter were accused of selfishness. Their steamers had special dredged berths and therefore avoided inconvenience and danger suffered by sailing vessels grounding in an irregular harbour. Their counsel at the House of Commons Committee considering the Bill retaliated with a salutary reminder that docks were not universally necessary or desirable, even for steamers:

> You may carry the system of Docks too far, if you do not want them; and we do not want them here . . . For one class of horses you want a particular sort of stable; you do not put a cart horse where you put a racer, particularly if it costs you more . . . those who want to get quick in and out will not use the Docks. Those include a large proportion of the trade of Aberdeen; and I have already shown to you, that if they use the Docks they will be great losers.[1]

Aberdeen did not get its dock, but places with a greater traffic soon found that goods could not be moved to piers, or loaded there, with the same convenience and expedition as passengers, and for normal commercial working it was essential that steamers be brought within the docks. However, since steamers had developed outside the docks they had been able, by the interaction of intense competition and technical advance, to grow in power and size to the stage where many of them were already too large to pass through the locks when it became desirable that they should do so. In Hull, for instance, where the locks had been designed with three-hundred-ton sailing ships in mind, the four-hundred-ton mark was passed by steamers in 1831, and by 1850 the largest, the *Emperor*, was 1,320 tons. Even that figure understates the predicament, since tonnage and official measurement are not an accurate guide to the overall size of steamers. When the master of the *Wilberforce*, officially measured at 179 ft × 24 ft 3 in, appeared before the Select Committee on the Hull Dock Bill in 1840 he declared the actual measurements to be 190 ft × 37 ft 6 in. The *Wilberforce* was not even an exceptionally wide vessel; the *Tiger*, running from the same port to Hamburg in the 1840s, was 188 ft long and 54 ft wide over the paddles.[2] The Humber lock at Hull measured only 158 ft 6 in × 41 ft 6 in, and the widest Liverpool lock was only 45 ft.

Owners and masters were reluctant to bring steamers into existing docks even where they could pass the lock. The *Wilberforce* needed three times her length in which to manoeuvre, and occupied an unprecedented length of quay. Steamers could not be crowded with other vessels as had been the custom with sailing ships. They wanted rapid ingress and egress, and demanded the same priorities as those they had hitherto enjoyed at piers, namely a specific place as their permanent berth. In 1840 it was calculated that a dock built to cater for 140 'normal' sailing ships of 200–300 tons could accommodate only 35 of these foreign-going steamers,[3] and dock authorities had little time in which to decide what to do. When, in 1837, the Hull steamer owners complained to the Dock Company there about the number of steamers that could not use the docks, they were told to build more prudently. But it was clearly imprudent to maintain such a stance when rival authorities might provide enticing facilities for steamers, and the major ports were soon engaged in another round of substantial dock building.

The remains of Railway Dock warehouse, Hull. The dock is to the right. Rails that ran down the public streets can be seen on the hydraulic bridge in the foreground, and the remains of the first railway goods station are beyond the warehouse.

c) The Coming of the Railways

Had the larger steamers been the only influence at work in the 1840s, ports might have satisfied demand temporarily by enlarging locks rather than by constructing new docks. The latter became necessary because of the physical needs of railways, and eventually because the increased traffic carried by the national railway network established in the 1840s gave a great boost to steam navigation.

The problem of introducing railways to ports was not at first the amount of additional business involved. Indeed, since the major ports were heavily dependent on water-borne traffic they were not seriously affected by rail-borne goods for a considerable time. Enthusiasm for railways was by no means uniform throughout the country, either in ports or their hinterlands. While it made sense to connect Liverpool with Manchester in 1830, there was no urgency about linking Leeds to Hull because of the latter's superb waterway connexions. Not until 1840 was Hull brought into the railway network and equipped, as it was said at the opening of the Hull and Selby Railway, 'to contend against advantages which other ports have hitherto possessed'.[4] In similar fashion London, with its vast domestic market and coastal trade, did not at first feel the need for rail connexions for freight purposes: nobody doubted the continuation of river working and coastwise activity, and long-distance distribution or collection by rail was not considered possible, particularly for coal which elsewhere was one of the main items carried by rail.[5]

Once the desirability of a rail link was recognised, port authorities had to face up to the difficulty of establishing it. As noted above, early dock estates were small in size and almost the whole of their activity faced inwards towards the water. They were not designed with land carriage

in mind and, since they were at the heart of port life, rails could only be brought to them with a vast amount of demolition of both residential and business property. Within the docks themselves an equal devastation of valuable property would have been called for. In Hull and Liverpool where the docks were more or less on public streets some attempt at railway access was achieved by running rails down those streets, but even here the routes were limited by local topography, and the square shape of the early docks required excessive use of turntables and bridges to get waggons round all their sides. A complete railway system was not possible in the old docks, and two partial answers — to carry goods by truck to a goods station some distance from the dock, or to bring rails into a limited area of the dock estate — involved such a degree of manhandling as to negate the speed, and therefore the relative cost advantages, of steam transport.

Quite apart from the costs involved, there was an objection to altering docksides to accommodate railways. While railway working ideally required transit sheds for rapid unloading and loading of both steamer and train, the traditional uses of the dock remained. There was still sugar and wine to be stored, and valuable cargoes to be guarded. An increasing specialisation of function appeared to be the most satisfactory solution to the various problems involved. The London docks had from the beginning been segregated because of their monopoly rights, and it was easily understood in London and elsewhere that new docks must be provided for the steamship and railway trades. However, while the argument that long thin docks were best for steamships also holds true for railway working, and while it seems logical in retrospect that docks should be constructed to accommodate both steamships and railways, the fact is that even as late as the 1850s the implications of this were not readily understood by port authorities. They could still, with some justice, think of steamers without railways and railways without steamers. Both were novelties, and the connexion between them was not overwhelmingly obvious to people who had seen steamers develop on the rivers rather than in foreign trade.

Hull offers the best example of short-sightedness. Railway Dock could not receive large steamers, while Victoria Dock could receive the largest steamers (her half-tide basin was larger than Railway Dock) but initially had no proper rail connexions. Railway and steamers were linked by lighters. In similar but less obvious fashion, Clarence Dock at Liverpool, though opened for steam-shipping in the same year as the Liverpool & Manchester Railway (1839), had no adequate rail connexion. Moreover, although it was the first dock opened specifically for steamers, the chief objective was their segregation for fear of fire rather than the provision of a new type of facility. Its lock was no wider — at 45 ft — than those of other docks catering for sailing ships, and the large entrance basin, allowing speedy turn-round in relative safety but without passing the lock, represents a half-way stage between river working and dock working that was still thought desirable for packet boats when Victoria Dock opened in Hull two decades later. It was Goole, in a desperate bid to win trade from Hull, that first provided special facilities for the reception of the largest paddle steamers in Steamship Dock, with its 210 ft × 58 ft lock, projected as early as 1827 but not opened until 1838. (When steamers were no longer a novelty, the name was changed to Ouse Dock.)[6]

d) New Docks for Old: Hull

Rather surprisingly the challenge from Goole was not taken up immediately by Hull, where the Dock Company was positively tardy in responding to the demands of local shipowners, and where continuing disputes about the siting of docks were not, at that time, resolved by the insistent pressures of expanding trade. It was not until the mid-1840s that these pressures made themselves felt, and resulted, as noted above, in Railway Dock, opened in 1846 to bring the Hull & Selby Railway into the dock system, and in Victoria Dock, opened in 1850 for steamships, but also for trade in general and timber in particular. Railway Dock, which appears to have been the first dock constructed in a major port specifically for railway working, was not in itself notable, being in fact only a small branch of the existing Humber Dock, with no independent entrance from the Humber. Its major feature — apart from the integrated railway — was the huge warehouse which ran along its south side. This warehouse undoubtedly lacked some of the convenience of transit sheds, but bearing in mind the small size of Railway Dock, the preponderance of sail among its users, and the inexperience of the railway in assembling and despatching cargoes, it made sense at the time to work from the waggon into the warehouse and from the warehouse to the quay in a fashion that would soon become obsolete for many types of goods. By comparison Victoria Dock had nothing distinctive on its quays but was itself one of those distinctive docks — of which

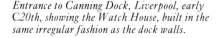

Carefully cut regular stonework of Victoria Dock Basin, Hull, c. 1850, with cast-iron ladder. Engineer, J. B. Hartley.

Entrance to Canning Dock, Liverpool, early C20th, showing the Watch House, built in the same irregular fashion as the dock walls.

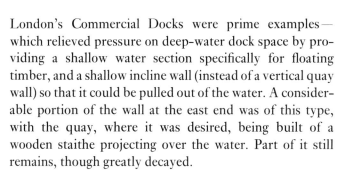

London's Commercial Docks were prime examples — which relieved pressure on deep-water dock space by providing a shallow water section specifically for floating timber, and a shallow incline wall (instead of a vertical quay wall) so that it could be pulled out of the water. A considerable portion of the wall at the east end was of this type, with the quay, where it was desired, being built of a wooden staithe projecting over the water. Part of it still remains, though greatly decayed.

e) Liverpool

In the year in which Hull's Victoria Dock was opened the tonnage of vessels frequenting that port was a little over eight hundred thousand; Liverpool in that same year received something over three and half million and, without going into the 'chicken and egg' relationship between the provision of docks and the advance of tonnage, it can fairly safely be argued that Liverpool's need for the former was greater than Hull's. In fact, the extent of dock building in Liverpool had been, and continued to be, quite staggering. Prince's Dock, completed in 1821 after recur-

ring delays because of war, had been expected to cope with the increase of trade for some time to come, but the tonnage entering the port rose from 839,000 tons in 1821 to 1,592,000 in 1831 (though the larger foreign-going ships accounted for only 404,000 tons and 719,000 tons respectively).[7] Faced with this remarkable growth the new Docks Engineer, Jesse Hartley, began work on a series of docks which were to earn him a secure place in the annals of dock engineering.

The first of these docks was Clarence, intended for steamers and therefore built some distance from the other docks for safety's sake. This was followed in 1832 by Brunswick Dock, which was the last of the old style designed by Hartley and the only one that he built south of the existing docks. Thereafter a pattern clearly emerged. Since large docks of the desirable, narrow shape would have meant too great an elongation of the river frontage, Hartley took advantage of the inward curve of the river frontage to project the sea wall outwards and thus provide enough room to turn the docks round in parade ground fashion to produce three short lengths perpendicular to the shore instead of one long length parallel to it. By linking them together and to existing entrance basins no new lock had to be made directly into the river, thus avoiding to some extent the broken river wall which would have caused excessive silting (and heavy expense). In this way the space between Clarence and Prince's Docks was filled by Waterloo (1834), Victoria (1836) and Trafalgar (1836), the three together containing some 29 acres of water.

A lull then ensued until the early 1840s, when work began on the first of Liverpool's bonded warehouse docks, the 7·75-acre Albert Dock opened in 1845 on the reclaimed land west of Salthouse Dock and again making use of an existing entrance, in this case the Canning entrance, which was now converted to a half-tide basin. There followed a period of frantic building as the sea wall was pushed northwards and further from the shore-line to allow for the constructing of another eight docks (Salisbury, Collingwood, Stanley, Nelson, Bramley Moore, Wellington, Sandon and Huskisson) containing something over 69 acres and entered via Salisbury Dock and Sandon Basin. They were opened between 1848 and 1852. Another lull in activity was followed in 1858 by the opening of Wapping and Coburg Docks, which were little more than infilling in the 'central' docks, and in 1859 by the 18-acre Canada Dock. Intended, as it name implies, for the timber trade, it was capable also of receiving the largest class of transatlantic paddle steamers. Indeed, one of the most important aspects of the continuous building was the increase in the size of the docks and of their entrances: Hartley's early docks had locks 45 ft wide, but this rose to 60 ft for Collingwood, Nelson and Wellington, 65 for Sandon, 70 for Coburg, 80 for Huskisson and 100 for Canada. The dimunitive Herculaneum Dock, built almost by accident in 1864, brought this phase of dock building in Liverpool to an end.

It must be emphasised that not all the docks built at Liverpool in this period were intended for 'modern' rail/steamship working. Sailing ships still made up the vast majority of vessels entering the port, and a diversity of docks was necessary for a diversity of vessels and trades. In particular the interlinked Salisbury, Collingwood and Stanley Docks differed from all the others in being projected backwards into the land (with Stanley Dock as the only one east of the main dock road, called Regent Road at this point) and forming the new terminal of the Leeds and Liverpool Canal. At the same time much traffic continued to leave the docks by road for storage in the extensive private warehouses that continued to be built in

the business area across the road; and for this traffic no modern facilities were required.

Important as were the larger docks for their acceptance of steamers carrying cargo, the fact remains that here, as in other ports, the very rapid turn-round of packet boats or ferry boats was not easy within docks of any sort, and it was generally felt that passenger boats should leave from some special central site rather than be muddled up with goods traffic along the length of the docks. The river wall enclosing the docks was not itself suitable because of very low—or no—water at low tide, but recent advances in technology which made the iron ship a possibility also enabled Sir William Cubitt to design a floating iron pontoon, 80 ft × 10 ft, linked to George's Dock wall by two 154-foot-long bridges. Its cost, at £50,000, was only a fraction of that of a dock to do the same amount of work, and it was so successful from its inauguration in 1848 that a more substantial pontoon, 1,000 ft × 80 ft, was positioned off Prince's Dock wall in the following decade when the larger transatlantic liners began to evolve. Here the passenger liners continued to berth for as long as they used the port. The pontoon itself—known locally as the Landing Stage—was actually rebuilt following a fire in 1874 and substantially altered and extended in the 1890s with the opening of Riverside Railway Station for the boat trains.

Much has been written about the Liverpool docks of this period and, inevitably, about Jesse Hartley who designed them. Liverpool is unique in the number of docks she built, and Hartley, who was the full-time engineer of the Dock Trust, consequently had a greater impact on this place than other engineers had on ports for which they were merely consultants. The sheer volume of Hartley's work was impressive, but so, to the modern observer, is the quality. Everything is on a grand scale, whether it is the vast length of wall on the landward side of the docks, or the sea wall on the other side which appears at low water as impressive as any medieval walled city. The gates are imposing, the clock-towers grand; and above all—quite literally—tower the warehouses that excite much admiration today, though a local historian described them a century ago as 'a hideous pile of naked brickwork'.[8] In fact the warehouses at Wapping Dock (now part of King's Dock) and at Stanley Dock are almost identical in design to those at Albert Dock, but the latter produce their visual effect by surrounding the dock with their five stories of grimy red brick and their great cast-iron pillars almost as far round as they are high. The Albert Dock obviously

Stanley Dock, Liverpool, showing a typical 'heavy' warehouse of the early C19th pattern.

The cast-iron pillars and fireproof floors of Liverpool dock warehouses in Wapping Dock, Liverpool. Also seen is Jesse Hartley's hydraulic tower of 1866 and the base of a chimney in typical irregular stone.

The floating landing stage, Liverpool, early C20th view with the magnificent dock office in the background.

owes its design to the influence of St. Katharine's Dock in London, but in one respect it was in advance of its model: Hartley used cast-iron framing and brick-arched floors which had not been used in the early St. Katharine's warehouses but which were copied for the central block erected shortly after the Liverpool work.

Needless to say, the configuration of the Albert Dock warehouses was not their only characteristic to attract attention. No less a commentator than Sir John Rennie, while declaring that docks must be classified by use 'in order that all the machinery and other conveniences may be adapted to carry on the trade in the most expeditious and economical manner', went on to proclaim (in 1854) the economical advantages of the warehouse dock:[9]

> As a general principle, the docks should be surrounded with warehouses having open sheds on the quays between them and the warehouses, or immediately under the warehouses; by this means the cargoes can be assorted under the sheds, and those goods which are not required for immediate exportation or inland use may be warehoused, and there kept under bond until wanted; whereas according to the system for the most part in use in Liverpool, the goods are carted at great expense to and from the private warehouses at a considerable distance from the docks; moreover, the loading and unloading cannot be carried on so economically as can be adopted where the whole is under one well-combined systematic management upon a large scale.

Having paid the customary tribute to Jesse Hartley and Albert Dock, a number of suggestions might be made about this whole business of assessing the 'importance' of docks. Firstly, the 'solid construction' and the use of granite in some of Hartley's docks, while interesting to the student of dock-building materials, is of no special significance: docks everywhere were as solidly built as they needed to be and engineers generally chose the most appropriate materials and designs for the purpose in hand. The major advances in building materials were not the choice of a particular stone, but the much earlier discovery of waterproof mortar and the later perfection of concreting techniques. Secondly, since the great bonded warehouses were inappropriate for many trades, to praise their construction as the major achievement of a dock engineer is to overlook his duty to provide for all trades. The question ought not to be 'Are the remains aesthetically pleasing to modern observers?', but 'Did they serve the purpose for which they were designed?' By this criterion it might be argued that Hartley's greatest contribution to the prosperity of Liverpool was not the relatively backward looking Albert Dock so much as the forward looking Canada Dock. By a similar token Liverpool's docks, despite their great number and aggregate acreage, are not noticeably 'better' than docks built elsewhere. All this is not to deny or belittle the achievements of Hartley or the Liverpool Dock Trust, but to suggest that Hartley's great achievement was the provision of an adequate mix of docks to suit all demands, and the achievement of the port was to provide them more or less in step with demand. Nor does it lessen the 'tragedy' of Albert Dock, the only survivor of the great bonded docks since those in London were destroyed, which is now (1980) in such a derelict state that all access is forbidden and the people of Liverpool, with neither the wealth nor the confidence that saw it built, can apparently afford neither to repair its buildings nor to pull them down. They remain the most visible evidence of a great era in British trading history, and a constant gaunt reminder of the inexorable changes which occur from time to time in both trade and shipping, to the great benefit or cost of individual docks or ports.

f) London

London was no less concerned with large ships than Liverpool and Hull, but there the problem was somewhat different because of the existence of the various Dock Companies, none of which was 'responsible' for answering new demands as were the authorities of the other two places. While it was generally admitted that the docks and the wharves between them already had an excess of warehousing, competition between companies after the abolition of monopolies severely limited their ability to expand water space. A partial answer to the problem came in 1838 with the amalgamation of the East and West India Dock Companies, the latter having plenty of warehouses and the former (after the abolition of the East India Company's trading monopoly in 1833) having plenty of water space, hopefully for the new steamers. But neither the new company nor the older ones were able to provide accommodation for larger vessels, and paradoxically the merger of the two companies was followed by the creation of a new one specifically to build an advanced type of dock. Very appropriately the Victoria Dock Company was led by the two greatest railway contractors, Peto and Brassey, and, not surprisingly, Victoria Dock, opened in 1855, was well equipped with railway connexions and could accommodate the largest steamers in its 80-foot-wide lock and at its half-mile-long quays.

The dock was distinctive in a number of ways, quite apart from its huge size, at 100 acres by far the largest dock in the country. Because of the ease of communications by rail and water, the Company determined to build down-river on the Plaistow marshes, where land was cheap enough to permit a massive dock estate, and far enough from the City to avoid the dangers arising from large steamers negotiating the most crowded section of the river above Bugsby's Reach. Moreover, since the land concerned was actually some eight to ten feet below the high water mark on the river, the dock could be constructed without full excavation: 'by making little more than embankments and entrances', in the words of Charles Capper, the dock's manager and historian of the port of London.[10] In consequence it cost no more than a million pounds, a fifth of the cost of London Dock and less than half that of St. Katharine's.

Victoria Dock had a number of interesting features. The most notable at the time, and long since removed, were the eight jetties projecting from the north wall almost to the middle of the dock, and looking very much like the 'finger piers' common in North American ports. Their principal purpose, as with the peculiar configuration of Liverpool's docks, was to extend the length of quay enclosing a given water area, and their success led to similar piers being added to the India Docks. There was at the same time a bonus, in so far as piers allowed cargoes to be unloaded from a ship on one side of the pier and concurrently loaded into barges on the other, a system which was speedier than one where barges could only be loaded when the ship had departed, and which was preferred by many people to the traditional over-side delivery into barges when the sorting of mixed cargo was involved.[11]

A second major difference between Victoria Dock and most of the other London docks was the absence of warehouses (though the company owned an 'uptown' warehouse in the Minories, on the Blackwall Railway line). Their place was taken by transit sheds integrated as far as possible with the railway system. 'The railways which encircle the Victoria Docks', wrote Capper,[12]

enable them to bring produce to their uptown warehouses, or to deliver it to the railway companies or to the London consumer, with greater facility and less loss of time — and in some cases even with less expense — than

the same goods could be carted to the railway stations or elsewhere, from the London and St. Katharine's Docks, which are connected with no railway.

It must be noted, however, that the jetties hampered railway working in Victoria Dock because they ran at right angles to the direction of the rails along the dock, and short of rebuilding the railway system to correspond to those operating in coal ports, there was nothing that could be done to avoid some manhandling of goods at the quayside and again at the railside.

Two further innovations were important for the modern functioning of Victoria Dock. The efficient operation of a dock some four miles from the heart of the port was assured by the introduction of the electric telegraph which, so far as communications were concerned, put Victoria Dock on an equal footing with the docks in the Pool, while the speedy handling of vessels within the dock was greatly assisted by the introduction of hydraulic power, which in London was first used effectively in this dock.

Victoria Dock could clearly compete with the facilities offered by its rivals, but too much should probably not be made of this so far as the early days are concerned. It is true, for instance, that large steamers favoured Victoria Dock, but the average size of vessels entering that dock was actually considerably less in 1860 than of those entering the London and India Docks. In other words, Victoria Dock was attracting all sorts of vessels and doing it chiefly, it would seem, by straightforward price competition. The Dock opened with an introductory 'bargain offer' which cut tonnage dues to almost nothing, and while the great increase in the tonnage of vessels using Victoria Dock in its first years did not cause a decline in the tonnage using the other docks, these were forced to reduce their rates to keep their shipping. As a result Victoria Dock Company continued to return 5 or 5·25 per cent on its meagre capital, London Dock Company's dividend fell from 5 to 2 per cent and St. Katharine's from 4·5 to 3·25 per cent between 1856 and 1861.[13]

Shipping frequenting the Principal London Docks, 1856–60

	1856		*1858*		*1860*	
	No	Tons	No	Tons	No	Tons
India Docks	1069	468,971	1099	451,865	1200	498,366
London Dock	1066	414,466	912	372,702	1032	424,338
St. Katharine's	902	213,797	904	202,740	905	223,397
Victoria Dock	1541	410,463	2420	849,360	2682	850,337

(excluding colliers and grain vessels)

Source: Capper, *Port and Trade of London*, p. 163.

Competition between docks was only part of the problem in the 1850s. The riverside wharves had never succumbed to the competition from the docks: the coal trade, for instance, had remained theirs, and many goods landed in the docks were still subsequently taken out and warehoused along the river, to the chagrin of the dock companies who made more money out of handling goods than they did from admitting ships. The wharves came into their own with the gradual relaxation of restrictions following the Customs Consolidation Act of 1853 which allowed them to handle dutiable goods. They expanded their role as cheap warehouses for a large volume of goods brought out of the docks by lighter, greatly assisted by the fact that neither lighters nor goods discharged over-side paid anything towards the upkeep of the docks. They also continued to receive their own shipping, chiefly coasters and near-European traders, and towards the end of the century they were still receiving approximately half of the total tonnage of shipping entering the port.[14] What they lacked in security and other advantages enjoyed by the docks, they made up in cheapness; and while all agreed that competition within the port kept London a cheap and therefore popular trading centre, it was, in the words of Broodbank, 'a grave question whether it did not also make the investment of capital in docks too precarious'.[15] By 1864 most of the companies thought that it did, and in that year the London, St. Katharine's and Victoria companies amalgamated to form the London and St. Katharine's Dock Company, and the Commercial and East Country Dock Company (formed in 1851) and the Grand Surrey Docks and Canal Company merged to become the Surrey Commercial Dock Company.

Competition remained, however, and was aggravated by the incorporation in the same year of the Millwall Dock Company and the opening, in March 1868, of the 36-acre Millwall Dock on the Isle of Dogs, complete with an entrance lock (450 ft × 80 ft × 28 ft) to accommodate the largest steamers. Faced with so much activity by actual and potential rivals, the East and West India Dock Company also sprang to life, and in 1866 began the conversion of their City Canal into South West India Dock. So reluctant were they to spend money, and so eager to open it (in 1870) that they neglected to build a new entrance lock, so that this dock, which for a time was attractive for vessels in the colonial trades, must be classed as one of the last of the old docks rather than the first of the new. Another 'lost opportunity' went when Surrey Commercial Dock

Company entered the competition again with their 16-acre Canada Dock, opened in 1876. Magnificent grain stores were built, and massive timber sheds, all to little avail once ships began to increase in size, since Canada Dock, like South West India Dock, could not happily receive vessels of more than five or six thousand tons.

The second phase of dock building in London had, therefore, created two railway-linked general docks—Victoria and Millwall—of considerable size and potential, and two—Canada and South West India—that served their purpose but were by Liverpool standards old-fashioned before they opened. Together with the older docks and river wharves and several minor works (East India Export Dock was also connected to the London and Blackwall Railway) they more than adequately served the current trade of the port so far as the simple volume of shipping and goods was concerned. But whether they served it in the most efficient manner is quite another question. London appeared to be a cheap port in which to trade, but Broodbank was not alone in following Mayhew by pointing to the high price that was paid in respect of the vast number of men employed—or under-employed—in the most over-capitalised, competition-riven and chaotic of the major ports.

*   *   *

The impact of large steamers on small docks had been severe, but at least the major ports were able in time to make the necessary adjustments. More serious were the implications for the remaining ports, particularly for those where facilities were not susceptible of easy improvement. Steamers had begun in a small way, owned very often by 'small' men for 'local' purposes that were as meaningful to bakers as to merchants. But as steamers grew in size and cost, and were adopted for long-distance trades, the spectrum of owners was narrowed to professional shipowners or shipowning companies, and the geographically widespread pattern of ownership of sailing vessels was not repeated for steamers. Steamers were to be found in a narrow range of leading ports where the concentration of business was most likely to offer them full employment and a speedy turn-round, considerations which were arguably more influential than docks until the second half of the century. Steamers were not yet tramps: they were more in the tradition of the regular liners, attempting to make ends meet, as international competition increased capacity and reduced rates, by securing regular customers and mail contracts, both of which tended to keep steamers in their 'home' ports or in thriving ports. It is a point of some significance, for several ports that were otherwise blessed with favourable resources were stifled for the simple reason that they could not attract regular steamshipping for their trade. Even some of the larger ports—Goole and Grimsby, for instance—suffered constantly because, for various reasons, established shipping companies would not operate from them. To some extent this situation was overcome later in the century as steamers became more common, and there were always vast numbers of sailing ships still available; but the fact remains that steamshipping helped to tie the bulk of the country's trade to a very small number of ports that had extensive internal communications and excellent dock systems.

2. THE RAILWAY AND MINERAL PORTS

The difficulty of introducing railways to established dock systems did not deter companies from making the attempt in all the major ports. They were, on the whole, successful, as the vast amount of traffic bears witness. Yet there remained an undeniable attraction, enhanced by the recently successful creation of Goole, in starting from scratch on a virgin site. Against the safety of lines to successful ports (where business communities promised instant returns) were the benefits accruing from avoidance of expensive encumbrances such as cramped and restricted sites, expensive land, vested interests and traditional working methods.

There was much to be said for new ports designed, organised and controlled by railway companies. Partly, of course, they were endeavouring to create—or avoid— monopolies, and in this they followed the precedent of port authorities which, except in London and one or two other places, enjoyed monopoly rights. Late-comers to the railways race were almost certain to avoid ports where other railways were already in possession, and, if they desired an outlet to the sea, to seek a decayed port or a new site. On the Humber, for instance, the arrival of the Liverpool–Leeds trunk route in Hull ensured that the Manchester–Sheffield railway would aim for Grimsby and the Lancashire & Yorkshire for Goole. Such exclusiveness was essential for attracting import and export traffic to their own metals.

a) The North-Eastern Coal Ports

For many railway companies the choice between an old or new port did not apply: they catered for trades created by themselves which could not easily or best be served by existing ports. Nowhere was the search for—and competition between—railway ports more in evidence than in County Durham, where railed waggonways were threading their way from colliery to coast long before 1825 when the most famous of them—the Stockton & Darlington— became, almost be accident, the first modern railway. Landowners and colliery operators were already in a state of excitement at the prospect of waggonways opening up the coalfield south of the Wear, and the next two decades witnessed intense rivalry between companies striving to penetrate the largest area and attract the most coal to their metals, and between port authorities—sometimes allied to railway companies—eager to attract the most coal to their staithes. The interplay of successful and unsuccessful promotions in the early days was, to say the least, confused, and it is not possible here to do more than indicate the general pattern of inter-port rivalry which led to the relatively stable situation existing in the north-east in the second half of the century.

The Stockton & Darlington Railway opened its first staithe for the shipment of coal at Stockton in January 1826, but it was soon apparent that Stockton's potential was limited by its distance from the deep-water channel off the coast. The old story was repeating itself: a harbour and river approach adequate for a small volume of trade may not be appropriate for more and larger ships. Within five years the railway company had pushed its line downriver, terminating—to the chagrin of Stockton—at 'Port Darlington', where they built a highly efficient set of eight steam-operated coal staithes. Partly as a consequence of the expanding coalfield, the tonnage carried by the Stockton & Darlington railway increased from 60,000 per annum in the late 1820s to 350,000 by the mid 1830s. At the same time industry associated with the smelting of the local Cleveland ore was quickly established in the shadow of the new port.

The Stockton & Darlington was soon followed by the Clarence Railway which was directly competitive, driving its line into the South Durham coalfield and terminating on the north side of the Tees, where Port Clarence was established opposite Port Darlington in 1834. However, many interested parties in the area immediately south and east of Durham city were anxious to avoid both the Tyne

Seaham Harbour, built by the Marquis of Londonderry in the 1840s. The paddle tug, Reliant, *is now in the National Maritime Museum.*

and the Tees. One logical alternative was Seaham Harbour, which was already under construction for the Marquis of Londonderry who was busy extending his waggonways into the hinterland. But it was too closely associated with the Londonderry collieries to be universally acceptable, and attention turned to the decayed fishing harbour at Hartlepool which had been mooted as a railway port as early as 1823.

Hartlepool Dock and Railway Company was authorised by an Act of 1832 to construct rails almost to Durham city, cutting behind the waggonways to Seaham and seriously inhibiting future traffic between the Durham area and Sunderland and Newcastle, whose Corporation, fearing the competitive disadvantage of expensive way-leaves, petitioned against the Bill 'to give to another Port an unfair and undue advantage over the river Tyne, long the principal Port for the export of coals'.[16] It was decided to convert part of the existing harbour—the Slake—into a dock, a prospect which was popular here and elsewhere (at Birkenhead and Lowestoft, for example) with those hoping to make large docks quickly and cheaply. But construction at Hartlepool was neither quick nor cheap, and poor foundations and funds —again a common combination in such schemes—delayed progress. The dock was abandoned, but a new harbour was opened for coal shipments from Thornley colliery in 1833.

The success of Hartlepool was not therefore assured. There was still the matter of competition and negotiation between rival companies, and for a time it looked as if the Clarence Railway might draw coal from the west of the coalfield down to the Tees. In the event the Stockton & Hartlepool Railway was promoted (from Billingham on the

Clarence railway to Hartlepool) and the new company agreed to use Hartlepool in preference to Port Clarence if the abandoned dock was built. With the prospect now of two coal lines bringing an estimated 400,000 tons per annum, work restarted on Victoria Dock, which was opened to shipping in December 1840. Hartlepool thus became the first proper railway port. Unfortunately only a meagre portion of the southern traffic arrived because Port Clarence offered lower charges, and recriminations between the Hartlepool and Stockton & Hartlepool companies became so bitter that the latter secured an Act in 1844 for the construction of yet another port, at West Hartlepool, a few hundred yards up the railway line from Victoria Dock in 'Old' Hartlepool. With few engineering difficulties and no serious delays, West Dock was opened in June 1847 when Hartlepool became unique in having two completely independent railway docks within the same port, a state of affairs only possible because, by historical accident, the 'port' of Hartlepool was still controlled by an ancient Harbour Commission which had done nothing at all to create the modern port.

An initial shortage of traffic for the new port was avoided by the Stockton & Hartlepool company taking over the Clarence Railway Company and diverting its coal traffic to West Hartlepool, where the water situation was vastly superior to that of Port Clarence. So great was this new traffic that a second west dock was started in 1849 and opened in 1852. By this time Hartlepool had on the east side of the bay the old original 25-acre harbour of the Commissioners and the Hartlepool Company's inner harbour and dock, each of 21 acres; and on the west side the West Dock basin of 44 acres and two docks together making 21 acres. Together they totalled 132 acres of water, and cost (with railways) one and a half million pounds. Something like a thousand merchantmen could take shelter in a port which only a decade earlier had been a neglected fishing village, and provision for working these vessels in the east harbour and dock alone included three steam cranes capable of handling 150 tons per hour and sixteen coal drops each capable of discharging 106 tons per hour (both for ten hours per diem). Although equipment at the west docks was inferior, together the docks exported 1·56 million tons of coal in 1850, of which 1·2 million went coastwise and the remainder abroad.[17]

While the two Hartlepool companies and the Marquis of Londonderry were endeavouring to extend their influence in the centre of the county, there were others just as eager to attract coal to the north and south. Sunderland, despite new coal staithes erected in the early 1820s, rightly felt herself vulnerable on all sides, and was only moderately relieved by the Durham & Sunderland Railway sanctioned in 1834, while the various schemes to construct a railway from Wear to Tyne were seen—as in the case of the Monkwearmouth & South Shields Railway—as attempts 'to detach the coal trade from the Port of Sunderland'.[18] In retaliation Sunderland planned a small coal dock in 1834 in Monkwearmouth, but it was not until 1850 that the substantial Hudson Dock was opened there by George Hudson, who had inspired it but lost his railway empire before it was completed. One interesting aspect of

Sunderland. When training the river Wear no longer sufficed, the 'Railway King', Hudson, initiated the building of small docks, seen here in the 1870s.

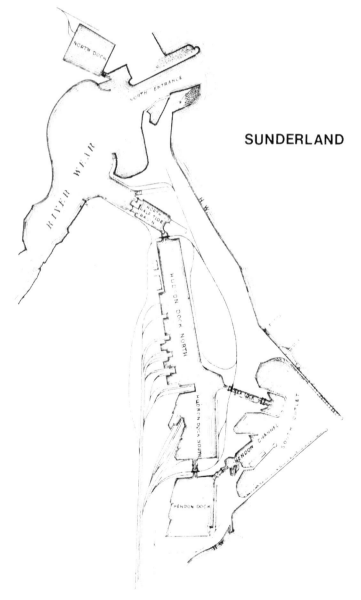

SUNDERLAND

port competition along the coast was seen after 1853 when Lord Londonderry began to send coal from his newer collieries to Sunderland rather than extend his own facilities at Seaham.

To the south the position of Port Darlington was seriously undermined by the opening of Hartlepool. Its coal handling equipment was inferior, involving the raising of each waggon in a manner that proved to be too expensive, too difficult in a tidal river, and too slow for an expanding trade. In order to remain competitive a group of local businessmen offered to build a nine-acre dock at Middlesbrough for the railway company, with an integrated rail system permitting the sorting and shunting of waggons on a fifteen-acre raised plateau, with double rails and inclines feeding the hoists (each assigned to a particular colliery or type of coal) and receiving back the empty waggons by gravity feed rather than horsepower and steam as hitherto. The initial result was a rise of some 29 per cent in coal exports between 1841/2 and 1844/5 and a rapid increase in the number of ships using Middlesbrough Dock to over 2,000 in 1844.

By contrast with the Tees, the Tyne had much to lose and an inclination to fight. New ports were not, at first, involved: it was merely a case of bringing waggonways to the river. But within a short time modern staithes had revolutionised activity, and the capacity of the railways to bypass up-river ports was threatening Newcastle as much as Stockton. The principal bid to capture the central portion of the Durham coalfield, the Stanhope & Tyne railway completed in 1834, avoided Newcastle altogether to terminate at a set of magnificent staithes at South Shields, and insult was added to further injury by the Brandling Junction railway, opened in 1839, which carried the Newcastle & Carlisle lines on to South Shields and also drove a branch to Sunderland, where coals could be delivered to the new Monkwearmouth Dock from the Stanhope & Brandling hinterland.[19] On the Tyne itself various proposals to build docks came to nothing because the river was long regarded as adequate and money was better invested in waggonways and staithes.

In contrast with Durham, competition for the shipment of Northumberland coal was slight. The only significant shipping place north of Newcastle was at Blyth, and though adequate for the shipment of local coal in the past it could only handle shallow-draught vessels. In the 1820s the Cramlington waggonway began to draw coal from the south of the river Blyth to a major staithe complex at Hay

Northumberland Dock, Newcastle, built by walling off a curve in the Tyne, for the Northumberland coalfield.

Hole on the Tyne, and this was eventually supplemented by the first section of the Blyth & Tyne railway (the Seghill Railway) opened in 1840. For many years it was a hotch-potch affair, but improvements in the early 1850s confirmed the Tyne as the outlet for Blyth coal. Indeed, the Bedlington Coal Company was so eager to ship from the Tyne that between 1842 and 1851 it employed an iron steamer called *Bedlington* which accepted 40 chaldron waggons at Blyth and 'tipped' them by ship-board steam crane into colliers on the Tyne.[20] Eventually the Northumberland side of the Tyne fell into line with the Durham ports when, in 1857, Northumberland Dock was opened by the River Tyne Commissioners as part of their scheme for straightening the river. A retaining wall was built across the shallow bay in which the northern coal staithes were situated, and a lock installed at the southern end, thus simplifying the loading process by removing tidal influences, and obviating the expensive necessity of removing the staithes to the new river bank. 'This', wrote Guthrie in his history of the Tyne,[21]

> was the first occasion on which any substantial improvement, or great plan for the benefit of the Tyne, had been undertaken and successfully completed by its conservators, and was a legitimate subject for congratulation. It seemed as if the stagnant waters of inertia were at last

being moved by the modern spirit of improvement, and that the Tyne was now entering in earnest on that path of progress and development on which hitherto such feeble and faltering steps had been taken. Not before time. The South Docks at Sunderland had been for some years in operation. . . .'

Two years later the south side of the Tyne gained a momentous competitive advantage in the Durham coal trade when a dock begun by George Hudson in Jarrow Slake, and abandoned on his downfall, was revived in the 1850s by the newly formed North Eastern Railway Company. Their magnificent Tyne Dock—sometimes called Jarrow Dock—was capable of accommodating five hundred colliers and of loading thirty at a time at the three great staithes fed by the latest system of inclined planes, involving almost 25 miles of rails, to avoid the lengthy process of raising and lowering individual waggons.[22]

The docks were 'eminently calculated to add to the commercial importance of the Tyne',[23] but the Tyne itself was in a parlous state. Though not necessarily worse than it had been in the past, Guthrie wrote of the year 1860,[24]

> relative to the trade carried on, and to its position as regards neighbouring rivers, it was at its very worst. Vessels of moderate size and draught were detained for weeks after loading unable to get to the sea *at the top*

of high water; other vessels were thumping and grounding on the bar in vain attempts to get to sea; and a state of things existed seriously detrimental, and which, if continued, would have been most disastrous — indeed ruinous — to the trade and reputation of the port.

Thus for Newcastle, more perhaps than for any other port, the arrival of the steam railway network demanded extensive river work if its full potential was to be realised. It was hoped at first that State assistance would be forthcoming with the recommendations of the Royal Commission on Harbours of Refuge in 1859, and though this fell through, the newly constituted Tyne Commissioners (1850) were able to borrow £350,000 under the Harbours and Passing Tolls Act of 1861 and begin work under the direction of John Ure, their new engineer appointed in 1859.

Unlike earlier engineers here and elsewhere, Ure did not put much faith in the efficacy of training walls, arguing that the river was too wide for it to scour its own channel. Instead he turned to dredgers, and by 1863 six were at work, shifting between four and five million tons of material per annum. By 1872, when a detailed survey was made, there were twenty-four or -five feet of water at low tide on seven shoals that had previously been dry (and one of which had been an island three feet high on which the women of South Shields had gleaned coal at low water). The harbour bar had disappeared completely. The river in what was commonly called Shields Harbour was around ten feet deeper than it was on the sills of the recently opened docks, and one happy consequence was the building of more river staithes and quays without the expense of further dock construction until the 1880s. A second consequence of extensive dredging was the new lease of life given to the up-river quays, as far as Newcastle itself, to which the deep-water channel had been deepened from an average of eight feet to twenty-two.[25]

b) The Ports of the North-West

In the north-west, the port owing most to railway development was probably Silloth.[26] It sprang from canal origins. Port Carlisle had been founded with the opening of the Carlisle Canal in 1823 to revive the trading interests of that place, only to find both canal traffic and port deprived by subsequent railway development along the Cumberland coast. Carlisle interests, believing that their 'own' port would preserve their marketing functions and capture trade between the east and west coasts and Ireland, formed the Carlisle and Silloth Bay Railway and Dock Company and in 1859 opened the new port of Silloth to replace the inadequate Port Carlisle. Here James Abernethy designed Marshall Dock and a 1,000-foot pier on an embanked site similar to Grimsby's, and equipped it with coal shutes, cattle lairages and hydraulic coal hoists similar to those he had recently installed at Swansea. In attempting to secure business the Company went so far as to finance coal explorations in the hinterland, but Silloth failed to secure the trade for which she was so optimistically planned. In 1862 the works were leased to the North British Railway Company, but no significant increase in traffic followed.

The principal reason for Silloth's stagnation was her inferior position compared with rivals further down the coast. The landowners of Cumberland were as eager as those of Durham to open up their coal and iron deposits with railways, and to extend and improve their 'private' ports: the Senhouse family at Maryport, the Curwens at Workington and Harrington, and the Lowthers (earls of Lonsdale) at Whitehaven. The Maryport to Carlisle Railway opened in 1845, aiding the Senhouse interest. The Earl of Lonsdale retaliated with the Whitehaven Junction Railway (1847) linking his port to the Maryport–Carlisle line; the Whitehaven and Furness Junction Railway (1850) linking it to the south; and the Whitehaven, Cleator and Egremont Railway (1855) opening up the mineral-bearing hinterland. 'Whitehaven', he declared in words similar to those used at the opening of the Sheffield–Grimsby railway (and no doubt others), 'possessed the finest harbour between Liverpool and Glasgow', and the port would instantly grow with a new Irish trade stimulated by the railways.[27]

Since the ports had reasonably good harbours, dock building in this area was not extensive. The small Lonsdale Dock at Workington was opened in 1865 for the coal and iron trades, its elevated coal lines in part still remaining, though performing no modern function. At Maryport Elizabeth Dock was opened in 1867 to supplement coal staithes in the river Ellen, and the larger Senhouse Dock in 1884, by which time Maryport had the most complex harbour and dock system in Cumberland, miraculously standing today almost as complete as in its heyday. Neighbouring Harrington was also brought into service by the Curwens, who supported the creation there of a small wet dock set back behind large piers in a small bay: it proved useful not only for the business of local iron works but also as a supplement to the inadequate facilities of Workington. However, despite the various exercises in port building, Whitehaven, with its range of piers and a small dock opened in 1876, remained the chief port of the region, and when viewed from the surrounding hills, is still one of the most impressive of the smaller British ports.

The Cumbrian ports were devoted to coal, iron ore and iron and steel in that chronological order. Elevated mineral lines threaded their way to them, and still criss-cross the coast road, though now lacking their rails and bridges. But for half a century or more the mining interests were overshadowed by the great iron and steel works adjacent to the ports. This new industrial enterprise was most in evidence in the Furness area. On the Duddon estuary the Hodbarrow mine was from the 1850s one of the leading British producers of iron ore and, in the absence of adequate local port facilities, built its own shipping staithes at a place called—as if to emphasise the new handling system—Borwick Rails. Over the Duddon, in Furness, the development of the Furness Railway Company by the Duke of Devonshire serviced the Barrow Haematite Steel Company (1859), which in turn (and with other later works) demanded extensive port facilities. In 1863 the Furness Railway began the construction of two great docks of 32 and 31 acres called, after the principal landowners, Devonshire and Buccleuch. A third dock—Ramsden, after the leading industrialist in the 'port'—was started in 1872.

More than the other north-western ports, Barrow shares with Middlesbrough the experience of local developments, based on iron working, which eventually became more important than rail-borne trade. Although the coastal and foreign export (and later import) of haematite was for a time impressive, the docks were really no more than expensive white elephants, and the southern parts of both Devonshire and Buccleuch were devoted to the shipbuilding and fitting business of Vickers.

c) The South Wales Coal Giants

To the south, the Welsh coalfield and ports benefited greatly from the building of railways: Newport, Cardiff, Barry, Penarth, Port Talbot, Swansea and Llanelli were all created or improved for railway-borne coal.

Cardiff owed its early prosperity to iron and to the Glamorganshire Canal of 1798 which brought it down to a basin and sea lock which replaced the old Town Quay on the inadequate river Taff. But the output of coal

(initially used to make iron) was growing rapidly in the valleys and, partly to exploit his mineral resources and partly to enhance his Cardiff property, the Marquis of Bute, the principal South Wales landowner, opened West Bute Dock in Cardiff in 1839. Almost inevitably the Taff Vale Railway, opened a year later, was forced to terminate at this dock, and Cardiff, which could never itself have built it (because the ironmasters were not interested and the coal trade was not yet developed), became the major coal port. No other place could rival its facilities and cope with the expansion of coal exports: Newport Town Dock (1842) was of negligible size, and Swansea did not acquire her first dock until 1852. As a result Cardiff rose from fourth place among the four coal exporters (Newport, Swansea, Llanelli and Cardiff) in 1840 to first place in 1851.[28] By then Bute Dock, originally under-utilised, was under intense pressure, and to avoid the possibility of a rival port emerging, the Bute estate opened, in 1855, the vast 46-acre East Bute Dock. At the same time business interests hostile to the Bute estate began work on a tidal harbour for the neighbouring river Ely and opened Penarth Dock in 1863, but since they could only work through the Taff Vale Railway, which leased the works, and since that company had a working agreement with the Bute estate, Penarth never became more than an overflow for the Bute dock system, though as such it was, of course, extremely valuable.[29]

What iron was to Cardiff, copper was to Swansea and Port Talbot, and since neither had so extensive a hinterland it was as well that they were able to maintain their connexions with metal industries to the present day. Nevertheless, it was coal again that provided the greater part of business in the middle of the nineteenth century and stimulated developments at both places. Swansea was fortunate in that the river Tawe, on which she stood, was better than many rivers along that coast, and also had a very convenient sharp bend for a mile or so above high water mark: following the example of Bristol this bend was cut off and in 1852 became a floating harbour as North Dock. With the continuing growth of business South Dock was constructed a quarter of a mile down-river from North Dock in 1859, but while she gained ground as a general-trade port—indeed, as the only general-trade port on the coast—Swansea never regained her early eminence in the coal trade.

Some years earlier Port Talbot also had made a floating harbour out of a lagoon associated with the river Avon, chiefly to serve the copper interests of the Talbot family, though it was not until the end of the century that extensive harbour works were undertaken. Similarly Newport, the principal coal exporter until the 1840s, was able to manage with little in the way of harbour improvements, apart from the 4.5-acre Town Dock opened in 1842 at the mouth of the Monmouthshire Canal, until the major extensions of the 1870s.

d) The Commercial Railway Ports

While most railway docks before 1914 were constructed for mineral traffic, there were some notable exceptions. The most important were Grimsby and Birkenhead. Almost exactly contemporaneous, both were designed by J. M. Rendel as part of joint railway and dock schemes. Birkenhead was built for what became the Birkenhead, Lancashire and Cheshire Railway Company, with high hopes of drawing traffic from Liverpool's heartland. Grimsby was transformed for the Sheffield, Ashton-under-Lyne and Manchester Railway Company, anxious to create an east-west trunk route south of the route based on Leeds and Hull, and the Grimsby Haven Company, composed of the cream of north Lincolnshire landowners eager to attract a railway to their decayed port and able to thwart any which shunned it.

Both were to be general-trade ports. The works at Grimsby, reported the directors of the subsidiary Great Grimsby and Sheffield Junction Railway, 'will undoubtedly make Grimsby the best steam packet and mercantile harbour and shipping port on the Eastern coast: and its importance in that respect, both to Lancashire and the West Riding of Yorkshire, cannot be too highly estimated'.[30] The prospectus of the Grimsby Dock Company—the revitalised Haven Company—was equally emphatic that 'the proposed additional dock accommodation cannot fail to render it by far the most eligible port of the east coast'.[31]

Grimsby was fortunate: by 1847 Birkenhead was being described as 'a splendid ruin', and while the former was opened by the Queen in 1852 amid a blaze of publicity to attack Hull's local pre-eminence, the latter had endless trouble involving Rendel's dismissal and reinstatement, and ending in 1858 with Birkenhead's absorption by the Mersey Docks and Harbour which, to the chagrin of Manchester Free Traders and anti-monopolists, drastically scaled down the plans for Birkenhead's rail connexions.[32]

Why did the two ports fare so differently in their early days? Partly it was because of their hinterlands. Although Birkenhead was nearer than Liverpool to the industrial south Midlands, she had no practical advantages to offer the hinterland already served by Liverpool (and, for that matter, by Garston). So unlikely had the success of a rival port on the 'wrong' side of the Mersey seemed in the early 1840s that the Corporation of Liverpool had actually sold the site of Birkenhead to the individuals who, much to the city's annoyance, subsequently formed the Birkenhead Dock Company. By contrast, the Manchester, Sheffield and Lincolnshire Railway (as the combined railway and dock companies were called) effectively tapped the southern part of Hull's traditional hinterland, a fact which had already caused consternation in Hull among those who saw the growing railway system as a reduction rather than an extension of that port's internal communications.

More serious, perhaps, was the difference in the two plans proposed by Rendel. His earlier (1843) scheme for Birkenhead involved the impounding of Wallasey Pool to form the 'Great Float', thus—in theory—providing the largest possible area of water at minimum cost compared with the more normal excavation of land as in Hull and London, or the embanking of foreshore as in Liverpool and the later Welsh ports. In order to provide immediate accommodation for shipping while the Great Float was being prepared, two docks—Egerton (4 acres) and Morpeth (11·5 acres) were rapidly constructed and opened in 1847. By then the money had run out. The original Dock Company was wound up, and though it re-formed it is doubtful if the Great Float would ever have been completed but for the intervention of Thomas Brassey, who had worked on various local railways including the Birkenhead and Chester Junction and who, having been born in Birkenhead, took a sentimental interest in the port. In fact the dam he built in order to work on the Float failed and he retired ignominiously from the scene, though some forty acres of the Float were serviceable. Shipping lines had begun to show interest, but not enough to save the beleaguered company, whose bankruptcy was only averted by the sale of the docks to the Corporation of Liverpool in 1855, for £1·1 millions. As an independent port Birkenhead had ceased to exist.

Birkenhead was not allowed to slip quietly away. The hostility between Liverpool and Birkenhead had been seen in the hinterland as yet another example of the monopolistic tendencies of ports which, it was supposed, reduced

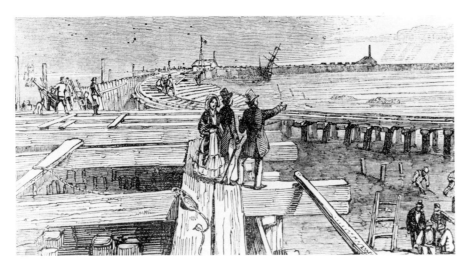

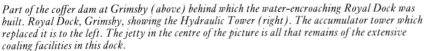

Part of the coffer dam at Grimsby (above) behind which the water-encroaching Royal Dock was built. Royal Dock, Grimsby, showing the Hydraulic Tower (right). The accumulator tower which replaced it is to the left. The jetty in the centre of the picture is all that remains of the extensive coaling facilities in this dock.

efficiency and raised charges. In particular, Manchester merchants objected to paying dues which Liverpool assigned to its civic coffers. This was the great decade of the attack on local taxation of trade, reaching its height in the Bill introduced into Parliament in 1857 by Manchester Chamber of Commerce and others to deprive the Corporation of Liverpool of its ancient rights over its own port. Liverpool objected but lost, and in 1858 the Mersey Docks and Harbour Board was formed to administer both Liverpool and Birkenhead docks. Nobody would dispute that they did their job well in Birkenhead, which was not neglected as some had feared it would be; by 1872 the Board had completed the impounding of around 165 acres of water and constructed nine miles of quay.

Birkenhead's troubles sprang from an over-ambitious plan supported initially by inadequate railway connexions and uncertain mercantile expertise. Large expanses of water commonly enticed engineers into works that were harder to construct and more expensive to fund than they imagined. Impounding havens looks sensible and easy: it rarely is. In many cases where it was tried it failed through insecurity of foundations or high cost of preparing adequate quays. The history of the Grimsby Haven, for which he prepared plans in 1844, should have warned Rendel of the dangers of impounding Wallasey Pool, but he went ahead and virtually ruined the company that employed him. The Hartlepool Harbour Commission had roughly similar problems when they tried to impound their Slake, and Peto's adventure in Lake Lothing at Lowestoft was never fully completed and never served the purpose for which it was intended. Promoters and engineers were too greedy when impounding standing water and allowed themselves flights of fancy that they would never have countenanced in the excavation of normal docks.

By comparison with his Birkenhead venture, Rendel's plan for Grimsby was a magnificent piece of compact engineering which went ahead almost without a hitch. Because of heavy silting the old Haven was ignored, and a long dock was built on reclaimed land stretching out beyond the low water mark. It was constructed behind a huge coffer dam which was one of the wonders of the age and which did not, unlike its fellow at Birkenhead, fall down.[33] But the real achievement of Grimsby was not the design or construction of its admittedly excellent dock so much as its superb integration with a railway, and this was reflected not only in the details of the railway system within the port, but also in the application of the second major element (after powered hoists and cranes) which linked together the steamship and the goods train: hydraulic power.

In this regard Grimsby's was the first truly modern dock in Britain. Admittedly hydraulic power had been applied to cranes in Liverpool's Albert Dock, *c.* 1847, but there were few, and no hydraulic *system* was involved. (See below, *p.* 99, for hydraulic machinery.) It was at Grimsby that a large, deep, adequately locked dock (in fact there were two locks of different sizes to save water on transit of small ships) was finally given a source of power which solved the two fundamental obstacles to the growth in the

Specialised quays for the fish trade, Grimsby, from a postcard, c. 1905.

size of both ships and cargoes. The difficulty was no longer the physical limitations imposed by the lock, since these had been adequately built as a matter of course since Rennie's day, and most problems with foundations could be overcome with deep piles or rafts. The limitation was now the difficulty of moving the huge gates required by large locks. At Grimsby the largest gates (of which there were four) each weighed 75 tons, and opening them— and the larger ones which followed in other places—was not at all the same kind of operation as opening a canal lock. The application of Armstrong's recently perfected hydraulic machinery was therefore more immediately useful for working lock gates than for any other purpose, and its success in this role was amply publicised by the huge Italianate campanile which was erected between the two locks to serve as the hydraulic reservoir. But its value for other purposes than opening lock gates in two minutes was soon recognised, and high pressure water was piped to fifteen cranes along the quays, thus removing the second obstacle to 'progress', namely the difficulty of handling large and heavy loads. For the first time a powered crane, making use of rails, terminals and connecting pipes, could be moved to the ships, instead of the ships, at great inconvenience, being moved to the cranes.

The Dock Tower at Grimsby was a brilliant advertisement for the port. As the publicity put it: 'When a steamer can run into a port as soon as it makes land, and can transfer its cargo to railway waggons, that cargo may be delivered 150 miles off before another steamer can grope its way up the intricate navigation of a river at night.'[34] It was a point that could be made of any of the railway ports, and the Manchester, Sheffield and Lincolnshire Railway appreciated the value of the connexion between its port and its railway for perishable goods by investing in fishing smacks and opening the first modern fish dock, thus creating the modern fishing industry and, indirectly, the industrial towns' addiction to fish and chips.

Grimsby was fortunate in having a general industrial hinterland providing an assortment of potential exports and demanding a variety of goods easily brought from the Continent. Just as Hartlepool, fed by the North Eastern Railway, was able to push the value of her exports ahead of the Tyne ports (which dealt chiefly in coal), so Grimsby surpassed Hull in two of her traditional trades: woollens and cottons. Machinery was added, and within little more than a decade Grimsby had become, by value of her trade, the fifth port in the country. However, even Grimsby had difficulty in establishing herself in competition with Hull, despite vociferous claims in Hull that a steamer there paid dues of £51. 12s. 6d. compared with a mere £2. 1s. 8d. in Grimsby, and that identical goods bound for Russia paid charges of £24. 11s. 5d. in Hull and £15. 18s. 0d. in Grimsby.[35] But the point is that the shipowners in Hull complained because they did not wish to send their ships to Grimsby, and so few of them did that there was no hope of regular liner traffic establishing itself there. The railway company was eventually forced to run its own regular steamers to the Continent.

It is important to stress this point that the performance of docks or of ports in the second half of the century was not determined solely by the quality of facilities offered either by the railway or the docks, or by the cost of working through them. General trade tended to follow established patterns associated with the large shipping companies (which were themselves situated in the major ports), with brokerage and insurance facilities, and abundant experience of handling cargoes. The old merchant communities, with their commodity markets, lived on. Those ports which succeeded as railway ports, were, therefore, those with very special rail connexions with manufacturing districts and coalfields. This was the formula for success in West Hartlepool and Grimsby, though neither place was able to maintain the initial boom following its opening.

3. THE PACKET PORTS

a) The Continental Packet Ports

The benevolent consequences of the interaction of railways and steamers did not end with the commercial ports. The old packet ports were also deeply affected, and several new ones were created to answer the distinctive needs of postal and passenger services.

There had always been certain ports, noted for their short links with Ireland or foreign countries, to which diplomatic papers were despatched for immediate shipment by special 'packet' boats unencumbered by the restraints inherent in the carriage of freight. These packets could equally serve the General Post when it developed, and their fast crossing and regular service attracted the better class of passenger. The Grand Tour, as likely as not, began at Dover, which alone of the Cinque Ports had survived into modern times as a considerable place on the strength of the short route to Calais. Its great advantage, so far as London was concerned, lay in the fact that traffic through Dover avoided the dangers of the Goodwin Sands and the long and potentially hazardous journey round the Foreland and up the Thames. In this respect external communications were more important than internal ones. Packet ports did not share the commercial ports' need for inland navigations: speed was the basis of their prosperity, and this was best provided by post roads and stage coaches.

A second characteristic of packet ports sprang naturally from the absence of general cargo, from the smallness of

their vessels, and from the speed with which those vessels turned round. They were able to cope with large tonnages without the additions to facilities required for similar tonnages of cargo vessels. The chief task of those responsible for maintaining packet ports was to build adequate piers or open wharves at which rapid turn-round could be effected. Access to deep water was not essential, though places with an adequate depth of water at 'Low Water Ordinary Spring Tide' were preferred. It was this ability to make do with relatively inferior situations, together with the desirability of obtaining the shortest sea crossing, that encouraged the growth and continuation of packet ports at otherwise unlikely spots on the coast.

So far as Dover was concerned, her link in the route to France was confirmed with the opening of the railway from London in 1844. The new eight-acre Wellington Dock did not bring the expected flow of goods, but the speed and convenience of trains and steamers encouraged the movement of passengers and facilitated a closer contact between Britain and the Continent. Businessmen were better able to explore their markets, and the middle class responded to the Grand Tour opportunities opening with the spread of the European railways. A second railway, the London, Chatham and Dover, arrived in 1861, further enhancing the port's status.

The tonnage of foreign-going vessels entering Dover rose rapidly, from *c*. 90,000 tons in 1841 to 500,000 in 1880, but whether Dover could itself have continued to cater for them is a matter for conjecture. The question did not arise because the government, concerned at the likely consequences of foreign steamers in the Channel, and dismayed at the absence of a decent port on the south-east coast, abandoned Ramsgate, so long the recipient of government largesse, and created a new harbour of refuge at Dover. Work began in 1847 on Admiralty Pier, planned by Ralph Walker to extend the western line of the bay and provide a greater sheltered area for both naval and commercial vessels. The pier itself provided berths for cross-channel packets on its lee side. Constructed of Bramley stone and concrete, it was originally estimated to cost £245,000, but its length and mass were periodically increased in keeping with naval ambitions. By 1850 it extended 600 feet from the shoreline; by 1871, when work stopped, it had reached 2,000 feet and cost around £2 millions. Thus, at little cost to itself or its shipping, Dover had acquired the first part of a major harbour. The second part was not completed until the end of the nineteenth century, when the Dover

Harbour Board built Prince of Wales Pier to enclose the Inner Harbour. The vast Outer Harbour of almost 600 acres was nothing to do with cross-channel traffic. The Admiralty built it as part of naval preparations for the First World War: it was completed in 1909. Having, for a variety of physical and strategic reasons, proved inadequate, Admiralty Harbour was handed over to Dover Harbour Board in the 1920s, and the eastern portion was used initially for exporting Kent coal and, more recently, for the Dover car ferries.

In the long run Dover gained a great deal from the acquisition of naval facilities, but in the early days there were several threats to its primacy in the packet business. What railways brought they—or their rivals—could also take away; and if railways set their rates to their own advantage the cheapest or fastest route to the coast could make the difference between the success or failure of a packet port. For Dover it was particularly serious that the route to the sea chosen by the South Eastern Railway Company reached Folkestone the year before it reached Dover, for the railway company also bought out the Folkestone Harbour Company, founded in 1807 to maintain a substantial fishing harbour the possession of which, it was said in 1845, 'is expected to prove of great importance in connexion with the traffic to France and other parts of the Continent'.[36] On a fine day it was possible to sight Boulogne from Folkestone, but in inclement weather Folkestone suffered more than Dover from gales off the Channel, and since steamers also ran from Dover to Boulogne the attempt to make a rival packet port at Folkestone was not entirely successful. On the other hand it was not an abject failure, and as cross-channel traffic began to build-up in the present century Folkestone was able to attract around a quarter of the tonnage operating from Dover.

Another potential rival was created at Newhaven by the London, Brighton and South Coast Railway Company which, having arrived there in 1847, agreed with the Western Railway of France to run ferries jointly between Newhaven and Dieppe in order to create a cheap London to Paris service. Unfortunately the longer crossing militated against a speedier through journey than was possible via Dover and, since it could compete only on price, the Newhaven passage soon acquired a third-class sea-sick image which it never entirely lost.[37] Moreover, there were difficulties over running steamers in the early days when routes were being established, and the harbour at Newhaven—the mouth of the river Ouse—was rather poor until

improved in the 1880s by the railway-financed Newhaven Harbour Company incorporated in 1878. Thereafter the number of passengers using the port rose fairly rapidly (with boosts provided by the growing number of International Exhibitions) from 75,000 per annum in the 1880s to 212,000 between 1900 and 1909. But in order to reach this level the London, Brighton and South Coast Railway Company had to invest well over £750,000 in harbour works and steamers, and the question must remain whether such expenditure was justified. This sea route was never a paying proposition: its purpose was to attract traffic between London and Newhaven, and this it certainly did, to the apparent satisfaction of both company and passengers. On the other hand, looked at from the point of view of national needs, Newhaven might be regarded as irrelevant; but that is true of many aspects of railway duplication of facilities resulting from inter-company rivalry. There was some slight consolation in the case of Newhaven in so far as a heavy-goods traffic developed in machinery, for which steam cranes and a 60-ton sheer-legs were provided. When W. Clark Russell visited the port in 1883 he was told that 50 carriages and 60 locomotives had been exported in the previous nine months, though trade was more commonly in fruit, silk and other fine goods for the fashionable market. He was also shown a machine capable of mixing 100-ton loads of concrete for filling jute sacks (41 × 8 × 6 feet!) which were sunk to form the foundations for the solid piers and breakwaters, at a cost of £58 per lineal foot compared with £360 at Dover harbour.[38]

While the routes to France lay through Dover, Folkestone and Newhaven, the route to the Netherlands ran through Harwich, standing on a sheltered peninsula in the Orwell estuary, one of the best harbours in the country and conveniently situated only a day's coach journey from London. Since the harbour was so good, and the water adequately deep, no major works were required beyond a small pier, and the 'port' of Harwich hardly existed as a topographical feature: in the 1840s it had only three main streets, and was little affected by the traffic passing through it. Necessary works in the harbour were paid for by the Admiralty because the Orwell had for centuries been a place of resort for the Royal Navy. Indeed, Harwich almost failed to survive into the modern period. The postal packet was removed to Dover in 1836, and while Harwich failed to attract a railway line Ipswich opened a 33-acre dock in 1841 and was linked to the rail network in 1846. Steamers ran thence to Holland, and even the arrival of the railway belatedly in 1854 did not re-establish Harwich's position. Eventually under an Act of 1863 the railway company—now the Great Eastern—built a new 'Continental Pier' and started steamer services to Rotterdam and Antwerp, but disputes between the company and the town (among other things over the very serious matter of the supply of water to the shipping) halted expansion. Following well established tradition the railway company then built a new port up-river from the old, reclaiming a large area between 1879 and 1883 and establishing the first real deep-water quay in East Anglia at a cost of over £500,000.[39] It was called Parkeston, after the chairman of the Great Eastern Railway, and it was here that the company established its chief packets, including, from 1893, the well-known one to the new port of The Hook of Holland. However, the distance between the two places—little over a mile—was too small for the new name to come into general use and, as at Hartlepool, the two ports merged in the public mind if not in local government maps.

Harwich and Dover were the two major outports for rapid transit between London and the Continent in the great buildup of traffic between the European countries in the half century before 1914. Because the passengers and the more luxurious passenger vessels tend to attract the most attention, it might be emphasised that figures of the real value of imports and exports which become available in the second half of the century reveal the very important role played by these two places in the importation and exportation of high value, low volume goods. By the end of the century Harwich had overtaken Grimsby in terms of trade value, and while Dover was a long way behind, it too was important.

b) The Irish Packet Ports

By comparison with the south-eastern packet ports, those on the west coast were of slight importance in terms of measurable trade and port facilities. The belief before the introduction of steamers that the shortest sea crossing was the best, whatever the cost in land travel, had led to the creation of four separate mail routes to Ireland: via Milford Haven to Dunmore (Waterford) for southern Ireland; via Holyhead to Howth (Dublin) for the capital; via Liverpool to Kingstown (the newer port for Dublin) for commercial purposes linking Lancashire with Ireland; and via Portpatrick to Donaghadee (for Belfast) for northern Ireland and particularly for linking that region with the west of Scotland. Doubts about their continuing usefulness were raised first by the advent of the steamer and secondly by the desire of the government to cut public expenditure and their apparently mistaken belief that mail contracts subsidising commercial vessels would be better and cheaper than state-owned vessels.[40]

The Milford Haven route was far from satisfactory. The road there was inconvenient, and the packet station was no better: it was so primitive during the period in question that both mail and passengers were conveyed between the open beach and the packets in rowing boats. The opening of regular steamer services between Bristol and Waterford removed the need for continuing at Milford, and in 1835 the Post Office packet was withdrawn. In consequence Milford Haven failed to become even a minor port on the basis of the packet business, though ironically a quay there was completed a few months after the packets were withdrawn.

The question at issue, once steamers proved themselves, was whether the packets should run the shortest routes from inconveniently situated places, or be transferred to the major ports—Bristol, Liverpool and Glasgow—where commercial agencies could operate the postal services without direct Admiralty involvement in the ownership of packet boats. This issue was very clear in the case of the northern packet port, Portpatrick. It was doomed for much the same reason as Milford, despite the fact that the piers, built by Smeaton in 1778 and rebuilt by the Rennies after 1820, were still in the process of completion. It was simply too difficult of access from Glasgow—or anywhere else that mattered—and the harbour, despite the genius of its engineers, was poor. 'Of all the harbours in Great Britain,' it was said of it in 1847, 'Portpatrick offers the minimum amount of shelter for the large amount of money that has been laid out upon it.'[42] Two years later the Post Office, seduced by the offer of Messrs Burns to carry the mail free on their Glasgow to Belfast commercial packets, closed down the packet station at Portpatrick, and the place gradually fell into the decayed state in which it can still be seen.

Arguments in favour of the shorter sea crossing revived when trains began running much faster than steamers. However, it took some time for them to penetrate the south-west of Scotland, and when Portpatrick was reached, in 1861, the harbour was so bad that the marine terminus of the Portpatrick Railway was pulled back to Stranraer in the sheltered waters of Loch Ryan, which had earlier been nominated by the Belfast Chamber of Commerce as the more suitable place. In 1863 railway packets began running thence to Larne which, unlike the more distant Donaghadee, was linked to Belfast by rail. Stranraer rapidly became—and has remained—a popular port for migratory workers, but no major works were required apart from the East Pier, erected in 1863 and later extended to give access to deeper water than could be reached from the small West Pier which had been built for local purposes in the 1820s.

In contrast to the vicissitudes affecting the other packet ports, the major route from London to Dublin was always through Holyhead. With the rising desire for economical government, and the recognition of railway potential, there were those who argued that Holyhead should be abandoned in favour of commercial ferries from Liverpool carrying the mails, but though the Post Office steamers were for a time run from Liverpool as well as from Holyhead, the latter station was saved by the opening of the Chester-Holyhead railway in 1848. Although Holyhead survived, the Admiralty's packets did not. In 1850 mail contracts were signed with the City of Dublin Steam Packet Company and, in contrast with the situation in most packet ports, where railway packets were essential to maintain the station, the City of Dublin packets were not replaced by those of the railway company until 1920.

Holyhead was—and still is—a very simple port. Admiralty Pier, built at government expense during the Napoleonic War for military purposes, continued to serve until the present century. The very impressive harbour built by the state between 1847 and 1873, at a cost of almost £1·5 millions, was intended as a harbour of refuge and was in no way related to the packet port which happened to be within it. (In fact it was largely a waste of money, since it was not completed before the adoption of steam power on the Irish Sea made it redundant.) Not until 1873 did the railway company, responding to increasing traffic and larger vessels, begin embanking the original inner harbour and constructing sheltered railway quays, though these could not be approached by large steamers until further modifications were undertaken in the 1920s.

In terms of passengers and goods carried, and shipping turned round, the packet ports handled large numbers and vast tonnages with the minimum of facilities and this, of course, had a profound effect on every aspect of port life. They did not require large numbers of dock workers or seamen, or a large-scale back-up service in ship-repairing

and victualling. Nor did they attract a mercantile community or sustain service and port-related industries of the sorts found in most commercial ports. Several of them combined resort activities with port activities, but even so Harwich and Holyhead each had fewer than 9,000 inhabitants at the end of the century, and Dover and Folkestone were both very much smaller than the railway ports of Grimsby and Hartlepool.

c) Inter-Continental Traffic and the Rise of Southampton

Much of the packet business, both in mail and passengers, originated in London, and the volume of traffic through the packet ports was a clear indication that the great port, so admirable for the general trade of the metropolis, was unfavourably situated for those special trades in which speed or comfort was at a premium. This was just as true of the long-distance routes, though here the troubles of the Channel were less important because of its small proportion to the total route from America or India, and because the volume of mail and passengers was not high enough in the pre-railway age to justify regular packets. The American colonies were, of course, an exception and government packets were transmitted there as they were to Ireland, with Falmouth acting for the colonies (as Weymouth did for the Channel Islands) on the grounds that it was a good harbour which avoided the Channel run though at very considerable inconvenience so far as the post road was concerned.

The transatlantic colonies and ex-colonies were developing rapidly in the first half of the nineteenth century, and the flow of trade, emigrants, travellers and mail was booming long before the steamship brought a revolution in communications with America. It was clear from the start, however, that steamers involved in the longer crossing would not be in the same class as those crossing the Channel, and that a packet port must be found that was conveniently situated for London yet capable of receiving large ships. Since Liverpool was hardly better situated than London as a terminus for the packet, and since Bristol was not really in the running because of its inferior harbour, it might have been expected that the development of the railway system would confirm Falmouth's position by easing the land connexion with London. But events took a quite different turn, to the benefit of none of the ports currently engaged in transatlantic commerce.

For a long time there had been those who favoured the creation of a new Channel port connected directly to the capital; but various canal schemes, of which the Portsmouth Ship Canal of the 1820s was the most promising, foundered on high costs. It was just as well, for the size of vessels and volume of trade for which the Portsmouth canal was planned would have rendered it useless for its intended purpose, while the harbour at Portsmouth, which was more or less the preserve of the Royal Navy, would not have been ideally suited to commercial traffic. Good sense prevailed, and railway projectors concentrated on Southampton, a decayed port which had lost its substantial medieval trade because it was too far from London and had no promising hinterland. The London and Southampton Railway (renamed the London and South Western) was founded to reverse this situation. It was opened in 1840, and the government soon recognised the superiority of the new port—only three hours away from London—by removing thither the American packets based on Falmouth.

The town itself—which in 1840 was more a watering place than a port—responded rapidly by forming the Southampton Dock Company, with London help, to build Outer Dock on land reclaimed to the south of the town at the confluence of the rivers Test and Itchen. Opened in 1842, it completed the facilities which proved irresistible to the new long-distance steamship lines and, for the time being, to the Post Office. The Peninsular and Oriental Steam Navigation Company secured the mail contracts to the Peninsula, India, the Far East and Australasia, while the Royal Mail Steam Packet Company was paid over £250,000 per annum to carry the mail to Central and South America. A third company, the Union Steamship Company, began carrying supplies to the Crimea during the war there, and then secured the mail to South Africa. Equally important in the early days was the fact that Southampton's excellent position on the Channel made her a natural port of call for the American companies (Ocean Steam Navigation and Vanderbilt) and the German companies (Hamburg-Amerika and Norddeutscher-Lloyd) steaming between the two continents.

Rapid growth of trade—the tonnage leaving the port doubled between 1840 and 1841 and rose by a further 40 per cent by 1847—encouraged further harbour works, and the enclosed Inner Dock, the only impounded dock to be constructed in Southampton, was opened in 1851. These two docks and Victoria Pier (later renamed Royal Pier) pro-

vided all the accommodation required by contemporary steamers, but it was soon doubtful whether they would continue to be required. The advantages gained from railway communications were diminished when the railway also reached Falmouth and Plymouth and those two ports clamoured for their share of the postal business, part of which was indeed transferred to Plymouth. At the same time rapidly expanding trade in Liverpool and London made it so much easier to obtain full loadings there that shipping lines began to look with disfavour at Southampton, which still had no adequate industrial hinterland. Cunard stuck resolutely to Liverpool, and in 1870 the P. & O. line had that port written into its mail contract. The Southampton authorities responded by offering to build a new river quay outside the docks on the Itchen, but it was too late. P. & O. withdrew to London in 1875 and other lines threatened to follow. For ten years or more it looked as if Southampton might not survive as facilities fell behind those of Liverpool and the Dock Company fell into bankruptcy. Not until the 1890s did the situation change radically and the modern transatlantic trade burgeon.[43]

4. POWERED MACHINERY IN PORTS

a) Manual Cranes and Hydraulic Power

Steamships and trains came together in the new railway ports, but they required a further element before they could work efficiently: powered equipment. Nothing has been said so far about handling devices for the simple reason that they were all so primitive as to excite little comment. Manpower was predominant. In the worst cases goods were still carried into and out of ships over ladders and gangplanks with back-breaking and time-consuming effort. Coal was literally dug out of the holds of colliers by 'coal whippers' and carried from ship or lighter to waggons by 'coal porters': their alternative name of 'coal backers' was an apt description of the job. Somewhat less dirty but equally arduous was the vast work of moving deals, a task performed in London and elsewhere by 'lumpers'.

There were many varieties of labourers, jealous of their particular 'skills' but lumped together by most casual observers who noted only the uniformly hard work and the insecurity that kept them lowly. 'The dock labourers', wrote Henry Mayhew of those who worked on the London quays,[44]

> are a striking instance of mere brute force with brute appetites. This class of labour is as unskilled as the power of a hurricane. Mere muscle is all that is needed; hence every human locomotive is capable of working there. All that is wanted is the power of moving heavy bodies from one place to another. Dock-work is precisely the office that every kind of man is fitted to perform, and there we find every kind of man performing it. Those who are unable to live by the occupation to which they have been educated, can obtain a living there without any previous training. Hence we find men of every calling labouring at the docks. There are decayed and bankrupt master-butchers, master-bakers, publicans, grocers, old soldiers, old sailors, Polish refugees, broken down gentlemen, discharged lawyers' clerks, suspended government clerks, almsmen, pensioners, servants, thieves—indeed, every one who wants a loaf and is willing to work for it.

The very ease with which strong men could take up dock work created an immense problem in industrial relations which carried through to recent times and was one of the chief factors inhibiting the development of modern working methods in the ports. Too many men tried to do too few jobs, bidding down the value of labour and creating a system of permanent insecurity. To make matters worse, the seasonal trade booms—for instance in timber—were sure to bring in the Irish, so that dockers never acquired even a seasonal scarcity value. Once the enclosed docks were built, the unseemly business began of men queuing for work at the gates, though this did at least take them out of the hands of publicans who had dominated the work pattern on the river Thames. So far as the port employers were concerned, it could be argued that abundant cheap labour encouraged too much reliance on manpower and too little concern for mechanical devices. As trade grew, docks in the major ports employed men in their thousands, though inevitably work slowed down as larger ships were introduced. Simply to increase the number of men was not enough to clear large ships quickly.

Dock labourers did not, of course, work entirely without mechanical aids. Although horse, wind and water power used in other industries could not be introduced to quays, the hand crane, capstan and winch had been used from time immemorial to assist muscle power in raising and

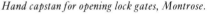

Hand capstan for opening lock gates, Montrose.

A simple wood and iron crane, of which very few survive. Rodel, Harris (1976).

pulling heavy weights. The chief advance had been the introduction at some unknown date of the treadmill crane. Joseph Glynn, writing in 1849, was of the opinion that 'the cranes of the last century, especially the first half of it, were rude and clumsy devices borrowed from the Dutch, many of them worked by men walking within a large hollow wheel. . . .'[45] Two years later Mayhew described such a crane working in London Dock:[46]

> The wheel-work is performed somewhat on the system of the treadwheel, with the exception that the force is applied inside instead of outside the wheel. From six to eight men enter a wooden cylinder or drum, upon which are nailed battens, and the men laying hold of the ropes commence treading the wheel round, occasionally singing the while, and stamping time in a manner that is pleasant, from its novelty. The wheel is generally about sixteen feet in diameter and eight to nine feet broad; and the six or eight men treading within it will lift from sixteen to eighteen hundredweight, and often a ton, forty times in an hour, an average of twenty-seven feet high. Other men will get out a cargo of from 800 to 900 casks of wine, each cask averaging about five hundredweight and being lifted about eighteen feet, in a day and a half.

The first major step forward came in the early nineteenth century with the substitution of iron for wood for the knees and collars of cranes, and eventually for the posts. Stronger materials and better cog wheels produced cranes capable of lifting five and ten tons, but manpower was still too slow. The search began for a method of driving 'self-acting' cranes.

There were three lines of approach to the problem. The most obvious was to adapt steam power. Bramah experimented with dock cranes fed from a central boiler house in 1802, and Joseph Glynn records seeing one at work in Dover harbour in the 1840s,[47] but they were not successful for general dock work. The second approach was through pneumatic power, and cranes working by this method were suggested for the new St. Katharine's Dock in London, though not accepted. For both systems the provision of consistent power was impossible and connecting linkages were difficult to maintain.

The only surviving treadmill crane in Britain, now an ancient monument. Harwich (1981).

The third system was hydraulic power, perfected in theory by Bramah in the 1790s, but again too far ahead of its time to be physically possible. The problem was how to convert hydraulic power into rotary motion, and in the absence of a satisfactory method hydraulic cranes also were rejected for St. Katharine's Dock. The first hydraulic crane that actually worked was constructed by William Armstrong in his native Newcastle, and in 1846 his Newcastle Cranage Company opened a factory to produce hydraulic systems. Orders flowed in, first from Liverpool and Glasgow, but principally from the two new ports of Birkenhead and Grimsby, as noted above.[48]

The central feature of the system was the creation of regular pressure, and this was first done by raising water to a great height with steam pumps. The most spectacular evidence of this short-lived method is the Dock Tower at Grimsby, a grand campanile that was too expensive to copy widely. Armstrong himself thought that the breakthrough in the application of power to dock systems was not his hydraulic drive mechanism, but his replacement of the hydraulic tower by the 'accumulator'. Water was still pumped into a chamber, but constant pressure was provided by weights rather than by the weight of the water itself.

Hydraulic power spread rapidly. By 1858 Armstrong had sold 1,200 cranes and hoists, and hydraulic stations were a feature of all the major ports, where the smaller towers containing accumulators are still generally to be seen. The way was open at last for a massive increase in the capacity of cranes, and trades in very heavy objects, particularly machinery, became a practical proposition. It was also possible to use hydraulic power to open and close dock gates, which were increasing rapidly in size as steamships grew during the middle of the century. From every point of view hydraulic power was the most important advance in the history of dock machinery before the 1950s.

Hydraulic power was so valuable, and so practical, that it dominated cargo handling for a century, and distribution pipes—distinguishable from normal water pipes by the large size of their couplings—spread out from the dock systems to the surrounding streets in the larger ports where commercial hydraulic power companies were formed. Electric power was introduced towards the end of the cen-

Large hydraulic coaling crane (above), Queen's Dock, Glasgow c. 1880. The heavy cranes were usually fixed and the ligher ones mobile on rails.

A small hydraulic crane, with operating tower on the left, Leith (1978).

Steam engines for generating hydraulic power, Glasgow 1905.

Hydraulic bridges played a great part in those ports where the docks were surrounded by streets. Humber Dock, Hull.

Hydraulic piston mechanism for working lock gates, Victoria Dock, Hull.

tury, but it offered few advantages in traditional working circumstances. It was, of course, more adaptable, but this was not a valuable feature until after the Second World War when working methods changed. Even then the downfall of hydraulic power in the major ports owed almost as much to the destruction of mains by enemy bombing as it did to any inherent superiority of electric power.

b) Coaling Equipment

Hydraulic power was particularly valuable in the coal trade. Once waggonways began to replace pack animals in bringing coal for shipment, the search for an efficient and speedy method of bulk loading began. Fortunately many of the northern coal ports and the West Country mineral ports had high ground abutting or close to their waterside, and it was natural that overhead loading should have been commonly adopted as the easiest answer to the problem of handling bulk goods on the quayside and, particularly, of raising them over the side of the vessels. At Whitehaven, for example, the introduction around 1813 of a new iron waggonway and self-acting inclined plane (on which loaded waggons descending from the colliery in the hills provided the motive power for raising empty waggons up again) was followed by the construction of a high-level staithe on the south pier. Waggons were thus brought to the quayside some fifty feet above the level of the decks of waiting colliers, and their contents tipped down shutes into the holds below, 'thundering downwards,' in the words of Sir George Head, 'like a cataract, and with the force of a battering ram'.[49] This system, following that on the Tyne and Wear, and similar to that along the Cumberland coast at Harrington, could, when working to capacity, load eight or nine colliers (with 500–600 waggon loads) in a single day. So great indeed was the speed of operations at what were appropriately called the 'hurries' on the south quay at Whitehaven that the rest of the harbour was used principally for sheltering vessels awaiting their loading rather than for actually loading them.

High-level loading in this or similar fashion seemed ideal. The use of gravity dispensed with the need for both steam power and expensive labour, and keeping waggons above quay level eliminated the confusion which would have arisen had waggons mixed with general traffic and, in some cases, did away with the need for a built-up quay. On the other hand there were undoubted drawbacks to this system which led to its abandonment, at least for a time, by railway companies seeking to establish modern facilities for their coal trade. It was difficult, for instance, to accommodate the rise and fall of vessels with the tide, and in many places the distance between the top and bottom of the drop was so great as to damage the coal severely. But more importance should, perhaps, be attached to the desire of the railway companies to move away from shipping places suitable for natural gravity feed in favour of ports on estuaries where the land was little higher than the water level. In fact few major ports are immediately surrounded by high land, even in coal bearing districts, and there was a general desire to find a system of loading which would eliminate excessive handling yet allow railway working at low level, especially in such new coal ports as Hull, Grimsby and Cardiff. Low-level working was essential where railways wished to develop full commercial ports catering for imports as well as coal exports, and particularly where modern dock working was involved. In other words, it was quite possible for a railway to make use of a high-level riverside situation specifically for a coal drop, but there was never any chance of adapting it for other goods, and where it was desired to develop a full port in a better water situation 'natural' coal drops were virtually impossible.

Since coal must be delivered at the ship's side at a sufficiently high level to avoid strenuous man-handling, some method of raising the waggons was inherent in low-level working, and the railway and dock companies adopted a variety of methods of raising and dropping coal with a minimum of effort and damage. The Stockton and Darlington Railway Company began the search for new staithes by offering a prize for the best method of low-level working which would take account of the rise and fall of the vessels at their Tees-side staithe. It was won by the Company's own engineer, Timothy Hackworth, with a design which won the attention of Sir George Head during his *Home Tour through the Manufacturing Districts* in 1835, and whose description of these and other staithes has been used by almost every writer on the subject since that date.

What he found at Port Darlington was a staithe parallel to the river, with a raised and covered gallery, some 450 yards long and 'nearly as dark as a coal pit', to which waggons were raised by steam-powered lift. Half a dozen waggons at a time were horse-drawn along rails within the gallery to one of eight drops, where the waggons were turned and pushed out one at a time onto a cradle suspended on arms that were pivoted and counter-balanced with

some four tons of pig iron. When the brake mechanism was released the waggon descended under its own weight, in an arc, to the deck of the collier, and when its load was discharged through flaps the counterweight raised it back to the gallery, where it was pushed across and out of a back 'window' where another cradle let it down (turning it ninety degrees in the process) to the rails below. The whole operation, from pushing out the loaded waggon to disposing of the empty one took about two minutes.

A variation on this curvilinear drop was introduced by the Stanhope and Tyne Railway Company to take account of the peculiar topography of its new 'port' on the Tyne. So high was the land above the water-line that a cradle pivoted in the middle of its swinging arms could not have descended far enough, and consequently the arms were pivoted at the bottom and could therefore reach lower vessels, though at the cost of swinging out for a considerable distance over the river. 'The effect is grand', wrote Sir George Head,[50]

> to see and hear this enormous mechanical power in action: first, the waggon, weighing, together with its load, four tons, not reckoning the frame or cradle on which it stands, and two men beside it, altogether slowly descending from a height of upwards of fifty feet, down upon the deck of the vessel below; and with the sweep of the radius of fifty-five feet, describing its graceful periphery in the air, as the stupendous bulk of the counter-balancing chain is dragged upwards, as it were, reluctantly, with a writhing motion. The creaking and groaning of timber, the stress on the machinery, the grating of the brake, the rattling of the huge links, the clash of the hammer against iron bolts, and the thundering crash of the coal falling through the bottom of the waggon into the hold of the vessel, are all sounds that excite the senses and rivet the attention; while a further source of contemplation arises by thinking that the same operation is repeated over and over again during every working day throughout the year, and yet, after all, that the whole established together is but as a speck in the balance, compared with the vast, incessant shipments that cross the bar of the Tyne.

Curvilinear drops appear to have been satisfactory so far as their mechanical operation was concerned, but they were not popular outside the north-east, and even there they had their critics. The arc described by their descending cradle limited their use where considerable fluctuations in water level occurred, unless, as at the Stanhope drops, the vessels were anchored some distance from the quayside; and there were those who thought that a more stable operation could be performed if the cradle descended perpendicularly. George Leather (who had been involved in the building of Goole) recommended perpendicular drops when Port Clarence was built, and subsequently one or other form was in use in the northern coal ports. Hartlepool followed the Port Darlington pattern, but, perhaps surprisingly, when Middlesbrough dock was built adjacent to Port Darlington it was the Port Clarence pattern that was adopted.[51]

The coal drops described above were ingenious, but they were by no means as efficient as the natural gravity-fed shutes of Whitehaven, the Tyne and the Wear, and though Head praised the 'remarkable' and 'singular' appliances at Port Darlington, he summed up the raising and lowering of waggons as 'a circuitous application of additional labour, than which it certainly appears a more direct mode might have been devised.'[52] Put simply, the speed with which

waggons could be dropped to the colliers exceeded the speed with which they could be delivered to the drops because there was a bottleneck between the railway system and the port system. The solution at that time (though not necessarily in the great coal docks built in the second half of the century), was to raise the entire train rather than individual waggons, and this could be done in two ways which might be illustrated from Middlesbrough and Cardiff. At the former, where ten coal drops were built into the western end of the dock, the whole of the waggon assembly area was raised as a great fifteen-foot-high plateau. It was, needless to say, an expensive exercise, using far more land than actually occupied by the rails to and from each drop.

The final stage in the development of coal-handling equipment came with the application of hydraulic power. It then became possible to raise or lower waggons at any desired height, and to tip them automatically, at far greater speed than was possible with gravity mechanisms. The

Coal drops on the Tyne (above), curvilinear pattern, with low pivot to allow for fluctuating water level.

Coal drops at West Hartlepool, working in curvilinear fashion, similar to those at Port Darlington and suitable for dockside working.

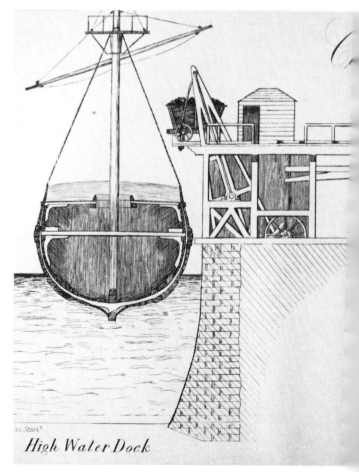

High Water Dock

tower coal hoist became a feature of all the major coal ports in the flatter regions of the country, while the most unusual variant, at Goole, allowed coal barges to be lifted out of the water to be tipped into ships alongside.

c) Mechanical Dredgers

Although not the same kind of machinery as dockside appliances, mechanical dredgers nevertheless played an absolutely vital role in encouraging the growth in the size of ships. The maintenance of deep-water berths was almost as difficult as their construction. The alternating disturbance and stilling of silt-laden water left deposits outside and inside docks which could in some places be measured in inches per month. Ross Johnson, in his textbook on port management, gave as a principal duty of dock authorities:[53]

> The preservation by dredging, scouring, or other means of the necessary depth of water in the docks and entrance

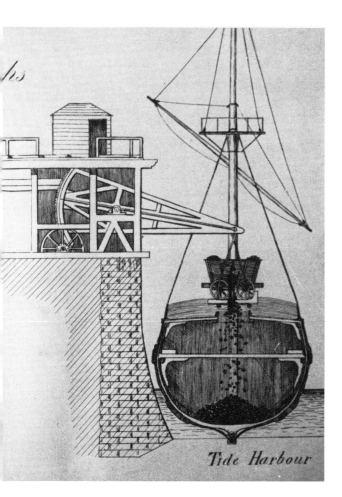

Tide Harbour

locks for ships using the port. Ports are not, of course, able or expected to offer an unlimited depth of water to any ship which may desire to use the port, but every port holds itself out in its public notices as providing a certain draft, which may, of course, be different in different parts of the port, and provided the ship obeys the orders of the dock master, who must know the day-to-day conditions of every berth, it has a right to expect to remain afloat, and has a cause of action against the Port Authority, which by accepting the dues has invited it to enter its docks, if it suffers damage from insufficient water or structural defect.

Wherever possible engineers had provided harbours and docks with a 'flush of water', but even so it was necessary to remove silt or sand from time to time. The ancient method was simply to dig away river or harbour deposits with spades at low tide or with long handled scoops from boats. Occasionally coffer dams were erected behind which digging could take place in relatively dry conditions. However, once docks were provided their 'cleansing' usually required their closure, and it was soon discovered not only that revenue was lost but that the sudden removal of water pressure revealed unsuspected weaknesses in the walls. Liverpool had an ingenious method of flushing, but even here a vast amount of manual labour was called for. 'All the docks', wrote Ayton,[54]

> communicate with each other by means of large tunnels under ground, through which each may pour its water for the purpose of washing out its neighbour. When a dock is to be cleaned, the water is drained from it as the tide retires, and the sluices are opened into it, when a number of men shovel the mud into the currents, and this operation renewed every tide for twelve or fourteen days, scours out a dock more effectually than any other means that have yet been tried.

The earliest mechanical devices were buckets dragged across the bottom, and at some unknown date these were joined to form the bucket-chain dredger which has changed little to the present day except in size and variation in the position of the buckets (initially placed over-side and now usually moving through the bottom of the hull). Hull Dock Company always claimed to have had the first power-operated dredger at work in its dock in the 1780s: literally a two-horsepower affair shifting 22 tons of mud per hour. John Rennie built a steam dredger when he planned the Humber Dock there, working 29 buckets and lifting 60 tons per hour, and it was later copied elsewhere.

About the same time Trevithick is credited with a steam dredger for the East India Dock on which Rennie also worked, and it may be that some sort of collaboration between the two men was involved.[55]

The increasing size of ships and depth of docks and river quays was matched by increases in the operation and capacity of steam dredgers. Hull, for instance, was shifting around 100,000 tons of material per annum in 1840 and 1·2 millions in 1880.[56] But the greatest concentrations of very large dredgers were to be found on the Clyde and Tyne where they were used for preparing the deeper river channels required to preserve the ports. The Clyde had five dredgers at work by 1841, and in the 1860s had the largest dredging operation in Britain. Still larger vessels were purchased towards the end of the nineteenth century as the docks were excavated in the city centre.[54]

The engineer John Ure worked on both the Clyde and the Tyne, and it was for the latter that he developed his largest machines. In 1840 the Tyne Commissioners' single dredger raised only 16,260 tons, and the average lifted yearly between 1840 and 1849 was only 36,519. However, between 1850 and 1859 the average was 169,869 tons, and by 1860–69 it had risen to no less than 3,261,420, with the quantity in 1866 standing at 5·27 millions.[58] Guthrie extolled the performance of the dredgers:[59]

> The result of these operations was, that the whole face of things was changed as by a transformation scene. The bar had substantially disappeared; the obstruction at the throat of the river, the "Narrows", had been widened and improved; a broad, fine, deep river had replaced a tortuous and shallow river; a sailing channel was made—with as much depth at low water as formerly existed at high water—right through Shields Harbour up to the docks. The wonderful phenomenon was seen of large vessels riding at anchor at places where just before had been sandbanks, dry many feet at low water; and four vessels were able to proceed to sea abreast, where previously one vessel had to pick her careful and hesitating way. The familiar story of ships being detained in the harbour after loading for want of water on the bar, ceased to be told; and a clear way in and out of the port at nearly all times of tide was provided for vessels of almost any size.

His point is well taken. In any list of factors contributing to the transformation of ports in the nineteenth century the humble mechanical dredger deserves a place of honour.

Double dredging machine, iron hulled, introduced by Tyne Commissioners in 1863. Dredged to a depth of 34 feet and between 1863 and 1879 moved 14·6 million tons of mud.

MARGATE, *Kent (above). Daniells' view of early river steamers making use of Margate pier. Increasingly they brought visitors for whom the pier, with its two levels, was an attractive promenade.*

SUNDERLAND, *Durham (below). Stone and timber pier, built as part of the training of the river Wear at Sunderland. The waggon rails were a feature of the northern coal ports long before the Stockton to Darlington Railway was opened.*

WHITEHAVEN, Cumberland. The country's most complicated system of pier harbours, here clearly visible from the hill to the south where the Lowther coal was mined. The outer harbour is seen to the left of the picture (1840s) and the small dock (1870s) is seen in the far distance, with a ship discharging acid which, with fertilisers, forms the bulk of modern traffic now the coal trade is in decline. The South Quay (left), with the remains of the coaling buildings. The line of the 'Hurries' is clearly visible down the hillside; the chimney to the right marks the shaft head of Haig Pit, with modern conveyor machinery in front of it.

WAPPING, London (above). Warehouses dating from the mid-late nineteenth century are to be found in the streets surrounding most of the docks and harbours in Britain. Although details varied, they generally followed this pattern, with a perpendicular set of doors and a pulley crane above them. PITTENWEEM, Fife (above right), while in no way a commercial port, is typical of the vast number of small places round the coast of Britain that shelter the country's inshore fishing fleet. IMMINGHAM, DOCK, Lincolnshire (below). Some of the original coaling equipment on the east side of this under-used dock points the way to the chemical and refining plants which now surround it; much of the business is now done at the pier outside the dock.

KIRKCALDY, Fife (above). The occasional grain ship is a lonely visitor in a small port once active in the linoleum trade, with aspirations as a coal port. As with most similar places, the facilities and buildings have been largely removed, though the basic functions of the small dock are maintained.

DYSART, Fife (below). The ruined lock gates of the small dock with which the ancient Royal Burgh of Dysart attempted unsuccessfully to regain a share of the Fife coal trade in the nineteenth century. The 'castle' in the background is in fact a fortified church.

BRISTOL, Avon. A recently refurbished warehouse in The Grove (left), shows an architectural style different from that of the other major ports, and also how surviving dock buildings can maintain the port atmosphere while serving modern purposes.

Brunel's Suspension Bridge (right) seen from his entrance to the Floating Harbour. The rich eighteenth century mercantile suburb of Clifton overlooks the Avon Gorge which rendered the harbour unsuitable for nineteenth-century developments and led to the building of Avonmouth down-river. Few ships today pass through the Cumberland Basin.

Ports are only as good as their dredgers. Here (below) the suction dredger Samuel Plimsoll is cleaning the Cumberland Basin. Behind it is the entrance to the Floating Harbour.

ST. KATHARINE'S DOCK, London. Its warehouses partly restored and now home for a growing collection of historic vessels.

CHAPTER FIVE

The Height of Prosperity 1870–1914

1. THE RISE OF THE BULK TRADES

The chief features of British trade were fixed long before steam power was applied to its carriage. Imported raw materials guaranteed a continuing high level of trade with lands where iron, timber, cotton and a multitude of vital commodities were to be found.[1] Luxuries were equally important for sustaining trade with their fortunate producers, and a large range of intricate manufactures were still required from Europe. Since the 1770s imported grain had played a mounting part in feeding an increasingly industrialised population, and any other foodstuffs that could survive the journey were eagerly sought. In return, Britain continued to send old and new manufactures to every part of the globe. Great changes occurred in the method of carrying and encouraging trade, but the routes were already established, and were already tied to the various British ports. The introduction of steamers on the Atlantic might work wonders for Liverpool, but had little to offer to Whitby.

It is true that there were few long-distance steamer trades that sailing vessels could not have undertaken, and the famous clippers, built when the steamship had already proved itself, remind us that there were some trades in which sail was still preferred. Nevertheless, it was the speed and convenience of the steamship and its back-up organisation that allowed long-distance trades to grow rapidly in the half-century before 1913. Moreover, it was the other aspect of steam—the railway train—which gradually opened up the corn lands and the cattle country of the developing temperate zone, and stimulated that rapid movement of goods within trading partners that had already been achieved within Britain herself. There was nevitably a time lag inherent in the process: steamers were trading regularly within Europe while they were still novelties on the Atlantic, and the widespread use of steamers in the Far East and the Pacific came only late in the nineteenth century.

Regular steamship lines were undoubtedly important in establishing long-distance trades on a modern footing, as the works of Hyde, Marriner and Davies have clearly shown, while Farnie has emphasised the contribution of the Suez Canal to the long-distance steamship trades.[2] Between 1880/4 and 1910/13 the average tonnage of shipping entering British ports from India rose by a factor of 1·8, from Australia by 3·7, and from Japan (though the total was less) by 33·0. Similarly shipping from West African ports grew by a factor of 3·1, and shipping from the whole of Central and South America by 5·0.

There is, however, a danger of over-emphasising these novel or exciting trades at the expense of the more mundane. While nobody would deny their importance, these new trades made no difference to the relative standing of the more traditional ones. Indeed, railways and steamers together so stimulated trade with Europe that shipping reaching British ports from the four nearest European countries—Germany, Holland, Belgium and France—rose from 38·8 per cent of all shipping entering Britain in 1880/4 to 45·7 per cent in 1910/13. Between these two periods shipping entering from the traditional areas (Northern Europe, Spain and Italy, India, North and South America) declined under pressure from the 'new' areas only from 90·2 to 89·0 per cent of the total: steamshipping and railways contributed to the general world-wide expansion of trade but did not raise, as might otherwise have been expected, the proportion of non-European trade in volume terms. This is of great importance for any consideration of the demands made on British ports, for it reflects the fact that exotic trades filled the headlines while European vessels filled the ports.

Whatever its origins or destination, there is no denying

the aggregate rise in trade in the half century before 1913. It is, of course, pointless to quote the value of trade for our purpose. The value of imports grew by no more than 14 per cent between 1870/4 and 1880/4, and by only 2·7 per cent between 1880/4 and 1890/4. Exports actually declined in value by 3·8 per cent between the former dates and remained static between the latter. Not until the present century was there a notable rise in the value of trade, by 71·5 per cent for imports and 102·3 per cent for exports between 1890/4 and 1910/13. This poor showing was largely the consequence of falling unit prices as the rapid expansion of trade and overseas investment reduced the cost of primary products and as these reductions, together with technical advances, economies of scale, and economic depression brought down the price and extended the market of manufactured goods.

Such matters were probably better understood by the contemporary Board of Trade officials, who drew up elaborate tables showing the movement of import and export prices, than by modern writers who do not always recognise that the declining growth rate in the aggregate value of trade masks a rising growth rate in the volume of trade. Moreover, quite apart from any significant movement in unit prices, the relationship between value and volume was upset by the disproportionate growth of trade in certain very cheap, bulky commodities such as coal which, despite a rapid rise in price just before 1913, was still worth only on average 14s. 6d. per ton in that year. (Graph on page 117.)

The spectacular growth in the export of coal of around fifty per cent per decade, from an average of 7·8 million tons in 1860/4 to 66·1 millions in 1910/13, was the chief factor stimulating shipping and overloading port facilities, but there were several other commodities whose growth, though less urgent, brought large aggregate volumes into trade. Manufactured cotton piece goods rose from 2,097 to 6,665 million yards during the same period, and imports of raw cotton from 947 to 2,290 million pounds. Imports of cornstuffs, with great influence on the major port-based industry of milling, rose from 2·8 to 9·8 million tons, and other foods followed suit. The table shows the extent of the growth in a select group of some of the leading imports. The major raw materials made great advances, but so also did an immense variety of less important individual items. To attempt to assess the total weight or volume of goods would be difficult if not exactly impossible; fortunately it is much easier to arrive at the volume of shipping required to carry it.

Quantities of Selected Principal Imports, 1870–1913

	1870/74	1890/94	1910/13
Bacon (000 cwt)	1,836	4,771	5,413
Butter/Margarine (000 cwt)	1,306	3,456	5,427
Cocoa (000 lb)	16,897	32,467	74,368
Eggs (000,000)	541	1,320	2,342
Sugar (000 cwt)	17,635	27,196	39,271
Tea (000,000 lb)	165	239	351
Tobacco (000,000 lb)	64	72	133
Cotton (000,000 lb)	1,524	1,754	2,290
Mineral Oil (000,000 gal)	12	137	403
Wood (000 loads)	5,111	7,184	9,374
Wool (000,000 lb)	314	696	799

Source: *Annual Statements of Trade and Navigation*

According to the *Annual Statement of Trade and Navigation*, from which most of the information in this section is drawn, the net tonnage of shipping bringing cargoes into British ports from foreign parts rose by 157 per cent between 1870/4 and 1910/13, from an average of 17·4 to 44·7 millions. The tonnage carrying cargoes out of Britain rose by 228 per cent, from 18·8 to 61·6 millions. This was not all owing to an absolute rise in the volume of shipping, since several millions resulted from changes in the method of recording shipping. Nevertheless, with rises of this magnitude there is no need to labour the point that facilities were likely to be stretched to their limits, and that continued growth would depend on massive dock extension.

As in former times, foreign trade was only part of the story. Despite railways, coastal traffic continued to grow (though at a diminshing rate) up to 1913, which experienced the largest coastal tonnages on record. It was not until 1880 that the tonnage of vessels carrying goods out of the country regularly exceeded that clearing coastwise, and not until 1895 that foreign tonnage inwards regularly exceeded coastal. Together the foreign and coastal trade employed over 37 million tons of shipping in 1870/4 and 94 millions in 1910/13.

Average Tonnage of Shipping Entering and Clearing with Cargo, 1870–74 to 1910–13

(000 tons)

	Foreign Trade		Coastal Trade		Total Trade	
	entering	*clearing*	*entering*	*clearing*	*entering*	*clearing*
1870–4	17,430	18,780	19,589	18,626	37,019	37,40
1880–4	24,608	27,674	26,293	23,791	50,901	51,46
1890–4	29,309	34,149	29,576	28,348	58,885	62,49
1900–4	38,055	43,108	31,228	30,844	69,283	73,95
1910–13	44,744	61,612	32,931	32,514	77,675	94,12

Source: *Annual Statements of Trade and Navigation*

Even this huge total of ninety-four million tons of shipping clearing from British ports is an inadequate statement of what was actually happening within them. While in the early days of expensive steamshipping it had been in the interests of owners to strive for cargoes both inwards and outwards, the growth of specialist bulk trades (especially coal, cottons and machinery), a mounting desire for speedy operations, and a general cheapening of freight rates (which were more than halved between 1870 and 1902), made movement in ballast not only necessary but almost acceptable. Naturally enough the tonnage entering Britain in ballast grew faster than the tonnage entering with cargo as the coal trade expanded, but what is more surprising is the fact that the tonnage clearing in ballast was also rising faster than the tonnage in freight in the 1890s. In other words, the complexities inherent in the unprecedented expansion of trade towards the end of the nineteenth century were such as to demand a proportionally greater expansion of shipping in order to carry it. This was even more the case with coastal vessels than with foreign traders: steamers were almost as likely to be in ballast as freight, though sailing ships were less so. Partly, of course, this was because vessels arriving in a port from abroad may well go in ballast to another port for a new cargo, especially coal.

If the foreign and coastal traders in freight and in ballast are added together, the total (which cannot easily be discovered before 1900 because certain types of coasters were ignored by the Customs) amounted to an average of around 108,000,000 tons per annum in 1900/4 and 136,000,000 in 1910/13. This is *net* tonnage, and is recorded because of the custom that ships paid harbour or dock dues only on cargo space. There is, therefore, a hidden increase in the total volume of shipping which occurred, as sailing ships, which were almost entirely net tonnage, were augmented and gradually replaced by steamers. In the 1850s and 1860s the engine room and other exempt accommodation might account for between 20 and 25 per cent of the gross tonnage, but as steamers grew larger in the 1880s and crew accommodation became more extensive, they could make up as much as 35 per cent of gross tonnage. By 1913 the net tonnage of the 12,602 steamers on the British Register was, on average, 60·3 per cent of their gross tonnage, and for sailing vessels the figure was 91·8. If, for the sake of argument, these figures were used to convert the net tonnage clearing from Britain into a very rough estimate of gross tonnage, we

should arrive at a grand total for the years 1910/13 of 223·3 million tons, and of 241·8 millions for 1913 alone. This, rather than the net tonnage, is the amount of shipping presenting itself at the dock gates!

While the aggregate tonnage entering the ports, with or without cargo and from whatever source, is likely to create simple overcrowding and therefore demand an extension of existing facilities, changes in the nature of trade and in the type and size of ships are more likely to demand new and more elaborate facilities. Nothing in this regard was more important than the growth in the size of steamers engaged in foreign trade. (Those in the coastal trade actually *diminished in size* slightly after 1875.) The average passed the 1,000 ton mark for the first time in 1875, and ten years later, when the average stood at 1,132, there were 1,378 active steamers in the 1,000 to 2,000 ton range, 241 between 2,000 and 3,000, and 32 over 3,000. By 1910 the average steamer in foreign trade was 2,298 tons but, while the largest of all — the transatlantic passenger liners — had passed the 20,000 gross tons mark with the *Celtic* in 1901, and caused acute embarrassment to certain port managers, the more typical large vessel was of the order of 3,000–4,000 tons. In that year there were 1,865 vessels between 1,000 and 3,000 tons, 1,954 between 3,000 and 5,000, 371 between 5,000 and 7,000, and 252 over 7,000.[3]

Average Net Tonnage of British Registered Vessels Employed in Trade, 1870–1913

	Home Trade*		Foreign Trade	
	sail	*steam*	*sail*	*steam*
1870	66·1	159·4	513·3	813·3
1875	67·8	195·9	586·3	1003·5
1880	65·0	179·5	647·3	998·3
1885	65·2	176·2	815·8	1132·5
1890	64·7	162·2	988·0	1267·2
1895	64·0	154·4	1263·6	1496·9
1900	61·1	143·4	1395·3	1837·9
1905	59·5	131·1	1459·8	2086·7
1910	56·8	129·3	1548·2	2297·9
1913	62·1	127·1	1567·7	2500·2

*In this table, Home Trade includes trade with nearby Europe from Brest to the Elbe.
Source: *Annual Statements of Trade and Navigation*

As an approximate guide to dimensions, it might be observed that a vessel of around 1,000 tons net would generally exceed 250 feet in length and 30 feet in breadth, while one of around 7,000 tons would exceed 450 feet and 50 feet. Larger ships were not always much longer (though exceptions such as the *Celtic* and *Mauretania* were 680 and 762 feet respectively) because of difficulties in manoeuvring and in filling so much space safely, but they became much deeper as third and fourth decks were added. A three thousand tonner would draw around 30 feet of water in the 1890s, though the relationship between tonnage and dimensions varied according to the trade (or port) for which a ship was designed.

One way of assessing the response of the ports in general to advancing trade, or, equally important, the encouragement to trade offered by improving facilities, is to examine the relationship between capital investment and tonnage of shipping. Admittedly there are difficulties on both sides of the equation. We have a comprehensive survey of investment for England and Wales but not for the remainder of the United Kingdom, while shipping figures for England and Wales are not easily extracted from United Kingdom figures. Moreover, there are no official statistics covering the full extent of the coastal trade, though this is of less consequence. Fortunately the foreign trade of Ireland was slight, and there is no reason to suppose that a comparison between investment for England and Wales and tonnage for the United Kingdom would be too misleading: Scotland was not proceeding noticeably differently from England.

Professor Kenwood has calculated that total investment between 1851 and 1913 amounted to £158·56 millions, falling in three waves of activity, the first between 1851 and 1870, with peaks in 1854 and 1866; the second between 1870 and 1892, with a peak in 1884; and the third between 1892 and 1913, with a peak in 1904.[4] The waves are not very closely associated with movements in foreign-going tonnage, as one might expect: the peak of 1884, the trough of 1892 and the peak of 1904 all followed fairly sharp upward movements in tonnage in the preceding years, and in any case one would not look for an exact chronological fit because of time-lags in building docks or opening new trades. The amplitude of the swings in investment, from the lowest trough of £1·25m to the highest peak of £4·43m, looks impressive, but is less so when set against the accumulating total of investment which is, after all, the foundation on which advancing trade is built up. Annual investment in port facilities is in fact small compared with existing investment (and would be smaller had we any reliable indication of pre-1850 investment), and we are left with a gentle and continuous rise in total investment, and a natural decline in the rate of investment until the present century.

Port Investment in England and Wales, 1850–1913

(£ millions)

Decadal	Totals	Running Totals	
1850–59	14·37	1860	15·88
1860–69	18·56	1870	34·18
1870–79	21·97	1880	57·57
1880–89	25·49	1890	82·97
1890–99	26·08	1900	110·36
1900–09	40·39	1910	149·43
1910–13	11·70	1913	158·56

Source: A. G. Kenwood, 'Port Investment in England and Wales, 1851–1913', *Yorshire Bulletin*, vol. 17 (1965), p. 157.

When the running total of investment is compared with the rising tonnage of the export trade (cargo *and* ballast) a fairly close correlation may be observed (Graph on page 117). An index based on 1870 = 100 shows both rising, but with tonnage lagging noticeably behind investment from 1883 onwards. It would be tempting to see this lag of five or six years as the time taken for investment to reach fruition, or alternatively as an inefficiency within investment. By their very nature, docks raise the provision of facilities at a stroke, whereas the tonnage to fill them grows more steadily. But some of the lag is no more than a reflection of the fact that investment in docks never catered for national trade *as a whole*, but only for that portion passing through ports where such an investment was necessary. Provision of dock space thus ran ahead of the national total of foreign-going shipping just as shipping at the major ports ran ahead of total national shipping. The point is supported by the coastal trade figures, which lagged very considerably behind dock investment because coastal traffic still, in many places, had little incentive to enter docks. Finally, it should be remembered that there was a qualitative as well as a quantitative advance in investment, in so far as the larger sums towards the end of the nineteenth century were for better facilities necessary to accommodate large ships.

*   *   *

If we turn from generalities to the conditions in individual ports, the role of the coal trade is immediately apparent.[5] Of the total growth in net tonnage of shipping active between 1870/74 and 1910/13 (52,668,000 tons), no less than 51 per cent was attributable to ports chiefly engaged in the coal trade: Cardiff, Newcastle, Newport Port Talbot, Sunderland, Swansea and the Fife ports which shipped little else; and Goole, Grimsby, Hartlepool

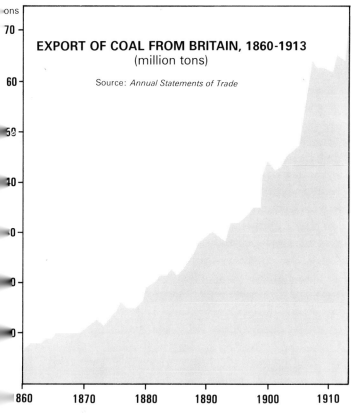

EXPORT OF COAL FROM BRITAIN, 1860-1913
(million tons)

Source: *Annual Statements of Trade*

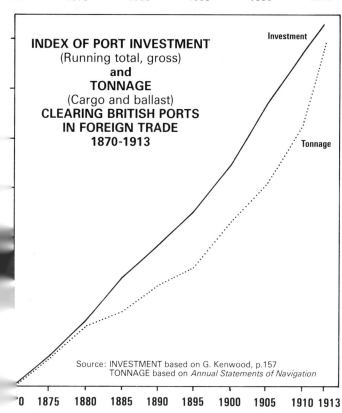

INDEX OF PORT INVESTMENT
(Running total, gross)
and
TONNAGE
(Cargo and ballast)
CLEARING BRITISH PORTS
IN FOREIGN TRADE
1870-1913

Investment

Tonnage

Source: INVESTMENT based on G. Kenwood, p.157
TONNAGE based on *Annual Statements of Navigation*

and Leith which, though they enjoyed a measure of general trade, were more deeply involved with coal. If account is taken also of Hull and Glasgow which, while concentrating on general trade, nevertheless between them handled a tenth of the national coal trade, the proportion of growth in tonnage attributable to ports strongly interested in coal would be around 63 per cent. In addition there were many smaller places shipping anything from a few thousand to a few hundred thousand tons of coal. (See Tables on page 139.)

It ought, in theory, to be possible to argue that since a steamer at the turn of the century would have a weight-carrying capacity of between two and two-and-a-half times its net tonnage, something of the order of 27 million tons of shipping would be required to carry the coal trade in 1910, a figure which is almost exactly half the total tonnage clearing with cargoes from British ports. There are, however, so many qualifications to be made about under-utilisation, mixed cargoes and ballast, that only the roughest of generalisations is justified.

One further general point might be made about the coal trade: it was also a major contributor to the growth in the *coastal* tonnage. Although most coal was carried by rail in the early twentieth century, some 22 million tons were still carried coastwise, including around 9 millions for the London market. Quite apart from shipping carrying coal as freight, the necessity of bunkering was the principal reason for many ships travelling coastwise in ballast either to their bunkering port or from that port to the port or ports in which they loaded their cargo. The demand for bunker coal must be borne in mind when considering the pressure on coaling facilities: the tonnage of coal carried out of a port was *not* the tonnage declared as exported for sale, but this quantity plus bunker fuel for consumption during the voyage. In the case of Hull, in the years 1910–12, bunker fuel was as much as 38 per cent of the volume exported for sale,[6] and, since the majority of Hull's exported coal went to the Continent, bunkering would presumably have been a higher proportion of the South Wales trade. In other words, at least one coal hoist in four was engaged in the loading of vessels with coal for their own use.

A second major area of growth, after the newer coal ports, was the newer packet ports. Between 1870/4 and 1910/3 Folkestone, Harwich and Dover all grew more than the national average, though the first two made their move forward in the first decade of the period and then followed the national trend. To some extent their more rapid growth was inhibited by the passenger services started in the Humber and Tyne ports, and by their own local rivals such as Newhaven. By contrast there was nothing to hinder the business of those ports which could attract the passenger lines. Part of Liverpool's advance was undoubtedly attributable to the great transatlantic liners whose constant coming and going contributed tonnage at a faster rate than any of the normal freight liners (which covered greater distances and sailed less often). But above all it was Southampton that gained from the liner trade, partly because of her deep water access, partly because of her position as London's southern outport, and partly because of her fortunate position on the route between the Atlantic and the Continent that made it worthwhile for foreign liners to call there on their way to and from America. As a result Southampton had the fastest growing trade of any of the major ports between 1890/4 and 1910/13, and by the latter date was exceeded in tonnage clearing only by London and Liverpool and the coal giants Cardiff and Newcastle. To some extent at least her growth was at the expense of Liverpool and London, both of which lost passenger traffic to her.

Two Channel ports in particular made very substantial gains in tonnage as a result of passenger or rapid-transit packet services. Apart from obviously new ports, Plymouth appears to have been the fastest growing port in Britain between 1890/4 and 1910/13, but the trend revealed by the statistics is false. Plymouth, more than any other place, 'gained' from changes in regulations which required vessels 'calling off' the port to land or embark passengers or baggage to be counted as if they had been 'brought to' in the immediate vicinity of docks and quays. (In consequence the tonnage clearing the port soared from 109,807 in 1906 (which was actually somewhat lower than it had been a decade earlier) to no less than 1,546,292 in 1907 and a staggering 3,778,427 in 1913, when Plymouth had the eighth largest tonnage of any British port. Southampton owed part of its remarkable growth to the same statistical change, when its tonnage leapt from 1,954,659 in 1906 to 3,571,389 in 1907. Similarly Falmouth, hitherto of slight commercial importance, entered the list of major ports for no better reason than the official recording, from 1910, of ships 'calling' there, in the days before radio, for orders from owners while proceeding up or down the Channel: 164,870 tons in 1909 and 594,988 in 1910. Which of these figures should be taken as the real trade of a port, representing the actual demand on facilities, is a matter

of debate. The smaller figures certainly indicate the tonnage trading in the usual manner, but there must have been an indeterminate overlap in which vessels 'calling off' the ports made use of the facilities. Fortunately all the ports in question had good natural harbours capable of accommodating large numbers of passing ships without straining their normal trading facilities.

By contrast with Plymouth, the second growth point on the Channel, Weymouth, was more directly associated with real advances in trade. Weymouth had suffered in competition with other places (particularly Southampton) earlier in the century because she had no adequate rail connexions, and it was not until 1889 that she suddenly burgeoned as a railway steamer port carrying holiday passengers and vegetables to and from the Channel Islands. In consequence her tonnage grew by 1,077 per cent between 1890/4 and 1910/13, the second largest growth (after Plymouth) among the older ports.[7]

Such a large-scale movement in the relative distribution of shipping in favour of the coal and packet ports could only take place at the expense of the two great general ports, Liverpool and London. For generations they had dominated British trade in terms of volume as well as value, but while the coal trade and passenger traffic made no serious inroads into the value of trade on the Mersey and the Thames, they most certainly presented a threat (if such a word is appropriate) to the *relative* volume of trade. Between 1870/4 and 1900/4 London's share of national export tonnage fell from 16·2 per cent to 14·9, and Liverpool's share from 18·6 per cent to 12·4: the leading port in the country was now Cardiff, with London second, Newcastle (incorporating Blyth) third, Liverpool fourth, Glasgow fifth and Hull sixth. In the import trade, where one would expect the commercial ports to have stayed ahead of the coal ports, London did retain a remarkably steady share (21·2 to 20·4 per cent) of national tonnage, but Liverpool again slipped dramatically, from 19·5 per cent to 13·9.

The fact that tonnage frequenting Liverpool and London was growing less rapidly than the national total is a timely reminder that advances in trade are not necessarily spread evenly round the ports, and that the modern period is no different from earlier ones in witnessing varieties of stimulus and response. The pre-war generation was the age of the coal trade, so far as national shipping was concerned, and those ports expanded fastest which catered for it. But, as noted above, part of this large increase in ncoming shipping was ballast tonnage heading for the coal ports, and we should not be surprised that it avoided the general commercial ports. Nor should we forget that volume had little bearing on value: in 1913 Cardiff handled ·7 per cent and Newcastle 1·8 per cent of the £1,404 millions of total national trade, compared with Liverpool's 6·4 per cent and London's 29·3 per cent.

Even where tonnage alone is concerned growth rates can be deceptive. There is a common tendency to regard the *peed* of growth as being of crucial significance, whereas n practice the growth rate is only meaningful in terms of he existing volume by which growth is measured. So far as the ports were concerned, a small place might double ts tonnage without straining its facilities or causing undue excitement, while a relatively small increase in a large port night demand a major construction programme. In the cases of London and Liverpool growth might have been slower than in some other places, but they still accounted or 27·4 per cent of the total national growth in tonnage between 1870/4 and 1910/13. In absolute terms Liverpool still had to accommodate 11·6 million tons of shipping in he years 1910/13, and London over 13·3 million tons, and he attempts to provide new works here, and in the other major ports, led to the most spectacular examples of port mprovement in the period under consideration. It would be a pity if the great achievements of the coal trade were allowed to detract from the equally extensive and economically superior performance of the general trades.

2. THE REVOLUTION IN THE MAJOR PORTS

The huge advance in tonnage between *c*. 1870 and 1914 was associated with a number of interlocking trends in port development. The first was obviously the growing interest n accommodating large ships which led ports already well endowed with 'old' docks to invest heavily in 'new' ones: n long, wide and deep locks; in long internal walls for berthing longer ships, and in vast areas of uncluttered space for turning them; and in advanced machinery such as cranes and hoists. At least one deep lock was essential f a major port was to placate its shipowners and fight off ts rivals, but at the same time a countervailing trend was observed in the increasing interest in riverside quays and pontoons outside the dock system: for short-haul rapid-ransit vessels in Liverpool and Hull and the newer packet

ports of the south-east; for the largest liners at Liverpool and Southampton; and, towards the end of the period, for oil tankers in many places.

Hidden within these trends were more specific subsidiary ones related to cargo handling. The aversion to dock-side warehouses that had been growing since the 1840s became, as far as is known, universal, with new docks favouring one- and two-storey transit sheds, often with built-in gantry cranes, and with more emphasis than hitherto on open spaces for the handling of minerals and machinery. According to the eminent engineer Sir John Wolfe Barry, giving evidence before the Select Committee on the Humber Dock Bill (1904),[8]

> the aim of all modern docks is to have a very large amount of quay space, so that the cargo can be discharged with the greatest possible rapidity, and cargo returned to take the place of the discharged cargo also with the greatest possible rapidity, so that the ship may get to sea and the heavy expense of working these large ships may be avoided.

In fact the largest buildings were now the grain silos required for the growing traffic from the prairies of America, Russia and northern India. The distinction between docks tended therefore to be seen in the sizes of ship rather than in the structure of the docks themselves. Deep docks were all very much the same whatever the cargo passing through them, with an increasing use of permanent berths which tied liners to particular sheds or specialist buildings such as cold stores, and consigned the smaller short-haul vessels and coasters to the older docks, which again were often assigned to particular trades to suit produce markets. The sifting out of fishing boats at Hull and Grimsby is a clear example, though these received their own shallow docks rather than redundant commercial docks.

Whatever the expected traffic, dock authorities were now spending a good deal less on bricks and more on concrete as the capital cost of long-term storage was assumed by other parties. Although some trades continued to use the grand old warehouses for cinnamon, or wine, there was a growing tendency for goods to be stored outside the docks, and for potential congestion to be alleviated by better integrated rail systems. Railways and docks were increasingly interdependent, a factor highlighted by the growing amount of traffic passing through railway-owned dock systems in some of the small ports, and by the necessary purchase by railway companies of the more or less bankrupt dock companies of Hull and Southampton. In 1904 the General Manager of the Great Central Railway, Sam Fay, was of the opinion that

> it is obvious from the history of the dock business on the east coast that a dock *per se* could not be exploited by any company or interest other than a railway interest, the railway interest having the advantage of an earning upon its railway. The dock is simply a mouth.[9]

The construction of large deep docks implied physical changes within the ports which are another trend of some moment, not least to those who lived and worked in them. Sites of several hundred acres with easy rail access could be obtained at reasonable expense only by going beyond the central waterfront already covered by old docks and buildings. Moreover, deep docks demanded suitable water access, and in most places this could be acquired only by jumping to the nearest point where a deep channel touched the waterfront. Few ports were as lucky as Southampton and Liverpool where deep channels were in the 'right' place for easy exploitation. Grimsby is a classic example of a port which was forced to build its deep dock several miles away from its shallow docks, while Bristol's new docks at Avonmouth and Portishead, and London's Tilbury Dock, were typical down-river developments in the same mould as Port Glasgow.

The building of down-river member-ports was really an admission of inadequacy and a warning that the old port might eventually succumb, as York did to Hull, or Norwich to Yarmouth. But in the late nineteenth century the more interesting development was in the opposite direction as new dredging techniques, and a liberal application of capital and gunpowder, allowed up-river places to assert or re-assert their position *vis-a-vis* down-river ports. The deepening of the Clyde, so well documented by Dr Riddell,[10] created the port of Glasgow after generations during which the commercial centre of Glasgow had worked through member ports; work on the Tyne created a vast new port of Newcastle; Goole built a 'Seaway' that brought larger—though not the largest—ships to its docks; and, most surprising of all, Manchester became, overnight, a major port with the construction of the Manchester Ship Canal.

Manchester's creation was the epitome of another theme in port development that was to have fairly serious consequences in the present century. Financial and organisational difficulties generated by the new deep docks raised once again the ire of those opposed to monopolies, and rivalries within ports and between ports were so carried away by the seemingly endless growth of trade that port authorities failed to recognise the fine line dividing adequate from excessive accommodation. Their folly was soon apparent as incomes failed to cover interest and maintenance charges in several ports, and amalgamations became more expedient, if not more fashionable, than competition.

Finally, while major ports enjoyed most trade and built deep docks, a subsidiary theme before 1914 must be the gradual extension of railway interests into the minor ports, and the creation of appropriate facilities that would never threaten those of the leading ports but would serve a useful localised function and, indeed, here and there pointed the way rather fitfully to very recent developments in motorship traffic between minor ports and the Continent.

a) Liverpool

Predictably it was Liverpool that led the way into this great era of dock building with the opening of Canada Dock in 1859 (see page 78) and Canada Half-Tide Basin in 1862, but the Mersey Docks and Harbour Board spent much of its first two decades producing order out of the chaos at Birkenhead, where Alfred Dock was completed in 1866 and Wallasey Dock in 1878. Only in the mid-1870s could the Board turn to a grand scheme of northern deep docks on the Liverpool side. 'What we need', said one of its prominent members in comparing Liverpool with rivals such as Hull and Grimsby, 'are deep water entrances coming from the sea on the Lancashire side and then we shall have surmounted our difficulties.'[11] Such a need was fulfilled, at least partially, by the opening in 1879 of Langton Dock, making use of its connecting passage with Brocklebank Dock (as Canada Half-Tide Basin was now called) until its own massive lock was ready. Alexandra Dock followed in 1881, and the northern group was completed in 1883 by Hornby Dock.

The Langton Entrance admitted the biggest ships to the whole of the northern deep-water system, but the docks as a whole—including the small Harrington (1883) and Toxteth (1888) docks at the southern end of the estate—were soon overtaken by the inexorable pressure of shipping. It was evident that the rising number of medium-to-large ships could only be accommodated if the dock system as a whole was up-graded, thus prolonging the useful life of all but the oldest docks and relieving the pressure on the most expensive deep-water docks. It could be done by altering the entrances, enlarging the passages between docks, and increasing the number of branch docks which, being long and narrow, gave maximum quay length while leaving turning space to the main dock on which they were built.

Those such as Forwood who advocated continuous, or at least regular, attention to the needs of progressively larger ships had, in fact, to fight hard to overcome the opposition of those cargo shipowners, led by Alfred Holt, who believed that ships would not in future greatly exceed the optimum size of vessels which they themselves found profitable. Fortunately for the port, the argument was swung by the transatlantic liner owners, clamouring for better facilities for their special requirements. The resignation of Holt as chairman of the Mersey Docks and Harbour Board in 1890 marks the beginning of a major refurbishing of the whole dock system on the Liverpool side which went on until 1906.

Work began, under an Act of 1891, at the northern end with the deepening and lengthening of Canada Lock, the re-shaping of the dock around its entrance, and the building of two new branch docks (1896 and 1903) and a massive graving dock (1899). The Canada-Huskisson passage was widened to ninety feet and a new branch dock was built in the latter (1902) over a series of redundant graving docks which had opened off the neighbouring Sandon Dock, which was also altered. And to improve access to the docks in this area, the Sandon/Wellington Half-Tide Dock was greatly altered (1902) in order to provide south facing locks as an alternative to the north facing Canada Lock which had caused trouble since its inauguration. (It was not finally removed until the 1950s.) To the south of the city, the old King's and Queen's docks were largely rebuilt in their present form, the former being united to Wapping Dock to the east and extending over the site of the old Tobacco Warehouse to the west (1906), while the latter received two large branches (1901, 1905), one of which had been its own half-tide basin. A new major entrance to the southern docks was built at Brunswick Dock (1905), again facing south to gain the best advantage from tide and wind. Finally, in the centre of the dock system, the Prince's Landing Stage was greatly extended and the river dredged in the mid-1890s to provide better accommodation for the rapidly growing passenger trades, both transatlantic and local. On the other side of the river, Birkenhead's eleven-acre Vittoria Dock was opened in 1909.

In this monumental burst of activity the Mersey Docks and Harbour Board had added some one hundred acres of new deep docks to their estate, modernised and greatly enhanced King's and Queen's docks, and rebuilt Prince's Landing Stage as the greatest structure of its kind in the world. In the process they spent something of the order of £24 millions between 1880 and 1909, or approximately a quarter of the total national investment in docks during this period.[12] On the eve of the war the Board's debts stood at £20 millions, but for this, and earlier expenditure, they presided over a dock system of approximately 450 acres, which was more or less the present Liverpool and Birkenhead docks with the exception of Gladstone and Seaforth docks.

The diversity of opinion for and against the building of ever-larger docks at Liverpool revealed the quandary facing most major ports at the end of the century: what should be done about large ships? It was not a new question, but the dilemma now was that any further growth in the size of ships would require vast expenditure for very few vessels at a time when the general-cargo trades employing medium sized vessels were also growing very rapidly. The *Mauretania* could enter the northern docks via the Sandon Lock, but there were those who thought that greater attention to the smaller timber and cotton ships would have done more for the port. In many places besides Liverpool it was beginning to be felt, as it was when paddle steamers were first introduced, that exceptionally large ships had no business entering docks at all: the latter should accommodate the great bulk of ships, while the ships of great bulk should remain outside at river quays or piers.

Giant oil tankers have so accustomed us to the idea of jetties that it now seems strange that anyone should have wanted to take the *Mauretania* into a dock at all, especially since New York was a pier port. The reason is partly the British view that docks are the best places for ships, and partly the fact that any port that wished to retain the great liners must provide dry-dock facilities. Since Liverpool's graving docks were traditionally within the dock system, there appeared to be no alternative to building at least one large dock or dock system and allowing other shipping to enjoy grand facilities, bearing in mind always that those who believed cargo liners had reached their maximum size were possibly wrong.

In Liverpool the expansion lobby won a limited victory in 1908 when the Mersey Docks and Harbour Board deter-

The Liverpool 'branch' docks provide a great amount of quay space without greatly increasing the river frontage and acreage of water.

Gladstone Dock is the only one with three-storey sheds. Here and in other ports ships are expected to use their own cranes.

mined to build a vast new dock to the north of Hornby, with a depth of water 30 feet below Old Dock Sill (which was still the local datum line despite the disappearance of Old Dock!), and with a graving dock for the very largest liners then under construction or contemplation. In fact within half a year declining dues and the desertion of White Star Liners to Southampton had frightened the Board to such an extent that the proposed dock was abandoned, and only the threat of losing more liner business to Southampton encouraged the construction of Gladstone Dry Dock, which was opened in 1913 as a wet/dry dock which could accept a single liner either for normal purposes or for repairs as the need arose. On the eve of the war advancing trade once more made the Gladstone Dock a feasible proposition, but with the inevitable delays caused by war it was not completed until 1927 (see below, p. 145).

Liverpool acquired its large docks more easily than most other major ports, for the same old reason: despite the various influences at work, the Mersey Docks and Harbour Board was the supreme authority with ample opportunities to borrow money on the strength of duties compulsorily levied on all ships entering the docks and, at a lower rate, on all ships entering the Mersey. It was, moreover, a body directly answerable to the mercantile community, and numbered interested shipowners among its members. London and Hull were less favourably placed in this regard, though the trade of each of them was growing faster than that of Liverpool.

b) London

In London, particularly, the old question arose as to how the existing rival dock companies could produce deep docks. Victoria Dock (1856) and Millwall Dock (1868) had

been built by new companies endeavouring to attract custom from older docks by charging lower rates; and neither company was wealthy. Indeed, the amalgamation of the Victoria Dock Company with the London Dock Company and the St. Katharine's Dock Company in 1864 had led to the new company—the London and St. Katharine's Company—keeping its head down in the matter of competition and investing as little as possible. However, the recent docks—including the improvement of part of the City Canal as South West India Dock in 1870—were incapable of accepting really large vessels at a time when the attractiveness of trading directly to and from the capital appeared to be growing. In consequence the London & St. Katharine's Company at last committed itself in 1874 to building an eastward extension of Victoria Dock, projected in the 1850s but dropped for lack of funds.

The new dock, planned by Alexander Rendel (son of J. M. Rendel who, like the senior Rennie, Hartley and Lyster, founded a family of dock builders), was opened in 1880 and called Royal Albert. (Victoria was renamed Royal Victoria at the same time.) It was, by any standard, truly massive, being, at 87 acres, the largest orthodox dock yet built in Britain. It was, moreover, notable in having straight sides for accommodating long ships instead of the irregular sides of Victoria Dock and the original Albert Dock plans. At approximately one and three-quarter miles long, it stretched from Victoria Dock to the river at Gallion's Reach, and so avoided some four miles of difficult river passage between the new entrance and the entrance to Victoria Dock in Bugsby's Reach. Despite its great size, involving a vast amount of excavation and the laying of 500,000 cubic yards of concrete and 20,000,000 bricks, the new dock was, according to Broodbank, one of the cheapest docks on the Thames (at £2·2 millions) because of the ease of building and the presence on site of gravel suitable for concrete. Nevertheless it was faced from the start with very serious problems, not least of which was another bout of competition.

Trade did not grow as fast as dock space, and Royal Albert appeared to fill its water with ships attracted from Royal Victoria and to a lesser extent from South West India Dock. The East & West India Dock Company were consequently faced with the prospect of losing all potential steamer traffic to the 'Royals' at a time when the company was losing business because of yet another modern invention. Broodbank has pointed out that the laying of ocean submarine cables after 1866 resulted in lower stocks of goods being held in London, with severe financial consequences for the warehousing dock companies which drew substantial revenue from this source. While the number of ships continued to grow, the India Dock Company found its income diminishing, and took the only course open to it, of investing more capital to save what it already had.

The old India docks suffered the same drawback as the old Liverpool ones: the benefits of their ample water area were discounted, so far as steamshipping was concerned, by inadequate locks, insufficient depth, and an awful clutter of piers—thirteen on the north quay of South West India Dock, eleven in West India Export Dock and eight in East India Import Dock—built to serve sailing ships and lighters. Whereas the Mersey Docks and Harbour Board could close any particular part of its estate for repair or reconstruction without loss of income, the competitive London companies faced ruin by the same process: closure denied them income, and major dock works were an exceedingly lengthy business. The India Dock Company had little choice but to build another dock, to rival the Royals, that would not, in its building, upset its existing dock system.

The site chosen, at Tilbury, avoided the difficulties and expense of lengthy Thames navigation and offered a depth of water which would allow vessels to enter at any state of the tide and find at least 33 feet of water. The 26-mile distance from London was not felt to be a serious impediment, since the London, Tilbury and Southend Railway provided a very adequate goods and passenger service, and the India Dock Company was able to negotiate 'London rates' with the leading railway companies whereby goods consigned to Tilbury were charged the same as those going to the central docks.

A very large estate (some 450 acres) was made possible by the cheapness of the marsh land, and the superior facilities were expected to poach the larger long-haul vessels from the Royals. To this end the lock, at 700 feet × 80 feet, was made the biggest on the river. However, the dock did not lend itself to easy and speedy operation. In contrast to the earlier London docks and those of Hull, Tilbury followed the recent Liverpool experiments with branch docks leading off the main turning area. Unfortunately, although this gave plenty of long berths and very good rail-to-quay links, it did not work so well in the London context as in Liverpool for the simple reason—overlooked, it seems, by the engineer—that London was a lightering port, and the three branches—between 200 and 300 feet wide—were too narrow for both ships and barges to rest happily. It was an important matter, since much of the bunkering in London was carried on by barges, into which the coastal colliers discharged. A river quay was provided outside Tilbury Dock for bunkering purposes, but it proved unpopular and was soon closed down.

It is debatable if much was gained in the early days from building at Tilbury. Large ships could avoid the city if they wished, but warehousing and marketing still took place there, and goods continued to move up-river in barges if not in ships. Tilbury's potential declined sharply when the London and St. Katharine's Dock Company, recognising its mistake in building too small a lock (550 × 80 × 30 feet) at Royal Albert Dock, began work on a second, larger lock which was opened in the same year—1886—as Tilbury. From the start Tilbury witnessed large ships, for which it had been intended, sailing past to enjoy the now equal facilities of the Royals. Shipping lines would not transfer their operations to Tilbury, and the lighterage companies boycotted the dock at first because they objected to the long distance involved. In desperation the Tilbury dues were reduced to secure a small number of shipping lines, but retaliation by the Royals led, in 1888, to the India Dock Company being placed in the hands of a receiver.

The impeding bankruptcy of this once proud descendant of two of the capital's richest trades was incontrovertible evidence that competing dock companies could no longer provide the service demanded of them in a sensible fashion. That the provision of long berths for large liners had—it was hoped temporarily—moved ahead of demand was not the point: it was the financial chaos which threatened the future of the port. To cut a long story short, in 1889 the two major companies came to terms under which their capitals would remain distinct, but their docks would be worked together, under the control of the London and India Joint Committee. The two companies were formally united by a further Act in 1900, having done no more in the interval than enlarge the entrances to West India and South West India Docks, in 1892 and 1894 respectively.

The two leading dock companies were not alone in their distress at the end of the century. Millwall Dock Company, which had built up a very substantial trade in Baltic goods and grain, was in serious financial difficulties. 'The policy', wrote Broodbank,[13] 'was to get business rather than to make profits', and the latter had, for some years, existed falsely on paper alone. The Surrey Commercial docks were also in trouble. Although they concentrated almost entirely on timber and grain, which were flourishing trades, and had seen fit to open the 16-acre Canada Dock in 1876 to receive timber from that country, the system of docks was unable to receive the larger ships now entering those trades. In 1894 the Surrey Commercial Dock Company was authorised to build the 22-acre Greenland Dock, and ten years and almost a million pounds later it was opened with a lock equal in dimensions to that of the Royals and a theoretical capacity to poach business from the amalgamated giant that was still struggling with its Tilbury problem. The latter promptly responded by undercutting the Surrey rates for timber, and the second 'minor' company faced bankruptcy.

As if the swirling eddies of competition were not enough to shipwreck the port, the river itself was in urgent need

River wharves continued to share in London's trade. Most were general wharves, but some, such as the Carron wharf, specialised in certain goods: this one dealt originally in ironmongery from the Carron Company's factory in Falkirk.

of more adequate conservation, particularly since many large ships and a vast number of lighters still used the Pool and the river wharves. By the turn of the century many eminent merchants and shipowners were convinced that the situation was as needful of investigation as it had been a century earlier, and in 1900 a Royal Commission was appointed. It reported in favour of a single port authority and, after years of jockeying between rival interests, the Government created the Port of London Authority which in 1909 took over the affairs of the Thames Conservancy Board and bought out the dock companies for a total of £22·4 millions. In fact the dock companies had done little in the way of improvement during the years of uncertainty about their future, and the Port of London Authority found that immediate remedial work would cost around £1 million, and that to bring the whole port up to an acceptable standard would cost something over half as much as had already been paid to the dock companies. But now the situation was more hopeful: there was a single undivided dock income, no competitive rate cutting, and a centrally and logically prepared expansion programme. Chief among the new works was yet another large dock projected to the south of Royal Albert but, as with Liverpool's Gladstone Dock, work was suspended when war broke out in 1914.

The London docks, as they existed in that year, were certainly impressive. Activity appeared to have been less frenetic than at Liverpool only because the London docks were of much greater size than the individual docks at Liverpool, and because a considerable amount of business was still done in the river itself. It could be argued that London had gained from competition between dock (and wharf) companies in so far as she was a cheap port, and little can be said in criticism of the quality of her leading

deep docks, or of her warehousing capacity.

Nevertheless there were by 1914 a number of disturbing features of London port which would lead to trouble eventually. Above all the port worked with a system which the considerate might call 'orderly chaos'. There were doubts about the continued viability of barge traffic compared with rail traffic, and barges certainly made dock working difficult. There were doubts too about the nature of labour usage in the docks: despite a variety of mechanical devices there was still a great deal of man-handling involved in the separation of docks and storage capacity and the inadequate rail linkages of some of the docks. Finally, there were doubts about London's continuing primacy as other ports nearer the Midlands and the industrial north made headway into the industrially-based trades. More attention should perhaps be paid to the effects of the London dock strike in 1889 which removed some at least of the port's financial advantages by necessitating a 25 per cent rise in charges.[14]

c) Bristol

For London the Tilbury extension was an optional extra which did not pay its way for a generation or more. For Bristol a similar move down the Avon was a matter of survival. Neither the Floating Harbour nor the Avon itself could receive transatlantic liners, and improvements were frustrated by the geological structure of the river bed, the Avon Gorge, and a greater tidal range than at any other port. It is, perhaps a pity that the Corporation of Bristol had never acted as that of Glasgow had done in creating satellites down-river, for this kind of civic imperialism was unpopular in the mid-nineteenth century. Since the Corporation was the Port Authority, member ports appeared to be out of the question until, to the chagrin of the Corporation, the work was taken in hand by private enterprise. Avonmouth Pier and Railway Company was established in 1862 to provide some sort of shipment place to the north of the mouth of the Avon.

As on the Thames, circumstances that vivified one company could do the same for another, and Portishead Pier and Railway Company emerged n 1866 to attempt something to the south of the river. Not to be outdone, the Corporation had also entered the fray in 1865 with an Act permitting the construction of the present locks into the Cumberland Basin and between that basin and the Floating Harbour. They went some way towards admitting

larger vessels to the town wharves, which were also improved and given rail connexions around 1866. Both private companies eventually went to Parliament in 1871 for authority to construct docks against the wishes of the Corporation, and they were opened at Avonmouth in 1877 and Portishead in 1879.

The new docks were substantial, though not unduly spacious compared with around 70 acres of the Floating Harbour which still held most of the water space, wharves and warehouses. Avonmouth Dock was *c.* 19 acres, including a small extension of 1894 devoted largely to the banana trade; and Portishead was 15 acres.[15] Their great advantage was their locks which, at 454×70 feet and 440×66 feet respectively, compared favourably with the reconstructed Cumberland lock which was only 350×62 feet. However, while Avonmouth offered a depth over sill between 28 and 38 feet depending on the season, Portishead was, at 24 to 34 feet, only a foot deeper than the Floating Harbour, and there must be reservations about regarding it as a modern dock.

There were certainly doubts at the time about the value of either dock to the bulk of shipping, and Bristol enjoyed a foretaste of Tilbury's bitter experience: despite the superiority of the docks for large ships, a considerable proportion of Bristol's growing trade was still carried past the docks to the Floating Harbour in small ships. It was attracted, among other things, by rate-cutting, and with increasing competition the Floating Harbour went into the red and the dock companies faced bankruptcy. The solution here as elsewhere was amalgamation, with the Corporation taking over the companies in 1884 and running the whole as a single non-competitive system and, incidentally, as the only important dock system operated by a Local Authority.

One reason for Bristol's ability to increase her shipping without massive dock building was, of course, the relatively small size of the vessels using the port and still being adequately served by the Floating Harbour. A second reason was the unique relationship between import and export trade. In terms neither of tonnage nor value would Bristol's exports merit her classification as a major port, and the proportion of shipping entering from foreign parts and subsequently clearing *coastwise* was the highest for any large port in the country. The reason was simply that ships entering with timber, wine or provisions left to load South Wales coal, and the result was that ships did not remain in Bristol for long or demand extensive facilities for loading cargo. In other words, fewer acres of docks could handle more ships because they traded only in one direction.

Avonmouth Dock could, therefore, cater for the largest ships using the port in the 1880s, but its lock proved inadequate for transatlantic liners introduced towards the end of the century and it was deemed necessary to provide facilities equal to those of London and Liverpool if Bristol was not to be forced out of her oldest and most profitable trades. As an interim measure Avonmouth lock was lengthened to 485 feet in 1898, and three years later it was decided to build a new dock with its entrance more suitably placed on the Severn rather than the Avon. The result, started in 1903 and opened in 1908, was Royal Edward Dock, offering 30 acres of water at 36 to 40 foot depth and able to accept the largest ships afloat through its 875 × 100 foot lock. It was this dock, linked to Avonmouth Dock and greatly extended in the 1920s, which carried most of Bristol's foreign trade, though it suffered the indignity of losing its name: few people outside the city know it as anything other than Avonmouth Dock. Coastal traffic continued for some years to go up to the Floating Harbour, and Bristol shared with other ports the tendency to ship non-bulk goods by barge from Avonmouth to the city for storage.

d) The Humber Ports

By contrast with London and Bristol, where competing private companies initially provided too much deep-water space for their own financial comfort, Hull found herself inadequately served by her single private dock company which continued to doubt the wisdom of raising large amounts of capital to secure a relatively small increase in income. Albert Dock, opened in 1869, had been designed for a long and narrow waterfront site, and proved so inconvenient in use that ships could not easily enter and leave it, and took a whole day to pass along it when it was teeming with continental liners, barges and fishing smacks. When ships began to get larger in the late 1870s they were too large for Hull. 'They are practically obsolete', C. H. Wilson, the leading shipowner, said of the earlier docks in 1880, 'and one continually hears that Hull is fifty years behind in that respect.'[16] The Dock Company's concession to increasing traffic—William Wright Dock, opened in 1880—was merely an extension of Albert Dock and suffered from all that dock's short-

comings, particularly in regard to provision for the expanding coal trade.

However, according to local opinion it was not the docks alone that were out of date. The North Eastern Railway's metals could not carry all the goods entering and leaving the port with the required speed, and that company was accused of diverting traffic to Hartlepool where there was less pressure on its metals and the docks, which it also owned. The railway monopoly joined the dock monopoly in the litany of the town's ills, and in 1880 the malcontents among the merchants and shipowners introduced a Bill to create the Hull and Barnsley Railway, a completely new line into the South Yorkshire coalfield, and a new dock to complement it. The 46·5 acre Alexandra Dock was claimed as the deepest (at 34 feet H.W.O.S.T.) on the east coast, and with three coal hoists and many cranes provided 'direct access from the colliery to the ship'. It was not an idle boast. Trains heading for the dock from the various collieries served by the railway were from their outset subject to an elaborate system of telegraphic communications, signalling and shunting in order to ensure a smooth flow of the right sort of coal for the right ship with the minimum delay. It was a wise precaution. It was common on the east coast for coal to be sent to the port before it was actually sold, and for it to be stocked there for weeks or even months in ever-increasing sidings that were often difficult as well as expensive to provide.

Alexandra's opening marked Hull's rise as a great coal port. 'Today,' said the Mayor, 'we crown King Coal in Hull, to reign for ever . . . But while we hail King Coal we must not forget that the railway line and dock cannot live by coal alone, and that, for complete success, they must take and bring other kinds of general cargo.'[17] So superior were the facilities of the new dock that it attracted more than its share of large ships entering the port. Within a decade it was handling a million tons of shipping per annum—half as much as all the other docks together—and Hull Dock Company was clearly out-manoeuvred. It hastily eased pressure on Albert Dock by building St. Andrew's Dock (opened in 1883) for the fishing fleet, but when the need arose for a second deep dock it could not provide the capital. Nor, for that matter, could the Hull & Barnsley Company. For many years the local interests argued and negotiated until finally, in 1893, Hull Dock Company sold out to the NER, and two years later the two railway and dock companies agreed to pool their

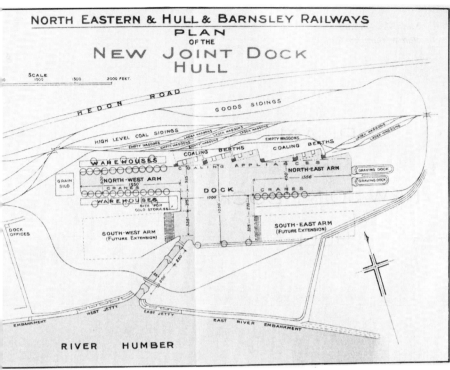

In the giant docks the size of the lock was almost more important than the size of the dock (above). The type of ship common in the North Sea trade has plenty of room in the $840' \times 90' \times 47'$ (H.W.O.S.T.) lock at Immingham, which rarely sees ships of the size for which it was designed.

King George Dock, Hull (left), opened 1914. Its complicated shape resulted from the attempt to cater for both general and coal trades. The south-east arm was finally constructed in the 1960s as Queen Elizabeth II Dock.

A modern view of King George Dock (below), now used extensively for the grain trade, and with the coaling quays replaced by straight quayage for large vessels.

resources and build a 'Joint-Dock'. So bitter were certain sections of the local mercantile community about this alleged reimposition of monopoly that it was a decade before the work could begin, and then it proceeded so slowly because of engineering difficulties that an extension was actually begun before the original dock was completed.

The final version, called King George Dock, was not opened officially until June 1914. At almost 43 feet it was some 8 feet deeper than Alexandra Dock and was fully expected to serve the port for decades to come, though to some extent the adequacy of these deep docks depended on various improvements elsewhere: the entrance to Albert Dock was remodelled in 1889, an extension to St. Andrew's Fish Dock was opened in 1897, and Riverside Quay was opened in 1906 to accommodate the fast turn-round vessels of the Continental produce trades. At the same time the Saltend Oil Terminal was built out into the deepest part of the Humber in order to receive the latest type of large ship.

New docks at Hull, especially for the coal trade, might have been seen as a threat to the survival of Grimsby and Goole, but both of these were controlled by forward-look-ing dock authorities which responded with alacrity when local needs arose. The situation in Grimsby illustrates the ease with which unfortunate decisions can be made and the lengthy time before they can be rectified. The Manchester, Sheffield and Lincolnshire Railway Company had just completed a 50-acre extension at Grimsby (called Union and Alexandra Docks, the latter built over the old Haven) in the year that the Hull & Barnsley Company obtained its Act, and had decided against a deep-water dock because potential traffic did not seem to warrant it and many people, as in other ports, did not believe that ships would go on growing in size. By the 1890s they were convinced of their mistake, but finding a suitable site and defeating the opposition in Parliament of the Hull & Barnsley Company took time. Add a further six years for building, and King's Dock as it was named, or Immingham Dock as it has always been known, was ready to ship its first coal, at the rate of 56,000 tons a day, in 1912: two years ahead of Hull's King George Dock against which it was racing.

For Goole there was no question of competing for deep draughted vessels since they could not reach the port. There was, however, a real possibility that greater facilities for medium-sized traders might attract more vessels up-river to link up with the canal-borne coal trade, which grew rapidly after the introduction of 'dumb' barge canal 'trains' by W. H. Bartholomew, the Aire & Calder's engineer, in 1868. Victoria Lock, opened in 1888, allowed larger vessels to enter the dock system and relieved pressure on the original Steamship Lock of 1838; Railway Dock was extended in 1891; and South Dock was opened in 1910 and West Dock in 1912 to accommodate advancing trade in their larger and less cluttered basins. Goole's interconnected docks remained something of a maze, with ships turning through all points of the compass in their progress through them, but the new works allowed the average size of vessel to rise from 288 tons in 1875 to 422 in 1913, and the largest to rise from 800 tons in the early 1880s to 3,000 by 1900.

Improvements did not end with the docks. Inspired by the Manchester Ship Canal, the Aire & Calder began work in the early 1890s on training and deepening the Ouse at a cost of well over a quarter of a million pounds, to provide the 'Ouse Seaway' which made South and West Docks worthwhile.

e) South Wales Ports

Despite the vast range of goods pouring in and out of the Humber ports, it was the coal trade which made the greatest demands, and this was even more the case with most of the remaining large ports. Significant dock build-ing was almost entirely confined to coal ports. In South Wales particularly, the construction of very large docks punctuated the period 1870–1914. In Cardiff, where the Bute Estate became rather tardy in the provision of further docks when revenue was uninspiring, rivals emerged as they did in Bristol and Hull. Penarth Dock and Railway Company constructed Penarth Dock (immediately leased to the Taff Vale Railway Company) on the opposite bank of the Taff in 1865 (enlarged in 1884 to 26 acres), and the Bute Estate retaliated (so far as Parliament would allow during the minority of the third marquis) in 1874 with the small Roath Basin (of 13 acres) which also afforded better access to East Bute Dock. By the 1880s the pressure of colliers in Cardiff was reaching crisis proportions,[18] and when proposals were published for the 33-acre Roath Dock (opened in 1887), colliery interests in the Rhondda were so disappointed with its potential and frustrated by the Bute monopoly that they went ahead with their own rail-way and dock at Barry, nine miles west of Cardiff.

Coal being loaded at Goole's unique barge hoists (above).

The construction of the Ouse Seaway was necessary because of the danger to shipping on the river. Here, the S.S. Altona *aground.*

Hydraulic coal hoist, Methil, recently removed.

The entrance to No. 3 Dock, Methil, running between two sea walls. Now used only for fishing boats: the dock is derelict and partly filled.

The vast 73-acre Barry Dock, opened in 1889, shared features in common with other coal docks, but among deep docks it was unique in one respect. Being constructed fairly easily by sealing off a lagoon between Barry Island and the shore, its quays followed natural geological formations and in consequence produced the only completely irregularly shaped deep dock in Britain. Such a neglect of long straight sides in an age clamouring for them was, within reason, of no importance in a coal dock where coal hoists did not require ships to lay close alongside a quay. A second Barry dock, opened in 1898 to the west of the first, compromised by having an irregular north quay and a completely straight south quay.

Together the two docks, totalling 107 acres, permitted the tonnage of shipping clearing from Barry to rise from 1·7 million in 1890 to 4·3 in 1910. It was not until 1907 that the Bute Estate's successor, the Cardiff Railway Company, responded by building the 52-acre Queen Alexandra Dock at Cardiff, the first dock there to admit really large ships, having a lock 850 × 90 feet, and a depth of 42 feet L.W.O.S.T. The Roath Dock was linked to it to make a unified system which was increasingly involved with the importation of timber (especially pit props at around half a million tons per annum), iron ore and provisions. Rather surprisingly Cardiff had become, by 1914, the third largest importer of frozen meat.

Elsewhere in South Wales problems were less intense because port authorities responded more rapidly to increases in shipping. At Swansea the Prince of Wales

Dock was opened on reclaimed foreshore in 1881 and extended in 1898, when it reached 28 acres, and the 70-acre King's Dock, with a lock very similar to that of Cardiff's Queen Alexandra Dock (875 × 90 feet), was opened in 1890. But perhaps the most ambitious port of all was Newport, where Alexandra (North) Dock was opened in 1875, and Alexandra (South) Dock was opened in 1893 and extended in 1907 and 1914, when it covered some 96 acres and had the largest lock in the world, at 1,000 × 100 feet.

f) The Scottish Coal Ports

Another region where the expansion of coalfields interacted with the development of ports was the east of Scotland. The Fife and Clackmannan field had its chief outlets at Burntisland and Methil. At the former, local Harbour Commissioners supported by the North British Railway Company built their first small dock (of 5·5 acres) inside a somewhat larger tidal harbour, in 1876. It proved too small, and the 11·5-acre East Dock was added in 1901, when the port had very extensive railway equipment and six hydraulic hoists. The limited nature of the trade is illustrated by the fact that the port never possessed more than six cranes, and four of these (electric cranes put into East Dock) were chiefly for the unloading of bauxite for the local alumina works.

Methil, though now less well preserved, was a more substantial port created by the Wemyss family, whose Wemyss

Coaling crane, Ayr, demolished in the 1970s.

A 'puffer' of the sort that carried goods around the west of Scotland and justified the hundreds of little piers. Seen here tied up beside a steam crane in the outer harbour at Troon, 1960. Puffers are no more and Troon is now derelict.

Coal Company owned much of the surrounding field, and whose waggonways to the harbours of West Wemyss and Methil carried the coal for export. The 4·75-acre No. 1 Dock was opened in 1875 for a few thousand pounds, but the second, opened in 1887, cost almost a quarter of a million because its position—to seaward of No. 1 Dock—involved a lengthy sea wall on a difficult site. Four hydraulic coal hoists—one in the old dock and three in the new—greatly increased the flow of business, but further development was delayed because the North British Railway, which bought the Wemyss transport interests in 1889, was already deeply committed to Burntisland. Intense pressure from Randolph Wemyss, including a threat to build a new port at Buckhaven, brought a response in 1907 when the North British Railway began building the 11·25-acre No. 3 Dock. Unfortunately the site to the east of the older docks involved the reclamation of some forty acres of sea-shore behind a vast sea wall which took several years to build. In the process No. 3 Dock was given the most unusual entrance in Britain. The sea wall was projected southwards for some 1,700 feet beyond the dock gates, roughly parallel with the sea wall of the older docks, and wooden piers formed the straight entrance channel between the two walls, linking the dock gates to the entrance channel of No. 2 Dock. A further five hoists and their attendant rails took a year or more to install, and the dock was not opened until January 1913. By then it was too late, and Methil, like Immingham Dock, never worked to full capacity.

Further south, Leith, though serving a flourishing general trade, was also the principal outlet for the Lothians coalfield, and it was the coal trade that encouraged the opening of Edinburgh Dock in 1881 and Imperial Dock in 1902 on an imposing water-encroaching site similar to that of Grimsby or Methil. By comparison Grangemouth, the principal outlet for the Stirlingshire coalfield, and closely linked to the Lanarkshire coalfield, was almost a one-commodity port, despite its connexion with the Forth & Clyde Canal. The port authority, the Caledonian Railway Company, opened Carron Dock in 1882 and Grange Dock in 1906 to keep the coal trade to its own metals, and in this it was largely successful.

g) The North-Eastern Coal Ports

The great north-eastern coal ports were exceptions to the rule that coal traffic required docks. It is true that both Tyne and Wear acquired relatively small ones—Hendon Dock, an extension of Hudson Dock, at Sunderland in 1868, and Albert Edward Dock at North Shields in 1884—but they accommodated their colliers largely at river quays. In fact it was the reconstruction of the rivers themselves, rather than the addition of docks, which allowed the northern coal ports to continue growing. The whole of the Tyne below Newcastle became usable for industrial as well as trade purposes following extensive dredging around 1870 (*supra*, p. 104), and major staithe construction was undertaken at Whitehill Point between

1871 and 1904. Indeed improvements to the river were such that coal staithes were opened up-river from Newcastle, at Dunston, in 1893. At Sunderland the continued use of river staithes was made possible by the building of new entrance piers between 1883 and 1914, and comprehensive training of the river by 1909.

At Middlesbrough the Tees was also extensively trained between 1888 and 1891, in association with dock extensions. Middlesbrough Dock, which had been specifically created as one of the first coal docks, was enlarged in 1874, 1885 and 1898, by which time it covered some 25·5 acres, but by then it was more concerned with the local iron trades than with coal, and it is not very accurate to describe Middlesbrough as a coal port at the end of the century.

h) Glasgow

The training or deepening of rivers to produce up-river ports was nowhere greater than on the Clyde. Work, begun in the eighteenth century, had been carried further in the nineteenth by the Clyde Navigation Trust, as noted above (p. 104), and some twenty feet was added to the depth of the river at low water between 1854 and 1886 when rock was blasted away at Elderslie, four miles west of the Broomielaw: a further eight feet was removed in the first decade of the present century. The last three miles of river — the 'Harbour of Glasgow' — was gradually canalised and a succession of quays built to accommodate rapidly expanding trade. On the north bank the old Broomielaw was joined in the 1870s by Anderston, Lancefield and Finnieston Quays and by Yorkhill Wharf; by Stobcross Quay in 1882; Merklands Quay in 1907; and Meadowside Quay in 1911. On the south side, two miles of quays were built in the 1870s (Windmillcroft, General Terminus and Plantation), and Shieldhall Wharf in 1886.

These river quays, though substantial structures, were soon inadequate, and supplementary basins were built behind them, fortunately at relatively little cost because the deep dredging obviated the need for locks. The 5·5-acre Kingston 'Dock' was opened for the West Indian trade in 1867, for a mere £128,000, and was only some ten feet deep at low water, and wharfed in wood until it was reconstructed following a fire in 1914. As with the other Glasgow docks it was not a dock at all in the normal sense, since it had no lock or gates. Needless to say it was unsuitable for large ships, which remained at the river quays until the opening of the 33·5-acre Stobcross (later Queen's)

The major ports required a large back-up operation to keep them going: here (left) is part of Clyde Navigation Trust's workshop, 1908.

The inverted brick arch was essential for providing a stable bottom for locks, probably first used by Rennie at Grimsby. Here (below left) the arch under one of the Govan Dry Docks, Glasgow, is seen under construction.

Monolithic construction, Glasgow, (above) showing a complicated pattern of pre-formed concrete cylinders sinking under weights, with walling constructed on top.

All docks and locks have massive underground drainage culverts which are never seen, except during construction, as here (below) at Govan Dry Dock, Glasgow.

Dock in 1880, and the 35-acre Prince's Dock (which cost around ten times as much as Kingston Dock) in 1892 and 1897. Altogether the available water space in the old Harbour of Glasgow was increased from around 70 acres in 1863 to more than 206 acres in 1907, and in the latter year the first major work outside the Harbour was achieved with the opening of the 20-acre Rothesay Dock at Clyde-bank which was designed specifically for the exportation of coal and the importation of iron ore, and was said to be the first dock in Britain to use the new electrically operated coal hoists.[19] Contemporary proposals for a dock at Shieldhall, on the south bank, were rejected in Parliament and not implemented until the inter-war period.

The Clyde Navigation Trust had spent around £8 millions on the eve of the First World War, and the port had almost 20,000 lineal yards of quay space. Increasingly this had, as in other ports, become specialised quayage. Over a third of it was appropriated regular berthing for liners, and around a fifth was devoted to coal export and iron-ore import, with modern hoists being introduced in the docks in 1903. A very extensive lairage for live cattle from Ireland and Canada was introduced at Merkland Quay in 1907, with the latter trade encouraged by the Canadian Cattle Importation Association, of which the Lord Provost was ex-officio chairman. Meadowside Quay became the focus of the grain trade, with a large granary which was periodically enlarged, most notably in 1960.

In keeping with Glasgow's position as a world leader in mechanical engineering, the Clyde Navigation Trust was constantly reviewing and renewing its equipment, of which a most impressive official photographic record survives to illustrate almost every aspect of dock building and cargo handling. In particular, the Glasgow skyline was punctuated up-river by the huge cranes used for the exportation of railway engines and other heavy pieces of machinery, and down-river by even larger ones associated with the shipbuilding industry. Glasgow, as opposed to Port Glasgow and Greenock, had grown up as the servicing centre for the Highlands and Islands, and in consequence there had always been a premium on open quays and rapid-transit working which kept Glasgow's quays, like the later quays in most major ports, devoid of warehousing. Only in part of Prince's Dock was there anything more than single storey sheds, and much of the smaller trade goods that required storage were accommodated in ware-houses scattered, as in Liverpool, throughout the centre of the city. Whisky bonds were, indeed, a notable feature of many of the riverside streets, but the whisky itself was never brought to the quays until shipment was pending!

Glasgow's harbour was more or less unique among major ports. Only Southampton, with a similar lack of tidal variations alongside, enjoyed a great traffic without great docks of the orthodox sort, but Southampton was not herself a great commercial centre as was Glasgow. What the latter had managed to do was withdraw to herself the shipping which had originally handled her trade some twenty miles down-river. When Glasgow's industry began to grow by leaps and bounds in the second half of the nineteenth century it was Glasgow herself which provided the shipping and the facilities and, of course, drew the profits. The city shared with London that blend of immense productive capacity with vast distribution services which made her the 'Second City' of the British Empire.

i) Manchester Ship Canal

The inspiration of Glasgow's endeavour in canalising her river was felt by none more than by the merchants and manufacturers of Manchester, resenting the profits, if not the pride of Liverpool. Their ambition to bypass their rival, long thwarted by the inadequacy of the Bridgewater Canal and the river Irwell, was given substance by George Hicks, newly arrived from the Clyde in 1875. 'Seeing the river there', he later wrote of Manchester, 'I wondered why it was doing nothing',[20] and he convinced his new friends that it might become another Clyde or Tyne (and for good measure Suez was also mentioned!). A seaway was out of the question because the land was not flat, but the alternative of a grand canal was taken up by Edward Leader Williams, sometimes engineer of the Bridgewater Canal, and enthusiastically supported in the town, particularly in the rising engineering trade. In 1885 an Act authorised the construction of a canal, 26 feet deep, from Eastham on the south bank of the Mersey to Manchester, a distance of almost 36 miles. Four sets of locks raised the canal 60ft 5in above sea level, and, incidentally, eliminated the need for docks to have their independent locks. Basins were therefore constructed after the Glasgow fashion, and the first three (now numbered 8, 7 and 6) were ready for use at the opening of the canal amid scenes of great rejoicing in 1894.

The Canal Company was unique among port authorities in being planned as 'the People's Canal', a private enterprise venture with neither local authority nor outstanding capitalists to divert it from the task of serving the town and its mass of small capitalists. Nevertheless its huge membership of some 39,000 shareholders—the largest roll of any private company—did not secure its financial independence, and following engineering difficulties in the 1890s the canal was only saved by the intervention of the Corporation of Manchester with a loan of £3m in 1891–2 and a further £2m in 1893–4, leaving the Corporation with a third of the shares and a dominant voice in the Company's affairs.

Though financial difficulties had eased, the rejoicing of 1894 was somewhat premature. As we have seen elsewhere, docks did not automatically or immediately make a flourishing port, and Manchester shared with Goole, Grimsby and Tilbury the frustration of being ignored by major shipping lines. The ships would not come, despite favourable rates, and deferred rebates offered by Liverpool lines to Manchester merchants ensured the latter's continued adherence to Liverpool. The cotton market remained in the senior port, and cotton exports continued to go by their old routes to foreign markets. Half the

tonnage leaving the port on the eve of the war was coal, though Manchester enjoyed only 0·4 per cent of the national coal trade in 1910.

By contrast with those who built Goole and Grimsby, the Ship Canal Company had spent so large a proportion of their funds on the canal and docks that they had little to spare for essential facilities or subsidising liners. They were rescued by Manchester Corporation, which erected a cold store (1895), lairages (1896) and oil storage tanks (1897), while Tyneside capital was brought in to build a dry dock, and another private company built the warehouses and grain elevator and leased them to the Canal Company. As a final blow to the latter's pride, No. 9 Dock, essential for large ships, was also opened by an independent company, in 1905.

By 1898 the Canal Company was virtually bankrupt, and was only saved by the continuing generosity of the Corporation of Manchester. In other words, the attempt to benefit Manchester merchants and manufacturers at the

Opening of Manchester Ship Canal to traffic on 1 January 1894.

expense of Liverpool was only achieved by income transfer within Manchester itself, and a casual observer might be tempted to view the port as a failure, or at least as unnecessary. It certainly could never compete with Liverpool's deep water facilities.

Fortunately three things saved the port before it was too late. The first was the creation of a direct link with Canada and the foundation of Manchester Liners Ltd. in 1898 to serve it. The second was the creation of Trafford Park Industrial Estate next to the docks in 1898, and the encouragement derived from the Co-operative Wholesale Society and others who established Manchester as the major distribution centre for Lancashire. The third was Manchester's undoubted superiority in terms of inland communications, especially after No. 9 Dock was constructed with an integrated rail system that was better than that in the Liverpool docks.

By the end of the nineteenth century Manchester's trade was beginning to respond to the improvements in shipping and facilities, and such was the economic importance of the city and its region that it rapidly increased its share of the national trade. By 1913 imports worth £35·3 millions were 4·6 per cent of the national total, and exports at £20·6 millions were 4·0 per cent. If value rankings are at all meaningful, Manchester's total trade had made her the country's fourth port by 1913: only London, Liverpool and Hull had a more valuable trade. While none of the rivals in the central region of England actually declined, it is presumably the case that some at least of the trade going directly through Manchester would otherwise have gone through Liverpool, Hull, Goole or Grimsby, and since the export of textiles also took place through Southampton and London those ports no doubt also enjoyed a slightly smaller trade than might otherwise have been the case. It was, however, in the inter-war period that the growth of Manchester really took off.

j) Southampton

Southampton was the other major port falling into the Glasgow, rather than any other, pattern. Progressive dredging of the Test and Itchen between 1889 and 1913 produced an adequate depth of water alongside for even the largest vessels. For a time in the 1880s it seemed as if new quays would be unnecessary, as P. & O. transferred to the Thames and other lines threatened to follow suit, but in a desperate bid to remain competitive the Dock

Company opened Empress Dock, behind the Itchen Quays, in 1890. As in Hull, the provision of modern facilities proved too much for the penniless Dock Company, which was bought up by the railway (the London & South Western), with attendant threats of monopoly. The Itchen Quays did indeed bring the liners, and the building of the Test Quays, to the west of the dock estate, provided accommodation for more. Moreover, Trafalgar Dry Dock (1905) was greater than anything Liverpool or London could currently offer. It was not, however, until 1911 that negotiations between the port authorities and the White Star Company culminated in the opening of White Star Dock and the removal of that company from Liverpool to Southampton. (This dock was later renamed Ocean Dock.) Her indisputable claim to be the best equipped port for transatlantic liners was recognised after the war when Cunard also transferred from Liverpool. Fears that Southampton would lose ground to Liverpool and London (after the opening of Tilbury) had proved false. The liners had remained; foreign liners increasingly called there; and trade with the Far East and Australia had grown considerably, to the discomfort of some of the more northernly ports.

3. THE MINOR PORTS

The theme of the decades before 1914 was the expansion of the large ports and the building of the deep docks. Developments elsewhere were very much minor-key affairs, though their local importance may often have been considerable. There was hardly a port which did not benefit from a measure of investment, chiefly by railway companies or stimulated by railway needs. Everywhere railway companies acted to attract trade to their own lines, the best example being the North Eastern Railway's investment in West Hartlepool, especially in the late 1870s, in order to draw trade from West Yorkshire which would more naturally have gone to Hull. Hull people saw it as a deliberate attempt to ruin them, and formed the Hull & Barnsley — the last major railway in the country — to save themselves from NER monopoly. The NER saw it as a rationalisation of their port and rail facilities. It was a fundamental divergence of interest that is bound to arise when one company 'owns' a number of ports but has a duty to its shareholders to maximise profits. Fortunately for ports there is a limit to which railways can divert trade.

Within that limit, railways could serve their inland

customers by finding cheaper alternatives to the major ports, usually small ports handling small ships on the near-European runs, for which expensive facilities were not required. The minor packet ports benefited in this way. Holyhead harbour was extended in 1880, and a pier was constructed at Heysham in 1904 for the Midland Railway to run ferries to Belfast. At Ardrossan the local Harbour Company, having bought out the Eglinton family who built the port, constructed a new ten-acre dock and two covered piers, opened in 1892, for the Irish trade. Finally, Harwich underwent considerable modifications with the building of Parkeston Quay, to the west of the town, in 1883.

The long-neglected ports of East Anglia were among those gaining from rail connexions.[21] Boston acquired a small dock in 1884, with coal hoists fed by rail from the Derbyshire coalfield. At Wisbech the Great Northern Railway opened a dock at Sutton Bridge in 1881 which proved a complete failure, though increased trade flowed over quays built along the river in the 1880s. Ipswich continued to flourish, and had a new lock put into the dock in 1881, and a new branch created out of the timber pond in 1897, though proper quays were not constructed there until 1904. Lowestoft benefited partly through normal trade and partly through the growth of fishing, attracted from Yarmouth where facilities were inadequate. The Lowestoft fish market and trawler basin were opened in the 1870s, and Waveney Dock, at the entrance to Lake Lothing, in 1883. Ten years later the fish dock was enlarged, under pressure from the booming herring fleet, and in 1902/3 Hamilton Dock was built as a northward extension of Waveney Dock.

The port in this area gaining most from railway connexions was undoubtedly King's Lynn, though it was not, technically, a railway port. In the early days there had been no response there to railway building and the threat of trade diversion to other ports in the region, and the King's Lynn Dock and Railway Company formed in 1865 was *not* a railway company as its name implies. Nonetheless its 6·5-acre Alexandra Dock, opened in 1869 on the site of the old fishing haven, attracted East Midlands coal on Great Eastern metals, and in consequence of expanding trade the larger Bentinck Dock was opened behind it in 1883. The cost of the works was negligible compared with the cost of deep docks: Alexandra cost a mere £81,000 and Bentinck little more than £165,000, though both were quite reasonably constructed small docks, easily answering the purpose for which they were built.

The minor north-western ports also gained briefly from construction work during this period. Marshall Dock at Silloth was extended to 10·5 acres in 1885 following the take-over of the Carlisle and Silloth Bay Railway and Dock Company by the North British Railway Company. (The extension, equipped with gates, remains as a dock; the original portion, now lacking gates, serves as an outer harbour.) The work was chiefly for the coastal and Irish trades, with Carr's of Carlisle among its principal users. However, despite local optimism the new works still failed to compete effectively with the West Cumberland ports, and Silloth prospered as a seaside resort rather than as a port. Maryport, which gained most at Silloth's expense through the Carlisle to Maryport railway, had the small Senhouse Dock opened in 1884 for the sake of the nearby iron works (the 1867 Elizabeth Dock was a coal dock). And Fleetwood's Wyre Dock, built by the Lancashire & Yorkshire Railway in the 1870s as a counterbalance to rival company dominance in Hull and Grimsby, was extended in 1909 for the sake of the fishing industry. Only at Preston, among the ports of this region, were extensive works undertaken to attract the trade of north Lancashire and, in particular, to poach smaller ships from Liverpool. The very large Albert Edward Dock of 40 acres, which with attendant works cost over a million pounds, was no more than twenty feet deep, and though minor trades (for example in timber and wood pulp) flourished, the more valuable trades did not follow the arrival of a small number of renegade Liverpudlians.[22] Preston was one of those places where, from the point of view of national requirements, such large scale investment was a waste of money.

Although many ports expanding during this period owed much to the railways, two of those situated north of the border catered almost entirely for extremely localised industry.[23] Dundee had long been a port of minor consequence when the rising world demand for sacking brought boom conditions to the already flourishing jute industry. King William IV and Earl Grey Docks (now completely covered by the approaches to the Tay road bridge) had been opened in 1825 and 1834 respectively, and Victoria and Camperdown Docks in the middle of the century, but though fairly extensive they lacked depth. The growth in the size and number of ships importing raw jute demanded a move away from enclosed docks, and consequently deep-water quays were constructed on reclaimed land in front of Victoria and Camperdown

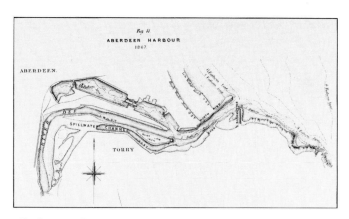

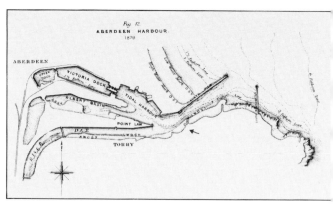

Aberdeen was able to serve its coastal and fishing trades by training the Dee to form Albert Basin in the 1870s and 1880s. The extent to which

old features often survive can be seen in the view across the harbour from the spot arrowed on map 2.

Docks in the 1880s. The continuing prosperity of the jute trade called for more wharves, which were built on the east side of the waterfront (avoiding shipyards) between 1903 and 1911. Finally, on the eve of the Great War work began on another wharf built over the river frontage between West and East Wharf; in common with other port works it was delayed by the war, and was not finally completed until the 1930s, when it was opened as George V Wharf.

While Dundee was chiefly concerned with jute, the much smaller east coast port of Kirkcaldy owed its rebuilding to the expansion of the local linoleum industry. The tiny dock opened in the 1840s no longer sufficed with the growth of important firms such as Nairns in the last quarter of the nineteenth century, but the situation was somewhat confused by conflicting railway interests. It was not until 1909 that a second, larger dock was eventually

opened. Though devoid of rails the port, sheltering behind its high sea wall, remains very much as it was in 1914, except that the handsome linoleum factory overshadowing the harbour is now derelict.

There were many other places where new works or extensions of old works improved the prospects for trade. Fowey, for instance, had eight railway jetties built for the china-clay trade; Exeter had a small dock built at Exmouth to obviate the use of the river; and Aberdeen built a new fish wharf and market on the north side of the Albert basin in 1888. In Scotland in particular, the creation of Harbour Authorities in the 1870s and 1880s in most of the smaller ports ensured the maintenance or extension of simple harbours and piers. Such works were generally on a small scale, and their contribution to the level of national trade was hardly measurable. In many places fishing boats were the chief beneficiaries.

Shipping is still vital for the Scottish islands, and their small ports continue to flourish. Kirkwall Harbour 1976.

Net tonnage of all vessels clearing selected ports for foreign parts, 1870–4 to 1910–13

(with cargo and ballast: '000 tons)

	1870–4		1880–4		1890–4		1900–4		1910–13	
	Tons	%	Tons	%	Tons	%	Tons	%	Tons	%
Blyth	*		*		*		1482	2·9	2074	2·8
Bristol	137	0·6	215	0·7	275	0·7	478	0·9	1093	1·5
Cardiff	1872	8·8	3971	12·8	6107	15·9	7568	14·8	9431	12·7
Dover	345	1·6	539	1·7	781	2·0	1119	2·2	2148	2·9
Folkestone	120	0·6	189	0·6	228	0·6	400	0·7	645	0·9
Goole	107	0·5	318	1·0	436	1·1	536	1·1	766	1·0
Grimsby	432	2·0	500	1·6	720	1·9	906	1·8	1920	2·6
Hartlepool	474	2·2	509	1·6	315	0·8	427	0·8	863	1·2
Harwich	155	0·7	357	1·1	546	1·4	700	1·4	932	1·3
Hull	1095	5·1	1329	4·3	1646	4·3	2069	4·1	3944	5·3
Liverpool	3969	18·6	4912	15·8	5034	13·1	6313	12·4	10617	14·3
London	3459	16·2	4708	15·1	5876	15·3	7549	14·9	11244	15·2
Manchester	–	–	–	–	–	–	713	1·4	1535	2·1
Middlesbro	274	1·3	490	1·6	678	1·8	833	1·6	2007	2·7
Newcastle	2870	13·4	4079	13·1	4952	12·9	4959	9·8	8048	10·9
Newport	361	1·7	1040	3·3	1213	3·2	1595	3·1	2405	3·2
Plymouth	80	0·4	122	0·4	107	0·3	118	0·2	3606	4·9
Port Talbot	–	–	–	–	–	–	–	–	1010	1·4
Southampton	658	3·1	861	2·8	919	2·4	1600	3·1	5632	7·6
Sunderland	914	4·3	884	2·8	1017	2·7	1193	2·3	1806	2·4
Swansea	548	2·6	777	2·5	824	2·1	1557	3·1	2487	3·4
Weymouth	30	0·1	117	0·4	104	0·3	101	0·2	1229	1·7
Glasgow	670	3·1	1286	4·1	1694	4·4	2503	4·9	4032	5·4
Bo'ness	151	0·7	199	0·6	202	0·5	278	0·5	–	–
Grangemouth	159	0·7	221	0·7	664	1·7	818	1·6	1064	1·4
Greenock	203	1·0	207	0·7	199	0·5	106	0·2	1024	1·4
Leith	389	1·8	478	1·5	692	1·8	945	1·9	1599	2·2
Methil	} 124	} 0·6	} 428	} 1·4	} 728	} 1·9	} 1366	} 2·7	{ 1143	1·5
Kirkcaldy										
Burntisland									{ 818	1·1
Dundee	95	0·4	83	0·3	88	0·2	59	0·1	209	0·3
Total U.K.	**21343**		**31141**		**38361**		**50803**		**74012**	

*Note: Blyth counted with Newcastle.

Source: *Annual Statements of Trade and Navigation.*

Net tonnage of all vessels entering selected ports from foreign parts, 1870–4 to 1910–13

(with cargo and ballast: '000 tons)

	1870–4		1880–4		1890–4		1900–4		1910–13	
	Tons	%	Tons	%	Tons	%	Tons	%	Tons	%
Blyth	*		*		*		922	1·8	1455	2·0
Bristol	382	1·8	509	1·7	636	1·7	793	1·6	1453	2·0
Cardiff	884	4·3	2248	7·5	3466	9·2	4738	9·4	6719	9·1
Dover	360	1·7	555	1·8	792	2·1	1127	2·2	2159	2·9
Folkestone	121	0·6	191	0·6	226	0·6	115	0·2	645	0·9
Goole	112	0·5	325	1·1	334	0·9	544	1·1	766	1·0
Grimsby	384	1·8	463	1·5	720	1·9	903	1·8	1812	2·5
Hartlepool	483	2·3	479	1·6	487	1·3	577	1·1	1116	1·5
Harwich	170	0·8	371	1·2	606	1·6	748	1·5	956	1·3
Hull	1258	6·1	1600	5·3	2077	5·5	2588	5·1	4360	5·9
Liverpool	4043	19·5	5139	17·0	5661	15·0	7023	13·9	11569	15·7
London	4410	21·2	6254	20·7	7860	20·9	10300	20·4	13284	18·1
Manchester	0		0		0		904	1·8	1920	2·6
Middlesbro	223	1·1	533	1·8	861	2·3	953	1·9	2228	3·0
Newcastle	1867	9·0	2710	9·0	3341	8·9	3789	7·5	6995	9·5
Newport	161	0·8	749	2·5	820	2·2	1028	2·0	1908	2·6
Plymouth	121	0·6	206	0·7	199	0·5	250	0·5	3653	4·9
Port Talbot	0		0		0		0		730	1·0
Southampton	729	3·5	963	3·2	1010	2·7	1820	3·6	5740	7·8
Sunderland	699	3·4	726	2·4	788	2·1	837	1·7	1477	2·0
Swansea	342	1·6	567	1·9	551	1·5	895	1·8	1868	2·5
Weymouth	26	0·1	116	0·4	104	0·3	107	0·2	1259	1·7
Glasgow	416	2·0	843	2·8	1091	2·9	1551	3·1	3271	4·4
Bo'ness	60	0·3	130	0·4	179	0·5	284	0·6	0	
Grangemouth	177	0·9	193	0·6	517	1·4	722	1·4	1013	1·4
Greenock	281	1·4	298	1·0	224	0·6	131	0·3	1105	1·5
Leith	480	2·3	621	2·1	800	2·1	1024	2·0	1640	2·2
Methil	} 59	} 0·3	} 189	} 0·6	} 446	} 1·2	} 865	} 1·7	{ 874	1·2
Kirkcaldy										
Burntisland									{ 528	0·7
Dundee	190	0·9	239	0·8	283	0·8	234	0·5	–	–
Total U.K.	**20768**		**30141**		**37666**		**50581**		**73541**	

*Note: Blyth counted with Newcastle.

Source: *Annual Statements of Trade and Navigation.*

CHAPTER SIX

Stagnation and Decay 1919–1980

1. TRADE IN THE DOLDRUMS, 1919–39

By 1914 the British were so used to being a prosperous industrial and trading nation that they had come to regard their predominant position and endless growth as part of the order of nature. Various Jeremiahs had commented on increasing foreign competition, but it was scarcely recognised that the current phase of massive exports—like the steel steamers that carried them—was no more than thirty years old and highly vulnerable. By 1918 the world had changed for the worse, so far as Britain was concerned, but politicians, industrialists and workers were so deeply and emotionally committed to a 'return to normalcy' that they failed to grasp, and to adapt to, the economic consequences of the war. No doubt had there not been a war Britain would have come to terms with the trends undermining her old basic exporting industries and altered production and trade aspirations accordingly, but she could not cope with the suddenness of the changes when war compressed perhaps forty years of economic evolution into four.

It was inevitable that Britain, as the major international trader, would suffer more than most countries from a weakening of the international economy. Import substitution cut into traditional British markets for cottons and metal goods. War-induced poverty and short-fall in population reduced the value of primary products and therefore cut back the purchasing power of Britain's customers in the less developed countries. At the same time the movement away from coal to fuel oil brought to an end the spectacular growth of the coal trade and turned Britain into an importer of energy.

The basic industries were in serious trouble, and the ports could not escape the effects of their decline. It is true that new industries were developing, but these were, on the whole, directed towards the domestic market, and other advanced countries were as capable as the British of supplying their own needs. In other words, expanding economic activity and reviving prosperity in the inter-war period were no longer reflected in the export trades. In terms of the value of trade, decline is all too apparent following the catastrophic slump of 1921, when the post-war re-equipment boom came to an end. Exports were worth £1,134 millions in 1920 but only £703 millions in 1921. However, it is fair to point out that current values did remain fairly steady between 1922 and the slump of 1929, and because international prices were falling the *volume* of trade was actually rising during the 1920s.[1] It was the early 1930s which witnessed the lowest export performance, and at no time before the Second World War did values recover to the 1930 level. On average exports in the 1930s were worth little more than half what they had been worth in 1913, in real terms.

If we turn from the value of exports to the tonnage of shipping required to carry them, the overall situation appears at first sight to have been even more serious as far as the ports and the shipping industry were concerned. Total tonnage clearing with cargo fell dramatically from 67·8 millions in 1913 to 36·4 millions in 1921, and though trade recovered to some extent, averaging 58·9 millions per year for 1921/25 and 61·9 for 1926/30, more than a tenth of the total tonnage was purely statistical gain occurring when trade with the Irish Free State began to be counted as foreign instead of coastal, in 1923. (See Tables on page 167.)

While there might be justifiable doubts over the export trades, there could be none about imports. Demand for foreign foodstuffs and raw materials continued to grow rapidly, and the continuous fall in the world price of primary products enabled Britain to import increasing quantities for a given volume of exports. In consequence the tonnage of shipping bringing imports into the country passed the 1913 figure in 1923, and thereafter was generally about twenty per cent higher, even during the slump of the early 1930s. The paradox of the inter-war period was that Britain did not have to work so hard at her basic exporting industries to buy the imports she required. High unemployment did not, therefore, prevent a general rise in the standard of living, and it was left for the next generation to work out, after 1945, how to pay for imports once they began to rise in unit value *vis-a-vis* exports.

The falling tonnage of vessels clearing and the rising tonnage of vessels entering Britain with cargoes was bound to have an important effect on the internal working of ports by altering the demand for facilities and labour. But it should be emphasised once again that the overall pressure on port facilities was much greater than implied by the movement of ships in freight: the tonnage clearing in ballast was rising steadily after 1924. It may well be that the declining coal trade reduced the ease with which ships could obtain return cargoes, but rather surprisingly the reduction of coal exports brought no decline in the tonnage of vessels *arriving* in ballast. Between 1913 and 1930 the tonnage clearing in ballast rose from 15 to 32 per cent of all clearances, while the tonnage entering in ballast moved from 33 to 34 per cent, so it looks as if the new types of trades evolving between the wars required something of the order of one ship in four to sail in ballast in both the import and the export trades. No doubt such a change was made easier by the declining freight rates in the early 1920s, which made owners eager for earnings at least in one direction and reluctant to accept coal and other goods at ruinously low freights if a voyage in ballast might secure a more remunerative return freight.

Whereas foreign-going shipping recovered fairly quickly after 1921, the same cannot be said of coastal shipping. Some 30 per cent was lopped off the tonnage of coastal freight by the war, and around 25 per cent off the total tonnage of coasters in freight and ballast. A further 20 per cent—around five million tons—was 'lost' when Irish trade became foreign in 1923. But it would be wrong to give the impression that the coastal trade was finished. A very large amount of coal was still carried coastwise, the average tonnage of coasters clearing the eight major coal ports being 7·9 millions in 1926/30 compared with 10·1 in 1913 (with 1926 being a particularly bad and unrepresentative year because of strikes). Comparisons are difficult to make, but it is worth noting, for instance, that the tonnage of coasters in freight was *increasing* steadily after

1926 while the tonnage of goods carried on the railways was declining. The expanding coastwise distribution of petroleum was partly responsible for this.[2]

Although activity was at a lower level than before the war, coastal traffic was increasing at many of the eastern ports, and was only failing to do so at the western ports because they lost ground heavily in 1923 through their Irish connexion. For a small number of ports, such as Greenock, Leith, Blyth, Sunderland, Hartlepool, Methil, Southampton, Falmouth, and above all London, the tonnage of coasters arriving during the slump of 1931–33 was actually *greater* than the tonnage active in 1913. All told, the tonnage of coasters was running at more than 50 million per annum after 1926, though the tonnage in freight was only half that amount. Nevertheless it was coastal rather than foreign trade which was responsible for much of the decline in *total* activity in the ports compared with the great days before the war.

So far as foreign trade was concerned, the inter-war period witnessed yet another of those changes in the composition of trade, with consequent adjustment between ports, which had occurred several times before and was to be repeated after the Second World War. It should have come as no surprise. The coal trade in particular had been dangerously over-extended, and far too much capital had been committed to it in the decade before the Great War. In so far as there was a collapse of foreign-going tonnage in the inter-war period, it was largely attributable to the inexorable decline of coal:

Average Annual Exports of Coal from Britain, 1911–1938

(million tons)

1911–13	67·5	1931–35	39·8
1921–25	56·2	1936–38	36·9
1926–30	47·4		

Source: Mitchell & Deane, *Abstract of British Historical Statistics*, p. 121.

It follows that ports did not suffer equally, and that the depressing effect of diminishing coal tonnage hides a substantial *growth* that was actually taking place in shipping involved with exports other than coal. If, for example, we compare the tonnage clearing from the principal eight coal ports with that from the principal eight general commercial ports in 1913 and 1926–30, we find the former falling by 20 per cent and the latter rising by 37 per cent. The commonly held view that the inter-war period was one of *universal* decline in the volume of the export trades is one that cannot be sustained, though equally it was far from being one of universal growth.

It was the coal ports, therefore, which bore the brunt of the inter-war troubles. By the 1930s the great Bute docks in Cardiff were shipping less than half their pre-war tonnage of coal, and more than half the locally-owned ships were laid up. Penarth Dock, specialising in coal, was closed. In Scotland the new dock at Methil, leading port of the Fife coalfield, was never fully used. The Tyne and Wear ports suffered from the devastating combination of declining exports and closed shipyards. On the Humber, Goole's foreign exports were shattered and the great new dock at Immingham, chiefly intended for the coal trade, never worked at anything approaching full capacity. In Grimsby, Alexandra Dock was partially closed and the Corporation Tramshed was built on quays at the shallower end. Everywhere coal capacity was underused, and even bunkering facilities were increasingly redundant as ships turned to oil firing. In many places coal quays lay empty, hoists unused and coal sidings rusting. But in others, where coal rubbed shoulders with general trade, it was possible to relieve pressure for general accommodation that might have arisen by spilling over into facilities originally planned for coal.

By contrast with pre-war experience, it was import trades which now demanded attention. In the past, and again after 1945, substantial shifts in the composition or direction of trade led to 'new' ports or to remodelling of existing ones. Any chance of this occurring between the wars was thwarted by the uncertainty resulting from the contraction of aggregate trade flows. There was less pressure on the port system as a whole, and for the first time in almost two centuries most of the major ports could relax, confident of accommodating their shipping for the foreseeable future without straining facilities to bursting point. It was just as well, for many port authorities were concerned that declining real income would impair their ability to pay charges on earlier investment, and were disinclined to invest further.

Expanding trade between the wars was likely, therefore, to be confined to those places which had equipped themselves for larger vessels and fast working in the years before 1914, and which already had a tradition of handling imports for very populous hinterlands. London, Liverpool, Hull, Glasgow and Manchester all gained substantially, with London's inward tonnage rising by 56 per cent between 1913 and 1926–30, and Manchester's by no less than 87 per cent as she confirmed her position as a leading consumer goods market for the north-west region. This was, in fact, to be the last flourish of the old major ports and their particular type of trade, and it owed a great deal to certain political and physical factors that were, to some extent, beyond the control of the ports themselves.

Firstly, the continued growth of the long-haul food and raw material trades, and the move towards Imperial Preference, greatly assisted the western and southern ports at the expense of the eastern ports. The last suffered further because their principal trades, with Europe, were upset by the economic consequences of the war and because hostility to Revolutionary Russia upset the Baltic timber trade at Hull, for instance, while encouraging the Canadian timber trade at Liverpool. In short, the degree of specialisation which had been encouraged by Free Trade worked in favour of some ports and against others when Free Trade was abandoned by the National Government in 1931.

Secondly, this trend towards longer-distance trades raised the proportion of vessels requiring specialised handling facilities or able to enter only the largest and most modern docks. Such a movement is seen in the rise in the *average* net tonnage of steam and motor vessels engaged in foreign trade from 2,500 in 1913 to 3,086 in 1923. Apart from other virtues, large ships were very much more economical of fuel and crews. A vessel of 25,000 tons deadweight capacity (i.e. about 12,500 tons net) required, in proportion to its capacity, only a third of the fuel of a vessel of 2,500 tons capacity, and only double the crew.[3] It was not simply a matter of large locks and deep docks. Such vessels also demanded a greater area of quay space or shedding and a greater concentration of handling apparatus, since larger vessels carried a greater tonnage of cargo per lineal foot than did smaller ones. A 250-foot-long vessel, it was estimated in 1921, had a cargo capacity of 5·55 tons per lineal foot, whereas one of 650 foot length (around 12,500 tons net) had a cargo capacity of no less than 40 tons per lineal foot.[4] The consequence, in terms of cranage, sheds and railway facilities, may be imagined. Catering for large ships was more expensive in every way.

So far as individual ports were concerned, the disparity in size of vessel increased markedly over time. For instance, the average tonnage of vessels paying tonnage rates at Liverpool rose by 42 per cent between 1913/14 and 1938/39, whereas the average at Leith, which was almost entirely committed to the northern European trades, grew by only 8 per cent between 1913 and 1937; and that at Methil, whose foreign coal trade was in trouble, *fell* by no less than 61 per cent.

It was not only large vessels that were attracted to large rather than small ports. There were financial savings to be made in shipping consumer goods to the major distribution centres only, and using road (or rail) transport for internal distribution over fairly long distances. Government control during the First World War had laid great emphasis on shipment through the most easily organised ports, and the continuation of a more rational system of ship operation after the war appeared to make sense. On the Humber, for instance, Grimsby and Goole never fully recovered the trade lost to Hull during the war, though both places maintained a very considerable barge traffic with Hull. Here as elsewhere the fall in freight rates encouraged owners to break bulk in the major ports and discouraged the practice of making several calls along the coast, each incurring dock dues and other handling charges.

This was particularly true of the liner and packet trades, which contributed a great deal to the growth of tonnage at London, Liverpool and Southampton. So far as the larger passenger liners were concerned, their concentration on Liverpool and Southampton brought a massive increment in terms of tonnage which was far less demanding of port facilities (given deep water) than freight traffic. Southampton in particular accumulated a large tonnage movement from vessels on their voyages between Europe and America calling and remaining in the port for hours rather than days. Indeed, here as elsewhere Customs recorded the 'calling' vessels in a way which distorts national shipping figures and gives the impression that trade between the wars was better than it actually was. A cursory examination of the statistics reveals Cowes as a major port because vessels anchoring in the Solent came within its jurisdiction, and Plymouth similarly had a recorded tonnage which was almost equally fictitious so far as real economic activity is concerned: ships called there so that passengers could proceed to London by train and save many hours over the Southampton route, and even more if their vessel was destined for Tilbury.

To some extent Britain was forced to look outwards from Europe in the 1920s, and even more so in the 1930s, but the collapse of German and Russian trade (which left Grimsby as the only major port with a declining overall tonnage between the wars) was not followed by decline in

other trades with northern and western Europe. These were increasingly channelled through the rapid-transit packet ports, which again were able to carry a very large amount of trade through relatively unambitious facilities by working them far more intensively than was possible in ordinary ports. Dover continued to be the principal port for French traffic, though she did not, in fact, recover the full extent of her pre-1914 trade. By contrast the tonnage of vessels at Folkestone grew by 36 per cent between 1913 and 1931–33, and at Harwich by no less than 181 per cent. Folkestone remained a smaller port than neighbouring Dover, but Harwich had overtaken her by the end of the 1920s both in tonnage and in value of trade. Indeed, by 1930 Harwich had overtaken Grimsby and ranked as seventh port in the country in terms of value of trade.

The phenomenal rise of shipping at Harwich was chiefly accounted for by the opening of the train ferry to Zeebrugge in 1924 and the building up of the Harwich–Hook of Holland packets with the development of the latter port in the early 1920s to replace Rotterdam as the gateway to western Europe. Regular services were also opened to Esbjerg for Danish dairy produce and to many of the smaller ports along the Dutch and Belgian coast. This was the route taken by perishables for the provisioning of London, cutting out the lengthy voyage via the Thames and also the additional man-handling of produce on both sides of the sea. This was an extra boon for the chilled trades (especially butter) which had previously required a fairly complicated handling system, but which now went from the collection centre to market in the same refrigerated railway van.

Dover benefited somewhat later from the introduction of train ferries which carried the London–Paris expresses from 1936, but also accommodated an increasing volume of goods traffic.

In both Harwich and Dover, facilities for running railway trains on board ferries could be adapted for motor transport, and motor cars were carried in growing numbers in the 1930s. Motor vans also made their appearance, but any precocious evolution of modern 'roll-on roll-off' traffic was thwarted by the appalling state of the roads to these, the most suitable ports for ferry operations. It really is quite remarkable that to this day no road communications equalling the old railways have been built to the major British ferry ports, though to be fair the approaches to Hook of Holland are not much better.

Finally, if one had to select a single commodity which

more than any other typified the transformation of British trade between the wars it must surely be petroleum. Total export tonnage was falling as Britain lost the resource advantages derived from coal's monopoly as the fuel for industry and transport. But total import tonnage was rising fast as crude and refined petroleum was drawn in to replace coal within Britain itself, and in 1936 the value of imported oil exceeded the value of exported coal. It was not, however, the value of the petroleum trade, or even its tonnage, which affected the ports most: it was the type of ship in which it was carried and the preferred method of unloading.

2. THE NEW BULK TRADE OIL

In turning to the physical changes within the ports between the wars it is as well to start with oil. Once the tanker had been adopted as the most economic method of transporting oil, it proved almost impossible to handle it in existing dock systems without ruinously expensive alterations. Oil shared with coal the need for large areas of quayside storage space, but whereas coal was carried by rail and spent a brief period in the docks, oil from tankers had to be stored in shore tanks, and since it was an imported material it was likely to be stored for longer periods than exported coal, which was kept at the pit if there was no call for it. The 'tank farms' thus became a feature of oil unloading which is now so common as to excite no comment. But in the early 1920s it was not only a cumbersome innovation but a distinctly dangerous one, running counter to the age-old tradition of keeping inflammable materials out of docks. Fortunately the use of pumps to empty tankers removed the need for normal quayside operations, and the use of piers connecting the tanker to the tank farm at some relatively isolated spot spread rapidly.

There were a number of important consequences of this system of unloading. Large quantities of oil and even larger tonnages of shipping could enter a port without using the docks, so that the rising importation of oil was not accompanied by the same sort of massive and expensive dock construction as was necessary for the earlier expansion of the coal trade. Piers, compared with deep docks, were easily and cheaply constructed, and once their adequacy had been proved it was not long before they were pushed out into deeper water in order to accommodate larger ships. As tankers were able therefore to grow larger the oil trade became concentrated almost, but not entirely, on the major ports, which were in any case the places most suitable for inland distribution by rail or barge. And finally, it became apparent as time passed that oil terminals did not necessarily have to be within a port at all, though the demand for port-associated services usually ensured that they were unlikely to be far away.

It was only to be expected that London would predominate in the oil trade, and in fact she already had three oil jetties and some seventy-five storage tanks at Thames Haven, thirty-five miles down-river from Tower Bridge; Thames Haven was the highest point up-river to which the wary port authority would allow tankers to proceed. Hull, also, had Saltend Jetty opened before the Great War, while Liverpool's Dingle Oil Jetty, immediately south of Herculaneum Dock, was built in 1922 and backed by the extensive 'Dingle Oil Installation' on an area originally purchased for further dock extension. Quayside working without piers was, of course, possible in places with a reasonable depth of water alongside, and landing stages and storage facilities were developed fairly easily at Bowling on the Clyde for Glasgow, at Ardrossan, where 'Ocean Tanker Berth' offered 38 feet of water, and at Fawley on the Solent for Southampton. The first two remain much as they were, but Fawley was later (1951) transformed into the modern terminal.

For a small number of ports it was impossible or unnecessary to work tankers at piers or open berths. At Swansea, for instance, there was a completely new dock — Queen's Dock — ready for service in 1920 but with no prospect of coal traffic, and this was converted into the first *dock* specialising in the importation of oil. It served the first British oil refinery, opened in 1922 by British Petroleum at Skewen, five miles north-east of Swansea. Although it is a true impounded dock, it never had any of the usual buildings associated with docks, and is unusual in that tankers are not worked alongside but at piers which are pushed out into the deeper water in the centre of the dock from the south and west sides.

Grangemouth also found itself with excessive accommodation when the coal trade failed to fill the Grange Dock and Basin, and the oil trade (already present before the Great War) was encouraged to use it. More importantly, for the future of the port, Scottish Oils Ltd. established a refinery in 1924 and built jetties from the south side of Grange Basin to the deep-water channel in the middle. The situations at Bristol and Manchester were slightly different, in that new docks were constructed specifically for oil tankers. At Bristol, where the tidal range demanded impounded working, a new arm of Royal Edward Dock, opened in 1923, was devoted to oil, with a special fire boom across its entrance to prevent floating fire from spreading through the rest of the dock. A vast tank farm developed over the coastline north of the dock, and Bristol, like Hull, distributed large quantities of petrol coastwise and by barge along its river system. Finally, Manchester was the sort of distribution centre that would obviously have a great demand for oil, but was too far from the sea to allow easy access by tankers, and too vulnerable, with its open dock system, to admit them safely. The solution to the problem was to ban oil from the city docks (where it had, in fact, been delivered in barrels since the 1890s) and establish an oil dock at Stanlow, near the mouth of the canal, in 1922. This new dock, it has been said, 'ushered in a new era in the history of the Canal by inaugurating a fundamental shift of activity from the Manchester docks to the Ellesmere Port section.'[5] A refinery was opened by Shell-Mex in 1924, and by the end of the decade Manchester ranked second only to London in the amount of oil imported. The canal was deepened to allow larger tankers as far as Stanlow in 1927, and a second oil dock was opened there in 1933.

Stanlow and Avonmouth were by far the leading importers of oil on the west coast, and they took on a still greater significance when the Second World War upset London's trade. As a result the two western ports were linked by pipeline in 1942, and by the following year pipes had been laid to the east of the country for the supply of oil to airfields there. It was an interesting development, since it implied that pipelines in future could be laid around the countryside from a very limited number of ports. Much would depend on the future size of tankers, but in the inter-war period there was no reason to suppose that they would ever require more than the thirty feet of water provided at Stanlow in 1927.

3. DIVERSITIES OF EXPERIENCE: NEW WORKS, 1919–1939

The examples of Stanlow and Avonmouth remind us that where specialised demands arose it was still necessary and possible to construct new docks. The 54-acre Gladstone Dock opened in 1927 at Liverpool is the best example of a 'super dock' built for the very largest transatlantic liners.

Its entrance, at $1,070 \times 130$ feet, also admitted larger vessels to the other docks in the northern system. On the other side of the Mersey the Birkenhead docks were no longer able to receive the largest ships passing through Suez, and here again a new entrance and deeper internal entrances were needed if the Far Eastern ships were not to be transferred to Liverpool. Work began on the main lock in 1922–23 and on internal work in subsequent years, culminating in the extension of the Western Float as Bidston Dock, opened in 1933.

The eagerness of the Mersey Docks and Harbour Board to increase their capacity for large ships owed more than a little to the knowledge that the Port of London Authority was still relentlessly pushing on with improvements for its growing share of the nation's trade. On the eve of the war the newly formed PLA had embarked on a programme of modernisation, and this continued after the war with almost no interruption. The most spectacular work was undoubtedly the new King George V Dock in the Royal Group, opened in 1921 at a cost of around £4·5 millions. Offering 38 feet of water, approximately three miles of unbroken quay and a massive entrance, it could admit all but a handful of the largest ships afloat; and a passage cut through to Royal Albert Dock greatly increased the size of vessels that could be admitted to it and to Royal Victoria. So far as George V was concerned, one of its most interesting features was an attempt to come to grips with a problem which had plagued several of the major ports since the eighteenth century. While the north side was a normal quay for working with rail or road transport, the south side was built as a series of seven long jetties *parallel* to the wall and 32 feet away from it. Barges were intended to lie between the jetties and the wall, allowing the sorting of goods to take place in the sheds erected on the jetties and, in theory, removing some of the confusion which had long been a feature of the docks admitting large numbers of barges.

The second main element in the London modernisation programme was the deepening of several of the larger docks. It was not an easy process, and deserves comment if only because it changed the shape of the docks. In the oldest docks the walls were curvilinear in shape, and dredging alongside was impossible because the walls underlay the mud. Even the more modern straight walls had a toe which projected outwards for many feet at the base to prevent them from slipping. The only way to dredge deeper without undermining the walls was to construct a

The remains of wooden wharfing above the typical sloping wall of Victoria Dock, Hull (1979).

'false wall' some distance into the dock, and allow a gentle upward slope of the floor to the original wall. Such a combination was not unknown in docks where a timber quay was built out over gently sloping dock walls, particularly in coal docks where the use of hoists did not require substantial quays. The best surviving example of such quays in a commercial dock—though in an advanced state of decay—is probably in Hull's Victoria Dock. The adaptation of the system for heavy working, and particularly for bearing sheds and warehouses, depended on the use of concrete cylinders in place of some of the piles, giving greater stability to the mainly concrete superstructure. The system was apparently first perfected in Dundee in 1913, and in the same year was used to build out the north quays of West India Import and West India Export Docks to allow the depth to be dredged from 22 to 26 feet. In 1935 the same method increased the depth alongside the north quay of Royal Albert to 34 feet, and in the following year attention turned to the north quay of Royal Victoria, still cluttered with the eight projecting piers which had long been unsuitable for berthing modern ships. They were gradually removed, and by 1938 had been replaced by a 45-foot-wide false wall. The main wall of the dock was never rebuilt in the places where the piers had been: load-bearing was now the job of the concrete quay.

Of the other works in London, the most important were undoubtedly at Tilbury. In 1921 the 1,000-foot reinforced-concrete cargo jetty was opened on the river frontage immediately south of the main dock to speed up the Continental traffic, and in 1929 the new 1,000 × 110 foot western lock, opening off the main dock at a far more convenient angle for both the dock and the river, was opened for passenger liners.

Expense and difficulty were considerably lessened by the use of monolithic construction. This system, apparently perfected in Glasgow by Deas, the Clyde Navigation Trust's engineer, and used for various quays and docks there and in other major ports, did away with the vagaries and inadequacies of wooden piling topped by stone or brick walls, a method of construction that usually involved extensive trenching for foundations and produced a result which was not always stable or adequately consolidated. Monolithic construction produced a solid mass. A short length of huge concrete cylinder with a sharp leading edge was sunk by heavy weights while the mud was removed from the core; further lengths were added until the required depth was reached, when the core was filled with concrete and the wall super-imposed.

The attractiveness of Tilbury was further enhanced by the deepening of part of the main dock to 38 feet and subsequently the Passenger Terminal was opened in 1930, in an attempt to prevent passenger vessels deserting to Southampton. One wonders how far it was all worthwhile, especially since Cunard were already thinking of still larger vessels for Southampton alone. The greatest gain appears to have been in the continued growth of the large cargo/passenger vessels in the Far Eastern trades rather than in the luxury end of the transatlantic services, which were in any case suffering in competition with foreign liners that ignored Tilbury and called only at Southampton.

The improvement of facilities was not restricted to the new docks. With the rapid growth of the transatlantic timber trade (and, to some extent, the food trade) it became clear that the Surrey Dock system would have to be upgraded. The dock estate was very extensive, but a large area of the centre (surrounded by Stave, Russia, Greenland, Canada and Albion Docks) was occupied by Centre, Quebec and Canada Ponds, and the north-east was occupied by Globe, Lavender and Acorn Ponds. The time had come to follow the example of most other ports and sacrifice the ponds. They had served their day when logs of unsawn timber were floated for convenience and carried in barges or towed around to sawmills; but an increasing proportion of imported sawn timber was seasoned in open sheds before milling, and the emphasis was now on covered quay space. In 1926 the central ponds were converted into Quebec Dock and additional storage quays; and two years later the northern ponds became Lavender Dock and further storage space. (Globe Pond, for instance, was completely built over.) There was, however, a difference between the two conversions. Quebec Dock was intended for ships in the normal fashion, while Lavender Dock continued to receive only barges and some floating logs. Lady Dock also continued to float logs.

North of the river, further work was undertaken to ease access to and passage through the West India and Millwall dock system. In 1926 Millwall Dock was connected to West India South Dock, thus allowing grain ships destined for the massive granaries at the northern end of Millwall Dock to enter by the West India locks rather than by the Millwall lock which was two and a half miles further up-river, in Limehouse Reach.

Equally important but less spectacular was the continuation between the wars of the modernisation of handling equipment in London. The unloading of grain by suction tubes had been introduced into Millwall Dock around 1904, and the 1920s witnessed the introduction of overhead rails for unloading imported meat, chiefly in Victoria Dock. Various quays and berths were altered to provide more space, and more transit sheds were provided for the rapid movement of goods that were not loaded into barges. Elsewhere there was a tendency for old hydraulic cranes to be swept away in favour of newer, moving electric cranes. The port also acquired a 150-ton floating crane, *London Mammoth*, for lifting such heavy loads as railway engines and machinery, and moved around the docks as the need arose. Finally, a work of great importance that was never directly visible resulted from the dredging of a deeper channel offering 27 feet of water at low tide as far up-river as the entrance to King George V Dock.

Although works at Liverpool and London were very great, it is arguable that the largest single work undertaken between the wars was at Southampton. The transfer of White Star vessels from Liverpool in 1907 had been followed by the removal of some of the Cunarders in 1919 and United States Lines followed in 1921; and both British and Continental vessels calling at Southampton continued to grow in size and number until the 'Old Docks' were no longer adequate. In 1927 work began on the 'New Dock', which again was not an enclosed dock but a huge deep-water (45 feet L.W.O.S.T.) quay along the Test, running some 7,500 feet from Mayflower Park to the new King George V Dry Dock, the latter the largest in the world to take the Cunarders.

Such a length of deep-water quay (like developments at Tilbury, Glasgow and elsewhere) would have been exceedingly expensive if not entirely impossible to build

by the traditional method of digging a trench in which to erect the wall, especially since the insecure foundations would have demanded a wall of gargantuan proportions. That of Ocean Dock, which was 75 feet from foundation to quay, had had to be no less than 40 foot wide at the bottom to prevent slipping. A similar problem with the new quay was avoided by building it on 146 of the largest monoliths (45 foot square) yet conceived, thrust down to between 70 and 100 feet below quay level by the weight of 4,000 tons of kentledge. Once the quay had been built, the mud to the seaward side was dredged away and used to fill in the landward side.

The King George V Dry Dock was opened in 1933, and the quay, with berths for eight or nine liners, in the following year. The new works confirmed Southampton's claim to the bulk of the transatlantic passenger traffic, and though London and Liverpool fought a rearguard action it was quite clear that they would eventually fail. What was not, of course, so apparent in the second half of the 1930s was that Southampton's future in this particular trade was also under threat from yet another revolution in transatlantic passenger transport!

Glasgow was the only other major port which found it necessary to engage in significant construction work between the wars. The drastic fall in coal exports, from around four million tons at the height of the trade to around two millions in 1933, was partly compensated by the continuing growth in the importation of iron ore, pig and scrap iron and limestone for the west-of-Scotland steelworks. This trade kept the south side of Rothesay Dock fully occupied while the north side, devoted to coal shipment, did not always exhibit its pre-war bustle. Proposals were made in 1929 to shift the importation of ore down-river to a more suitable deep water site which would also have given access to the major iron and steel works, but the general economic situation was against such action, and it was not until recently that the Hunterston Ore Terminal was finally built.

Glasgow's problem was similar to that of London, namely a growing general trade carried in vessels that were finding increasing difficulty in moving up-river to the old shallow docks. In response to this demand for deep berths, the 20-acre George V Dock was opened in 1931, offering 43 feet at mean high water, neap tide. Since there was no lock, the entrance, at 350 feet, could admit any size of ship, and while the 2,088-foot eastern quay was divided into four berths, the west quay was not so divided before the war and, at least in theory, offered a maximum berth length of approximately 2,700 feet. In reality it was not occupied by giant liners, and neither shedding nor railway was provided before the war. Nor was there anything approaching the modern provision of cranes on either quay, though this, to a large extent, reflects the sort of ships for which the dock was intended. Many of the larger, long-distance liners called at places in Africa and the Far East that did not have adequate harbour facilities, and they carried their own highly efficient derricks. Indeed, if photographs from the inter-war period are anything to go by several other areas of the port, including the more recent river quays and Queen's Dock, had few dockside cranes. On the other hand there were, scattered around the docks and river quays, a number of exceedingly large cranes suitable for heavy machinery, including the products of the locomotive works which had always provided one of the most spectacular sights in the port. On the eve of the Second World War, there were two 35-ton electric cranes in Queen's Dock, a 75-tonner on Plantation Quay, 130-tonners at Prince's Dock and Finnieston Quay, and a 175-tonner at Finnieston Quay. The last two were associated with the tradition of engine building in the Finnieston area, harking back to the days when engines were not fitted in the shipyards which only acquired their own gigantic cranes towards the end of the nineteenth century.

While the increase in the volume of many of the long-haul trades demanded ever larger and more expensive docks, the equally dynamic short-haul trades with Europe, and especially the packet services, were able to expand with a minimum of construction. At Harwich, for instance, the building of a simple steel structure allowing trains to run on board ship (in 1924) brought a growth of traffic that was quite out of proportion to the effort involved. The Parkeston Quay end of the port had been rebuilt in stone and concrete and equipped with a battery of electric cranes between 1909 and 1911, but the expansion of the Hook of Holland traffic led to an extension of the Quay (in the new ferro-concrete pile construction) in 1934, and the erection of a new passenger terminal, Parkeston Quay West.

Provision for more traffic was not quite so easy at Dover, since the tidal range made it impractical to attempt to ship trains via a sloping connecting bridge, while the swell generated within Admiralty Harbour would in any case have made it extremely difficult to hold a ferry steady enough to make and hold the vital rail connexion. In this case the solution was a small Ferry Dock, large enough

to hold a vessel for hours rather than days. Problems arose in the building because of water rising through the chalk, with the result that the foundations had to be laid underwater. In his report to the Institution of Civil Engineers, the engineer, Ellson, claimed that this was the first occasion that concrete had been poured under water,[6] though wet concrete had been laid in bags, and stone foundations had been fixed under water, when occasion demanded, since the eighteenth century, Smeaton having developed a diving bell to assist the operation. Stevenson refers to the pouring of concrete under water in his *Design and Construction of Harbours* published in 1874.[7]

The remaining packet ports required little modernisation, and only three of them had anything done that could be described as a major work. On the south coast Weymouth acquired new quays for the Channel Islands trade in 1933; and Shoreham, lying mid-way between Brighton and Worthing, was so involved with coastal traffic associated with the growth of residential property in that area that a new lock (Prince George Lock) was built at the entrance to the impounded Aldrington Basin in 1933, and decaying wharves were refurbished. On the west coast the only development was at Holyhead, involving the dredging of the old Inner Harbour so that the Irish packets could tie up at Station Quay instead of at the exposed Admiralty Pier.

The success of the leading importation and packet ports was abundantly obvious between the wars, but it would be a mistake to assume that all the other ports were uniformly depressed. A few were still expanding, and even those that were not discovered that changes in the composition of their trade created a pressing need for new works: aged quays and redundant equipment could not always be adapted to new purposes for which they had never been intended. On the Tyne, for instance, the general merchandise trades continued to grow despite the stagnation of the coal trade, and since coal staithes were useless for anything else the 1,100-foot-long Tyne Commission Quay was opened, chiefly for the Norway trade, in 1928. So fast did this particular trade grow that a 400-foot extension, taking the quay to the entrance to Albert Edward Dock, was opened in 1937. Similarly, a 1,062-foot general-cargo quay—Corporation Quay—was opened on the river Wear below Sunderland, in 1934, and a further quay, specially for fish, was erected in 1938 on the south side of the river and a short distance from Corporation Quay.

Fishing was another of those food trades that flourished

between the wars, a fact that is obscured to some extent by the collapse of the ephemeral herring boom of the early years of the century. Discounting herring, landings of fish grew by 18 per cent between 1913 and 1933, and most of the fishing ports or harbours were kept busy, though not necessarily prosperous since the value of the fish rose by only 13 per cent at current prices. The demand for new facilities was not great. The fishing harbours such as Scarborough and Girvan continued to use their primitive and often ancient piers and quays with very little change, and the fishing ports, such as Aberdeen, Peterhead, Fleetwood and Hull had plenty of surplus capacity left over from pre-war expansion, especially since the herring fleet had declined so drastically. Grimsby was the only port where facilities were inadequate, plans for No. 3 Fish Dock having been abandoned because of the war. After lengthy delays, caused chiefly by financial questions, No. 3 Dock was eventually opened in 1934, offering a further 33 acres where trawlers could lie between voyages, and, equally important, three slipways for repairing trawlers and three coaling jetties for more speedy loading of the 900,000 tons of coal which the trawlers annually consumed. The slipways remain, but the coaling towers, which were as interesting a feature as the Grimsby Dock Tower, have, with their 4·5 miles of coal sidings, been swept away in recent years to make room for frozen-fish factories.

Grimsby reminds us that even within the coal trade there might still be modernisation within a situation of general contraction. Alexandra Dock, which had been equipped for the coal trade, was difficult of access for shipping, but there was no room for coal quays in Royal Dock. The problem was solved by the erection in 1934 of a large overhead electrical conveyor which carried coal over the main dock railways and along a new pier built in the middle of Royal Dock. Four ships could be loaded simultaneously, and subsequently Alexandra Dock was used chiefly for unloading timber and Humber barges.

Blyth was another port where coaling facilities were extended, principally because its coastal trade was still growing. New staithes were opened in West Blyth by the London and North Eastern Railway in 1928, providing two electrical conveyors capable of shipping up to 800 tons per hour into vessels of up to 10,000 tons. In 1934 the Cowpen Coal Company, which shared the port with the LNER, also built its Bates Wharf staithe with more of the latest appliances. But the most substantial work was probably at the small west-coast port of Workington, where the old tidal harbour and dock were supplemented in 1937 by Prince of Wales Dock, again equipped with coal conveyors, long since abandoned. (Minerals at Workington are handled now by grab cranes!)

For many small ports, all that was necessary during the inter-war period was the building or extension of quays for an increasing number of smallish vessels engaged in the near-European trades. In some cases, even in large ports, these extensions were to be found outside rather than inside the dock systems because of the faster turn-round that was possible. In Dundee, for example, George V Quay was built on the waterfront in 1926, and extended in 1932 to 1,460 feet, complete with shedding and eight new electric cranes. In Ipswich a fear that larger ships might not be able to use the dock had led, before the war, to plans for a new quay on the Orwell, and, despite a cut-back in trade, Cliff Quay was built in three stages opening in 1925, 1930 and 1937. It rapidly became the centre for the local timber trade, but made its mark chiefly in association with an oil-storage depot established by British Petroleum, Shell and National Benzole in the 1920s and a fertiliser factory opened by Fisons in the 1930s. Even ports such as Boston, which was in serious trouble because of the collapse of its coal trade, thought it worth while to construct River Quay on the Witham; and King's Lynn rebuilt its Boal Quay, on the Great Ouse, in 1927, as well as making improvements to its two docks.

*   *   *

By comparison with the earlier period, dock building between the wars was comparatively slight, but very effective. Several of the largest and most useful British docks were opened or fully constructed between the wars, and many improvements were made both in ports that were booming and in those that were, relatively, stagnating. Quays were extensively remodelled to provide longer berths, greater open space or deeper water. Electrification of cranes and other equipment eased operations, and even where hydraulic power remained supreme (for certain cranes and gate machinery) it tended to be produced more easily with electric motors than with steam power. Conveyors for coal, carcasses or bananas became fairly common. Outside the major ports cosmetic changes of this sort often produced spectacular results, especially in short-haul trade, where large vessels were not necessarily more economical to operate than small ones.

*   *   *

The ease with which the country as a whole handled its trade after the Great War resulted from a decline in some parts of that trade rather than from the provision of new facilities, and some of the trends observable in the larger ports caused worry to dock engineers, traders and interested observers alike. Continuing growth in the size of ships had the effect of writing off smaller docks, at least for overseas trade, so that the acreage of usable docks was actually decreasing over time. Many of the most recent large docks were unsuitable for 'modern' trade because they were in the wrong place—the coal ports. But new docks in the major commercial ports were not being built as rapidly as some thought they should be.

On the one hand there were those who saw a rising average size of ships and argued that docks must continue to get bigger to accommodate them. Liverpool shipowners—or some of them—had been saying it for a century or more, and now it was taken up by the Liberal Industrial Enquiry of 1928:[8]

> The question is . . . not so much how to accommodate existing traffic too great for existing capacity, but how to meet the demands which will be made within a few years. Shipbuilders in recent years have been laying down larger keels. . . . Hence it is necessary to look ahead and plan for these future requirements, both by the reconstruction and "modernising" of old docks and the construction of new ones. That some of the port authorities are alive to the needs of the times is evident by the carrying out of large development schemes in recent years, for example, the Gladstone system of docks at Liverpool, where the biggest vessels, built or likely to be built in the near future, may be accommodated in ease.

The principal obstacle to progress, it would seem, was the diversity of authorities responsible for docks. In the United Kingdom as a whole there were, in 1938, some 255 places described (in some cases loosely) as ports, and of these, 114 were owned by trustees, 59 by municipalities or county councils, 35 by railway companies, 23 by private companies, 17 by private individuals, 4 by the Admiralty and 3 by the Northern Ireland Ministry of Commerce.[9] Nobody was responsible for taking a long-term view of national needs, or for investigating the best sites for either docks or ports. And each of the authorities noted above had shortcomings when it came to long-term planning of this nature. Du-Plat-Taylor, the leading engineering consultant with experience of both Liverpool and London, was not alone in suggesting that the only way forward was through state ownership, as in France and other countries:[10]

> State ownership enables the design of ports to be considered from the national or imperial, instead of from a purely local, point of view. To some extent it does away with competition between ports, and to this extent it may be disadvantageous to traders through preventing any competitive cutting of rates. On the other hand, it enables the accommodation to be provided wherever it is most required, instead of being dependent on schemes prepared by local bodies.

Whether or not it was politically advisable to look to state ownership for salvation, there were good grounds for doubting the advisability of any widespread construction of very large docks, or, to be more precise, of docks for very large ships. What was the point of all the major ports equipping themselves for the proverbial 'largest ship' when there were in fact only a dozen such ships, devoted not to normal trade but to the transatlantic luxury passenger run? Taking all costs into account, these ships were not economic propositions: shipping lines ran them for prestige rather than revenue, and governments subsidised them for reasons that were nothing to do with trade. They were ruinous for dock companies, since dock dues were paid on *net* tonnage, and passenger liners had much lower net to gross ratios than cargo ships. In the 1920s, for instance, the 56,551-ton *Majestic*, requiring a 1,000-foot lock and deep dredging, actually paid duty on only 26,259 net tons, or 46.4 per cent of her gross tonnage. The slightly shorter (884-foot) *Berengaria* paid duty on only 40.9 per cent of her 52,226 gross tons. By contrast, general-cargo vessels and oil tankers in the 1920s were far less demanding on lock and quay length but had net tonnages of approximately 63 per cent of gross tonnage. The general run of small vessels were thus paying for length and depth of facilities which they did not themselves require and were subsidising the largest vessels which did not pay dues commensurate with their vast size for which the grand facilities were required!

Economic considerations alone would reduce the number of ports which could provide super docks, but a further question which arose was whether docks were appropriate places for large ships, especially passenger liners. Their great length produced severe turning problems inside docks and required a great deal of dead water which was expensive to enclose. Du-Plat-Taylor calculated

Steam crane for heavy goods, Dundee. The heyday of the man-sized parcel; the warehousing of small units in Glasgow, 1926.

that to construct a 1,000-foot berth with 41 feet of water would cost, at that time, £900,000 inside a dock but only £480,000 as an open, double-sided pier. For a single-sided river wharf with railway lines and all necessary equipment but without shed or passenger terminal the cost fell to as little as £195,000.[11]

The easiest and cheapest way forward would appear, therefore, to require the concentration of the largest liners at Southampton (which suited their geographical preference anyway) and the ending of the race for ever-larger docks. Any serious expansion of trade in larger vessels might be accommodated at open berths or in extensions to existing docks, thus avoiding the vast expense associated with locks. There was an alternative, namely to work the docks more efficiently. The pressure of trade and the low level of wages in the 1930s were not such as to provoke any serious approach to modernising the handling of general cargoes, and on the eve of the Second World War they were still being loaded and unloaded in labour-intensive confusion that had change little since the Crimean or even—if one excepts railways and hydraulic power—the Napoleonic War. But the cost of deep docks, and the difficulty of finding suitable sites for them, were now so great that any sizeable rise in general trade would bring on a crisis in the ports that could only be resolved by a revolution in working methods: advances in civil engineering were no longer enough.

4. THE SHIPPING REVOLUTION

During the two centuries prior to 1945 the dominant theme in port history had been the continual struggle to provide adequate facilities for the larger class of ship. Engineering and entrepreneurial skills had, by and large, succeeded in providing the docks, locks and quays necessary to cater for them, but in one fundamental respect there had been little advance between 1845 and 1945. The deepening of water and the lengthening of berths had not been accompanied by any substantial modification in the system of loading and discharging general cargo.

Advances in handling goods in the nineteenth century had all been associated with specific trades where bulk handling was an essential ingredient of expansion. The coal trade called for larger cranes, hoists and conveyors; the grain trade demanded grabs and elevators; the heavy machinery trade could not have occurred without the largest cranes ever used in commercial docks; the meat trade relied, in best practice, on overhead conveyors; and the banana trade (and some others) made great use of the canvas-sling machine with its ingenious ability to wend its way from the hold of a ship to the quayside. The miscellaneous trades could rely on no such devices. Most goods still, in 1945, came or went in 'man-sized' boxes, barrels and packages that were stacked loose in sheds, on quays and in holds, and trundled endlessly around. Thirty-hundredweight cranes were all that were generally required because that weight equated roughly to the volume of goods that could be removed by hand or hand-barrow if deposited on the quayside at intervals of two or three minutes. The number of cranes on a quay was limited by the danger of collision, and they did not usually work at night.

The handling of general cargo was never as confused or haphazard as it appeared to observers and still appears in photographs. But there was no denying that it was a labour-intensive and time-consuming business which could not cope with the vastly increased tonnage of goods per lineal foot of the largest ships. Here, rather than in the locks and docks *per se*, was the chief barrier to the use of more economical vessels in general commerce: it was physically difficult, if not impossible, to unload them. Larger cranes could not help significantly. A long time would certainly be required to load or discharge large ships, which must remain in port incurring demurrage when their owners wanted them on the high seas earning freight. Indeed, the speed of handling was inversely proportional to the anxiety of owners of ever-more-costly vessels.

The changes of the post-war period are sometimes thought of in terms of dockers' wage claims, strikes and militancy provoking port employers to devise means of doing without them. Industrial relations may never have been very good in docks in the major ports, and it appears to be the case that some shippers bypassed unionised ports because they wanted cheaper labour and more efficient working methods. But his had little bearing on the long-term trend, in which the militancy of dockers and the relative inefficiency of their employers appear as very subsidiary influences. The object of shipowners was to get rid of the system as a whole, to achieve the highest level of efficiency by applying bulk-load principles to general cargo. The militancy of dockers was in no small measure a panic reaction to the disappearance of their traditional role in the ports. It was no comfort to them that many of the traditional employers also were redundant, and that the great and glorious Port of London Authority would soon lose its *raison d'être*.

The greatest revolution in the history of ports was achieved through three roughly parallel developments: palletisation, Roll-on Roll-off (Ro/Ro), and containerisation. Like so many spurs to revolution their functions are so simple as to require only the briefest outline here.[12]

a) Palletisation

Palletisation owes its origins to two inventions: the fork-lift truck and metal banding. Once trucks were used in docks, from 1950, it was a fairly logical extension of their work to strap drums, boxes and other loose items to a wooden pallet which could be unloaded by crane and moved and stacked by truck. A later modification increased operating speeds by allowing trucks to enter through the side of ships and receive goods via internal lifts or ramps. But whatever the mechanism of transfer between ship and quay, the port

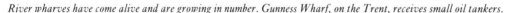

River wharves have come alive and are growing in number. Gunness Wharf, on the Trent, receives small oil tankers.

to many small ports such as Shoreham and even to places that were not, properly speaking, ports at all: for instance, New Holland 'dock' on the Humber and wharves on the Trent. Secondly, there was a tendency, now that timber could be stowed more easily on board ship, for it to arrive in much larger ships, especially in the long-distance trades, and be dealt with in the giant docks as normal cargo rather than through the smaller and shallower 'timber' docks. Specialised timber berths soon became a feature of the largest and most modern docks.

b) Roll-on Roll-off

'Ro/Ro' and containerisation had both been foreshadowed in pre-war railway usage. To speed the loading of trains and encourage certain types of custom—with house removals among the most obvious—containers had been developed which would fit both a railway waggon and a horsedrawn cart or motor lorry. (In fact at an earlier stage the Great Central Railway had even developed a container system for carrying live fish from Grimsby to Billingsgate!) The logical step of loading containers on board ship was not taken because of the physical and organisational problems involved, but, as we saw in the last chapter, whole trains of loaded waggons were rolled onto specially built railway ferries at Harwich and Dover between the wars. These, together with the beginning of motor traffic through Dover in the 1930s, and above all the success of 'landing craft' during the invasion of Normandy, led the way to Ro/Ro after the war. If tanks could be shipped in this way to France, commercial vehicles certainly could. All that was necessary in the ports was an angled quay so that ships could be loaded via the stern (or bow) and, in tidal water, a floating pontoon or adjustable ramp of some sort. Fortunately these were relatively cheap to construct, and could be added to an existing dock or pier without too much difficulty. The second generation of Ro/Ro vessels had their own ramps, sometimes with side-loading (as in the case of ScanAustral vessels) to allow normal berths to be used. Since Ro/Ro cargo is by definition mobile and self-propelled, little of the usual quayside apparatus was required, and the movement of cargo was so rapid that one berth could accommodate several ships in the same day.

Because Ro/Ro vessels were highly specialised, they generally ran only on predetermined ferry routes, adopting a timetable precision which enabled them to carry large

Capital intensive port operation: Roll-on Roll-off in operation at the King George Dock, Hull.

authorities were immediately called upon to provide level concrete roadways on hitherto cluttered and irregularly surfaced quays. Moreover, another blow was struck at the low-level warehousing system by the truck's ability to stack goods to a greater height than was previously feasible.

Even more important in its widespread consequences was the adoption of metal strapping for sawn timber, so that this particularly awkward commodity, now cut in approximately equal lengths, could also be handled mechanically. There were, in fact, two divergent results. Firstly, since timber was now less laboriously handled, there was a tendency for small ships to bring it from Scandinavia

amounts of trade through limited but selected facilities. It follows that shipowners usually chose the most convenient short sea crossing, and this meant, in practice, that most Continental Ro/Ro services were based on a few eastern ports, of which Hull, Felixstowe, Harwich, London and Dover are the principal, though others were involved to a lesser extent. The Danish bacon trade, for instance, was concentrated in a Ro/Ro connexion (replacing the old 'Butter Boats') through Grimsby, where the east side of Royal Dock was modified to receive it; Immingham and Goole received imported cars in this fashion, Goole concreting over the old Half-Tide Basin to receive them; and King's Lynn has its Hamburg connexion through the Ro/Ro terminal opened in Alexandra Dock in 1966.

Ro/Ro was stimulated almost as much by the development of road transport as by the interests of shipowners and, in particular, it owed much to the expansion of trade within the European Common Market. It is suited to 'do-it-yourself' distribution by motor lorry because it offers the possibility of 'door to door' service with no intermediate handling or agency, thus cutting costs and pilferage. But while Ro/Ro is extremely efficient over short distances, it is, after all, a ferry service rather than a cargo transportation service, and it is too wasteful of shipping space to be attractive over longer distances. The logical step was to follow the pre-war railway container system and carry only the cargo part of the motor vehicle, but this raised two almost insuperable obstacles: the unsuitable shape of most ships and the inadequacy of existing handling equipment.

c) The Container

That the container system was eventually successful owes much, in fact, to the exigencies of war. With shipping space at a premium, American supplies commonly crossed the Atlantic as deck cargo carried in tarred crates, and when the war was over the demands of the American armies of occupation spread around the world were so great as to provoke what was probably the first serious thought ever given to establishing a planned and efficient system of sea transportation of general cargo.

By about 1950 it was also becoming clear to the leading shipowners and port authorities that the only way to accommodate any further increase in the volume of world trade was to adopt some form of containerisation. The oldest docks were worn out or unsuitable for modern traffic. Many of the newer ones in Britain and Europe had been seriously damaged during the war. Many ships also were worn out, and owners were eager to increase the size and operating efficiency of their vessels. Yet the adoption of containerisation could proceed only slowly, and then only with the collaboration of all interested parties. Containers that had to be carried by ships, trains and motor lorries to the ends of the earth required a degree of standardisation unknown in a commercial world which had previously set greater store by individualism and competition than by co-operation.

In fact little could be done during the 1950s to speed the introduction of containerisation. It was still in the experimental stage along the American coast, and it was not until 1965 that the Port of London Authority commissioned the 'Martech' Survey of its trade and began

*Early containerisation (far left): transport of
live fish from Grimsby to Billingsgate by the
Great Central Railway, 1913.*

*Transport changes (left): barges still 'dock' in
the mud of the river Hull as the bridge nears
completion which now speeds the flow of
container lorries to the eastern docks. The
'gateway' is the boom erected in the 1970s to
stop flooding along the banks of the Hull at high
water.*

*The container revolution (right): terminal at
Manchester Docks for Montreal and
Mediterranean trade.*

negotiations with customers, including P. & O., who were persuaded to invest in suitable ships if part of the new Tilbury extension, then under construction, was equipped to handle containers. As a result the first container ships involved in short-haul to Europe began to work from Tilbury in the first month of 1968. Transatlantic trade began in June, and Australasian trade, in a shipowners' consortium called Overseas Containers Ltd., began in 1970, after a year's delay through strike action which helped to strengthen Rotterdam's position *vis-a-vis* London in this trade.

Variations on the containerisation theme soon emerged. LASH (Lighter-aboard-Ship) was a logical development on the Humber and Thames which had always made great use of barges. Standardised dumb barges, of the sort pioneered by the Aire & Calder Navigation Company at Goole, were floated into the open stern of special vessels and lifted to the appropriate deck. The largest of these vessels, the Lykes Line's 'Seabees', were introduced to the transatlantic trade in 1972, and, as 'intermodal' vessels, were able to carry large barges, containers, and palletised cargo.

Whatever form it took, the success of containerisation exceeded the wildest dreams of port and ship operators. Container berths could handle ten times the cargo of conventional berths with only a fraction of the work-force. A ship of a size which might previously have taken between a week and a fortnight to unload and reload could now be turned round in a couple of days. It is easy to understand why every port authority wishing to remain in business in a serious way began equipping container berths, and why

in some places the berths were moved out of the original port area to more open sites where containers could be laid out, sorted, and loaded onto trains or motor lorries. Since very large vessels—30,000 tons or more—were often involved, only the deepest docks or berths were suitable, so London extended Tilbury Dock, Hull built Queen Elizabeth II Dock as an extension of King George Dock, Southampton extended its deep-water quays, and Liverpool built the gigantic Seaforth Dock at the northernmost end of the dock estate. At Glasgow the Container Terminal—as these sites were soon called—was also moved down-river, to Greenock, thus reversing the move in the nineteenth century when the Clyde Navigation Trust had moved heaven and earth—and a fair amount of rock—to bring the contemporary 'big ships' to the city quays.

The new container terminals were not restricted to the current leading general-cargo ports, since little in the way of conventional port infrastructure or expertise was required. With rising Continental trade the deep-water Orwell Haven was particularly well suited to expansion, and the most spectacular growth in the post-war period has been at Felixstowe, a decayed port when the Felixstowe Dock and Railway Company was bought in 1951 by an East Anglian corn factor, H. G. Parker. In 1956 the refurbished dock was opened to vessels drawing eighteen feet of water and engaged in such things as the corn trade; but the port was seen as an investment as well as part of Parker's business. In 1964 an oil jetty was pushed out into deeper water, and in the following year a Ro/Ro terminal was added. The breakthrough came, however, when

Parker and his advisers, free from the financial and human restraints inhibiting the major ports, decided to build a full-scale container terminal to share in any benefits accruing to the neighbouring port of Harwich/Parkiston Quay. Both ports opened their container terminals in 1968, only shortly after Tilbury; and both benefited from a distaste for Tilbury and its work-force that was not uncommon among shipowners looking for 'private enterprise' ports that were not subject to traditional working patterns, restrictive practices and labour militancy. The point should not be exaggerated, of course. Traffic for London's northern hinterland could be carried through the Orwell estuary almost as easily as through Tilbury: Harwich had, after all, been the northern London route to the Continent for a generation or more, and transatlantic vessels bound for Rotterdam found it easier to call en route at Felixstowe than at Tilbury. But the crucial factor was Felixstowe's easy communications with the Midlands, which made it their natural outlet once the container berths were open.

Equally serious for the major ports was the growth in the size of vessels carrying the bulk trades such as coal, ore and oil, which tended to move from medium to deep-water sites, generally deserting docks for estuary terminals, as at Tranmere on the Mersey, and Thameshaven, Corton and Canvey Island on the Thames. The giant supertankers had, however, tended to concentrate on Fynart on the Firth of Clyde, Milford Haven and Fawley, with overland pipes linking these deep-water berths with inland refining and distribution centres. Similarly the giant ore carriers now come to Hunterston on the Clyde rather than to Glasgow's General Terminus Quay, though slightly smaller vessels can still use Immingham, Teesport and Port Talbot. The

Heavy machinery for the unloading of bulk iron ore, General Terminus Quay, Glasgow. Demolished 1982.

export of coal, which had been growing during the 1970s, is also concentrated, as a matter of Coal Board policy, at a small number of well equipped ports which has led to Immingham Dock, for instance, replacing all the other coal docks on the Humber as the outlet for the Yorkshire, Nottinghamshire and Derbyshire coalfield (though some minor shipment of coal brought by barge still takes place from Goole).

5. THE CONCENTRATION OF ACTIVITY AND COLLAPSE OF THE PORT SYSTEM

The urgent application of bulk-handling to most traffic (including such things as sugar and wine) in the 1970s was, without doubt, the most important influence on ports since the coming of the railways. The latter brought wonderful increments in trade that could almost—so far as ports are concerned—have been measured by the acre. To this vast panorama of water and warehouse the container and other systems of bulk-handling brought disaster.

In the first place, the collaboration between port authority and shipowner over the provision of highly specialised berths meant that a large proportion of the trade henceforth committed to containers could only go through the handful of favoured deep-water ports which were equipped to handle them, a fact which may have prevented a potential drift away from the major ports with the development of more efficient inland motor transport. Indeed, the latter increased the power of the great ports to poach in the hinterland of the others, though it also increased the level of competition between ports. Shipowners could shift their operations from one suitable port to another (as the passenger liner companies had done) with little concern for the state of inland transport which in the past had been of prime importance. As a result ports were brought near to bankruptcy by their inability to charge a truly remunerative rate for the use of that portion of their total facilities required for modern cargo handling.

In the second place, most ports, and certainly the major ones, were seriously distressed by the concentration of activity within them. Ro/Ro, palletisation and containerisation rendered most of the old general-cargo berths redundant, whatever the quality of their facilities and the depth of their water. Old docks were visited by a dwindling number of ships, but for the sake of which they had to be kept operational. Not all general cargo was—or is—carried in containers or large vessels, and many of the traditional berths offered specialised services, particularly in the storage of grain and refrigerated produce. It was recognised soon after the Second World War that many docks were likely to be underused—especially those catering for the coastal trade—and that they would act as a financial drag on better-quality facilities. However, many pressure groups opposed their closure because of the serious ramifications so far as local business and employment were concerned, and for a couple of decades or so the docks were left to empty gradually of their own accord.

The end, when it came, was quite sudden. All the 'town' docks were closed in Hull, all the 'southern' docks in Liverpool, all but part of one of the city docks in Glasgow. Elsewhere, on the east and west coasts small or interconnected docks remained open and little changed because of the expense or difficulty of closing down part of them; but everywhere they were underused. The atmosphere of ports had changed completely. Hitherto one could expect a dock, no matter how large or small, to have at least a small number of coasters alongside, and the export drive of the post-war period—and the later 'import crises'—had filled berths on end with foreign-going vessels. By the late 1970s one could visit Boston or Preston, or certain docks in most ports, without seeing a single ship. Of course they still came, but they were now rarities in an environment lately their own.

Nowhere was the run-down of port facilities so obvious or so tragic as in London. At the end of the war the port was in considerable disarray, having lost around a third of the PLA warehouses to bombing and several locks through bombing or semi-permanent closure associated with the building in South and India Docks of caissons for the 'Mulberry Harbour' used in the Normandy landings. However, by a monumental effort the trade which had been dispersed to the Clyde and Mersey was brought back to the Thames; the mess was cleared up; and all the docks were brought back into full service with the exception of East India Export Dock which was unusable (its wall had partly collapsed when the water had been removed) and which in 1947 became the site for Brunswick Power Station.

London's share of national trade continued to grow after the war, and by 1958 the 'up-river' docks from St. Katharine's to the Royals were enjoying the greatest volume of trade in their history. Yet within a decade the future of

the oldest docks was in question. In 1967 the East India Import Dock was sold to the Central Electricity Generating Board. In the following year St. Katharine's was closed, and London Dock in 1969. By 1970, with modern timber-handling systems in operation at Tilbury, the whole of the Surrey Commercial Dock system was closed, and the situation was becoming so serious in terms of lost employment and devastated communities that the Government began to show interest. London Docklands Study Team was set up in 1971 to plan the redevelopment of the entire up-river dock estate, on the basis that the above-mentioned docks were immediately available (some had already been partially filled since the early 1960s), that the West India and Millwall Docks could be closed *c.* 1978, most of Victoria *c.*1983, and the rest of the Royals *c.* 1988. In fact the PLA proposed to close the India and Millwall Docks in 1976, but they were reprieved because of Trade Union action, and opposition then and again in 1978 from the Government. In the latter year the PLA decided to close all the up-river docks because they were losing money at a ruinous rate and the work could be done by Tilbury. Sadly, it took the virtual bankruptcy of the PLA to persuade all parties concerned that the upper docks must be closed if the port was to survive at all.

The drastic action required for the docks, and the unhappy consequences for the local communities, were indeed only part of the story in London. The PLA, like port authorities in other major ports, did not monopolise warehousing facilities. In Liverpool and Glasgow goods were carted from the docks into the warehousing sector of the city. In London goods were largely, though not entirely, lightered out of the docks to the Thames-side wharves. These now suffered dreadfully, with companies going bankrupt, wharves decaying, and workers dispersing. All the major ports suffered far beyond their dock gates, and it is an interesting question whether, at the end of the day, the country as a whole made a net gain or loss from the apparently 'cheaper' handling of goods through limited modern facilities.

The consequences of these recent changes in cargo handling have been very great so far as physical remains are concerned. Until about 1960 one could have assumed with confidence that most of the harbours and docks and much of the equipment described in this book still existed. It was not always in its original form, or in pristine condition, but changes had usually been of a cosmetic nature, involving minor repairs and alterations to quays and locks, and the periodic modernisation of movable equipment. By 1970 it was equally reasonable to assume that many of the oldest docks were unused or only partially used. Their decay has not, however, meant that they have remained as monuments to a great past, a sort of vast industrial archaeologist's paradise.

In the major ports the situation varies considerably from place to place, and is constantly changing. For some years to come it will be impossible to draw up anything approaching an authoritative gazetteer of remains, and it seems likely that outside the currently working docks little will remain to show how ports looked before *c.* 1960. Generally speaking the very oldest docks have already been filled in, and, as at Liverpool and Hull, have totally disappeared. Others are in the process of being filled in or are being allowed to accumulate silt, while decisions are being taken about their future. In many cases this planning will again lead to the total destruction of the docks and associated works apart from odd features which may be kept for aesthetic rather than academic reasons. The truth is that preservation of major port works would be almost as expensive as maintaining ports and, in the absence of any national co-ordinated policy for the preservation of this kind of historical monument, little if anything will eventually survive.

It is not simply a matter of site values. So far as equipment is concerned there is often a desire to realise second-hand or scrap value which has removed all but a tiny handful of early cranes and hoists (though, to be fair, much of it went in the days when it was still being replaced by more modern working equipment). Even more recent equipment disappears with remarkable speed when it becomes redundant. For instance, the massive ore-unloading machinery at Glasgow's General Terminus Quay was dismantled within weeks of its closure, and London's *Mammoth* floating crane was sold abroad. The best chance of survival at the moment appears to be enjoyed by small bits and pieces of equipment in unused or little-used docks for which an alternative use has not yet been found; but it can only be a matter of time before both docks and machinery are swept away.

In the middling rank of ports, where smaller docks are still in use, the position is hardly better. Modernisation has in most cases destroyed the old character of these docks more than it has in the major ports where small docks were not considered worth modernising. Many of the smaller east coast ports, now deeply involved in Ro/Ro traffic with

Scandinavia and the Continent, have been affected in this way. Grimsby in particular has lost all its dockside building and equipment that distinguished it as a railway and coal port, though it retains a dockside ice house left over from the great days of fishing. West Hartlepool, however, probably holds the record as the most devastated port in Britain: apart from a few embankments associated with the banished coal hoists, and a number of minor buildings, the dock area has been razed to provide standing room principally for timber. Although the docks and dock gates remain, nobody wishing to know what ports were like in their heyday would find the place worth a visit.

In the two ports that would most obviously be worth exploring—London and Liverpool—there are, unhappily, immense difficulties. Both have enclosed docks, and the massive walls, distinguished in London by their immense height and in Liverpool by their apparently unending length, are among their most impressive features. But these walls were built to keep out unauthorised people and, though less well guarded than they once were, they still perform this function to an inconvenient degree. It is just as well. It cannot be emphasised too strongly that docks, whether working or derelict, are *extremely dangerous places.* The fact that a dock is closed to trade does not mean that the public has right of access to it, while a working dock is likely to be closed to the public in any case. Male trespassers may find themselves suspected of smuggling or thieving and females of plying an older trade.

6. A SURVEY OF DISASTER: CHANGE AND DECAY

In a brief survey of the current situation, the port of London can be divided into at least three different sections. Firstly there is the down-river working port consisting of Tilbury Dock and the Oil Terminals, which are closed to the public, and which in any case contain little of historical interest. Secondly there are the up-river docks, in varying stages of decay. As noted above, East India Docks were sold to the Central Electricity Generating Board, and the remaining water area was filled in almost immediately once the Export Dock was closed. Elsewhere work began tipping demolition rubble into the docks in order to provide a consolidated base for future construction once a plan for the docks evolved. The Wapping Basin and Eastern Dock of the London Dock system were filled, and most of the

Surrey docks suffered a similar fate, though they were not open to public use, despite reports from time to time of squatters and 'farms' on the Surrey docks. John Pudney, in his marvellously evocative *London's Docks*, commented that 'Even in death the Surrey Docks and London Dock were concealed from the public they once served while plans for resurrection were debated'.[13] In 1981 the work was in progress building over the site of London Dock. The closures of West India, Millwall and the Royal Docks are too recent for much alteration to have taken place, but they are still occasionally used for specific berths and again they are not open to public inspection. Plans for their future will no doubt change from time to time, but if the plans of the London Docklands Study Team ever come to fruition they will disappear, and all that will remain of the greatest of the British dock systems will be tiny water areas kept for landscaping purposes.

In the midst of decay one attempt was made to salvage something of the country's trading history for future generations, namely the well-known St. Katharine's project. Despite bomb damage and decay, St. Katharine's was the best preserved—or rather the least altered—of the original docks, and it was sufficiently small to be manageable without high level funding. It was sold by the PLA to the local authority and subsequently 'developed' in a way that illustrates the best and worst of this country's attitude to certain types of monuments. The part of the dock most likely to excite interest for all the 'wrong' reasons—the ivory house—was refurbished. Part of the warehousing was rebuilt in a very sympathetic manner, almost indistinguishable from the original. Part was still recently quietly decaying. But any attempt to create the atmosphere of the enclosed warehouse dock was ruined by a completely unsympathetic hotel development on the riverside of the dock. No attempt was made to recreate the southern basin and, to make matters worse an alien building was imported and re-erected simply because it happened to be old and surplus to another place's requirements. With trees and bollards scattered in pretty patterns, it is an example of the English middle class's unwillingness to preserve working class monuments as they actually were when working, and their equal desire to sanitise and recreate them as expressions of their own 'artistic' sensibilities. Future generations of Londoners will no doubt think that dockers queued at the gates for work because docks were such pleasant places in which to work! There is, however, a saving grace: the magnificent ship collection of the Mari-

time Trust is now to be seen in this dock.

The third element in the port of London are the miles of river wharves, especially on the south bank, which had once been the centre of commercial activity in and around the Pool. In the post-war period wharves continued to function here more than in any other British port, with lighters bringing goods from the docks for warehousing and distribution long after the ships themselves had deserted the river. As late as the early 1970s a trip on the river would reveal a great amount of activity at buildings which were among the most picturesque—and ancient—in the port. Indeed, for most visitors—and perhaps for most Londoners—the city wharves offered far greater visual evidence that London was a port than did the carefully hidden—and forbidden—docks.[14]

Since the lightering companies and the warehouses—of which Hay's Wharf was probably the best known—were an integral part of the dock operations, they were equally affected by containerisation and the rise of Tilbury. Their prime site in the centre of London has made them an obvious target for developers anxious to fill the south bank with offices and hotels, and most wharves have gone or are about to go, though the large warehouse at St. John's Wharf has recently been sympathetically restored and converted into flats. One of the finest examples, the derelict Cole and Carey warehouse at St. Mary Overy Staithe, has recently been classified as a listed building and may survive. It will no doubt show how a river staithe looked but will no more reflect the real atmosphere of London's working river than a single house would retain the glories of a Nash Crescent. Ironically this particular south bank area is being redeveloped by European Ferries Ltd., one of the firms whose success down-river is a principal reason for the closure of the facilities up-river.

The attempt to rescue as much as was economically possible of St. Katharine's Dock compares very favourably with the situation in Liverpool. On the one hand there are still many ranges of warehouses in the streets to the north of the docks which exude the atmosphere of the port. On the other hand the southern docks remain closed to the public and will continue to decay until some alternative use can be found for them. It is in fact possible to enter Wapping Dock without let or hindrance, and some may think it worth trespassing in order to view the general outline of one of the oldest docks and the magnificent range of warehouses along the east quay. However, the general outlines of even older docks (Canning Dock, Canning

Half-Tide Dock and Salthouse Dock) can be seen safely from the Strand now that the sheds have been demolished, and the equally impressive range of warehouses in Stanley Dock may be seen from Waterloo Road where the road bridge crosses the entrance to the dock.

Nothing in Liverpool or any other port can bear comparison with the magnificence of Albert Dock, but to describe its present condition as a national disgrace would be rather charitable. The major obstacle to its survival as a warehouse dock is that very magnificence which makes it so important a monument to Britain's two centuries of dominance in world trade. Potential tenants are not easily identified, and the cost of restoration and sympathetic conversion would be enormous. But maybe those from the industrial North might prefer the expenditure of public funds on the preservation of part of the British heritage which made the wealth in the first place than on the preservation of old Italian paintings. In the meantime access to Albert Dock is extremely hazardous, and permission to enter is unlikely to be granted by the port authority. Unauthorised entry would be foolhardy.

Even if London and Liverpool were more accessible to the public, Hull would remain incomparably the best place in the country exemplifying the various phases in port history. The old Haven is still crowded with vessels berthed in the mud at low tide, as it has been for the past five hundred years. They are barges rather than sailing ships, but the impression of the past is still strong, especially at dusk. The west bank of the Haven still has its old wooden staithes, and here and there eighteenth century warehouses remain (with at least one in the process of restoration). Beyond the warehouses lie the eighteenth-century merchants' houses and the mercantile quarter around High Street. The first dock, opening off the Haven to the north of the old town, has completely disappeared, though its outline can still be observed in merchant houses and warehousing surrounding Queen's Garden; and the lock, rebuilt by John Rennie, still serves as a dry dock, guarded by the original dock offices. A few yards south of the lock, in High Street, a museum is housed in three merchant houses, preserved largely because one of them happened to be the birthplace of William Wilberforce, whose people were Baltic merchants here.

A few minutes' walk westward along the line of the first, or Queen's Dock, brings us into the early nineteenth century, with Rennie's Humber Dock and Prince's Dock, somewhat spoiled by a new road built between the two,

but still having the original Humber lock with its hydraulic gate machinery and road bridge intact. (Remains of the hydraulic mains system are to be found in many of the dockside streets.) The docks are, and always have been, completely open, with sheds (now mostly demolished) standing between the quays and the public thoroughfares where those goods which were not loaded into barges were carried away by sled or cart. When eventually the railway system was introduced rails were laid in the streets where they can still be seen, with an elaborate arrangement of hydraulic turntables to get waggons round right-angle bends. One or two of the contemporary warehouses remain, with one of them, Moxon's, restored in a very imaginative manner.

Leading off Humber Dock to the west is an example of the next generation of docks: Railway Dock, built to bring the railway and ships together, with the remains of a grand range of warehouses on the south quay, and with rather interesting low-built railway sheds to the north. The lack of interest in this dock since the war is evident from the unrepaired bomb-damage on the north quay. The bomb just missed the hydraulic machinery for working the road/rail bridge over the entrance to Railway Dock, and this can be clearly seen in its well, now lacking its protective

Many ports still have their ancient 'port centre': High Street, Hull, was the focus of mercantile activity until c. *1800.*

over. To the south of Railway Dock lie the remains of the first goods station, and to the south of that, on the river Humber, can be seen the small inlet where goods were exchanged between railway and barges in the days before the later docks were fully connected to the railway system.

Railway Dock was a small affair for handling rapid-transit goods. Almost contemporaneous was the larger Victoria Dock, which was Hull's first big dock. It stands on the east side of the river Hull, and is again completely open to inspection. Nothing remains of the buildings, though it was chiefly a timber dock with open quays for storage. The entrance from the river Hull has long since been closed (though it can be seen from the Hull), but the Half-Tide Basin on the Humber, which was the place of resort for early steam packets, can still be seen. The dock was unusual in being built partly with a gently sloping stone wall topped by a timber wharf, and this remains, though the timber structure is in a fairly dangerous condition.

Hull's modern working docks to the east are not, of course, open to the public, but an excellent view of Albert Dock, Hull's first deep dock, can be gained from the bridge which takes Commercial Road (at the west end of Railway Dock) over the goods yard mentioned above. In the distance are the empty St. Andrew's Fish Docks, ruined by the EEC which has done so much to bring life back to the smaller east coast ports.

There are two further features of central Hull which illustrate general port activities. Riverside Quay stretches along the Humber Bank immediately south of Albert Dock entrance, and is typical of river quays for rapid handling of fairly small ships involved in Continental trade. It was best seen from the doomed Humber Ferry. The second feature is the Ferry Pier itself, which has existed in one form or another for several centuries. The present Corporation Pier was a partly wooden construction with a promenade superstructure added in the days of cast-iron pleasure piers. A floating pontoon was added between the wars to provide Hull with a Roll-on/Roll-off facility for the Humber Ferry, but the old wooden structure is still visible. Most of the cast iron work has been removed in recent years and something of the old splendour has been lost. The floating pontoon has been removed since the Ferry was replaced by the Humber Bridge in 1981.

There is one final aspect of the port worthy of comment. Hull was the first of the major ports to provide herself with dock offices to match her growing wealth and pride. Though not large by PLA, Mersey Docks and Harbour Board, or Clyde Navigation Trust standards, the Dock Office standing at the junction of Prince's Dock and Queen's Gardens is nevertheless a listed building of great quality which now houses the city's excellent maritime museum.

Hull has been described at length because its compact size and open nature make it the best witness to the past, even if most of the warehouses and all the non-hydraulic machinery have gone from the 'city' docks. But as it happens the other Humber ports also have a great deal to offer the historian. Goole's intricate dock system is more or less open to the public streets, and many interesting examples of nineteenth-century port facilities can easily be seen. All the docks survive (though the original Half-Tide Basin was recently filled in to provide standing room for packaged timber) and the original relationship between Barge Dock and Ship Dock, as well as the later elaboration of the docks, can be traced out. The disused Steamship Lock of 1838 (later called Ouse Lock) which survives immediately south of the later Victoria Lock, was in its day—and has remained—one of the finest examples of its genre. But the chief features remaining at Goole must surely be unique coal hoists for lifting canal barges ('Tom Puddings') from the water and delivering the coal on board ship: there is one in South Dock and one in Aldam Dock. Goole also has one of the few surviving railway hoists, in Railway Dock, with its incline running across the main road through the dock system. Goole was never a warehouse port of any significance and little in the way of port buildings remains. It was, however, a 'planned' port town. Unfortunately almost all of the Aire & Calder's Company town, directly to the north of the docks, has been pulled down since the war, and little remains to show the original plan.

Grimsby offers a wider contrast in remains. The eighteenth-century Haven can still be seen, though the seaward end was converted into Alexandra Dock and joined to Royal Dock. Traces of Rennie's lock can be seen from both the dock side and the sea shore at Lock Hill, while at the other end of the Haven the 'River Head' is still distinct, though most of the old warehouses have given way to a shopping precinct car-park. Half-way down the Haven (which stretches the whole length of Victoria Street) the 'Corporation Bridge', built by Head, Wrightson & Co. of Stockton at a cost of £5,200 in 1873, is probably the most spectacular dock bridge in Britain. Alexandra Dock has lost all trace of its coal hoists, and the overhead electrical conveyors carrying coal to the peninsula quay in Royal Dock no longer dominate the scene, but the razing of dock-side buildings to provide standing room has tended to emphasise Grimsby's greatest asset: the Dock Tower which alone is worth a visit to the town. In no other place was hydraulic power so triumphant in its architectural achievement.

Grimsby's other distinction as a port lies in her provision for the fishing fleet. The Fish Docks here are much easier to visit (and probably more active) than those in Hull, and more worth a visit, not so much because of the docks themselves as because of the fish market. It is held in a long winding quayside shed incorrectly called the 'Pontoon' (the original floated) where fish is landed on one side, laid out and auctioned, and loaded into the railway waggons (and increasingly into motor lorries) on the other. The distinctive coal appliances, with their great arms projecting over the water, have long since totally disappeared, as have the miles of coal sidings, traceable now by acres of ballast and discarded sleeper nails. Some idea of the extent of the land reclaimed for the Fish Docks and Royal Dock can be gained by walking along the embankment from the end of Suggitt's land (in Cleethorpes) to the Royal Dock piers, and down the west side of the dock to the old Haven. The last bit is technically trespassing, but it is doubtful if anybody will worry on a summer Sunday, when it can be a pleasant walk.

By way of contrast with the impounded docks on the Thames, Mersey and Humber, Glasgow's Harbour, with its river quays and open docks, is still visible in general outline. Kingston Dock no longer appears on the Glasgow City Plan (Bartholomew), but it can be found easily enough between Windmillcroft Quay and the magnificent SCWS headquarters in Morrison Street. The dock entrance was almost obliterated in the construction of Kingston Bridge, but its line can still be traced by the large coping stones

between Windmillcroft Quay and the river. The sheds are now privately occupied, but the dock basin itself has turned into a jungle already sporting sizeable trees.

A bird's eye view of the partially filled and wholly derelict Queen's Dock, together with its Italianate hydraulic pumping house (1878) and Yorkhill Basin, can be had from the Clydeside Expressway, but the best way to investigate the remains of the port is to proceed westwards from Windmillcroft Quay along the south bank of the Clyde. The street, criss-crossed by railways and still having *in situ* several hydraulic capstans for hauling waggons, passes behind General Terminus Quay, Mavisbank Quay and Plantation Quay. General Terminus Quay is now completely razed, but the back-up railway system can still be made out on the opposite side of the road. Mavisbank Quay has little of interest to show apart from the derelict but still impressive rotunda (1890–96) of the Clyde Vehicular Tunnel, at Plantation Place. (Vehicles were lowered to the tunnel on hydraulic lifts.) At the corner of Mavisbank Road is yet another Italianate hydraulic pumping house (1894), this time for Prince's Dock, which has its main road entrance at this point. The pumping house is now a motor repair shop, as are many of the buildings at the east end of Prince's Dock and, indeed, many parts of the river quay sheds. The east end of the dock is filled in, the abandoned cranes standing forlornly against a background of weeds.

The west end of the dock still functions, if only for tugs and fire vessels, and one heavy crane is still in position. The end of Plantation Quay is, in fact, at the river entrance to the dock, which has a derelict harbour master's office topped by the telegraph which signalled ships in and out. From this point, or from an open stretch of Plantation Quay a hundred yards to the east, a panoramic view of the Harbour of Glasgow can be obtained. On the opposite side of the Prince's entrance are the Clyde Navigation Trust's three Govan Graving Docks (completed in 1875,

Hunterston ore 'terminal', 1981. Such rural surroundings now witness the traffic that went to Glasgow's General Terminus Quay. Ore is landed by the devices on the pier to the left of the picture and carried by conveyor to the rail head on the right.

886 and 1898), the largest of which, at 880 feet, can still accept a fair sized ship. In the distance down-river is the huge silo on Meadowside Quay, and on the opposite side of the river is Yorkhill Quay, the Queen's Dock pumping house, and Queen's Dock, with its half-demolished sheds. Up-river lies Finnieston Quay on the north bank, with its huge crane still usually surrounded by large items awaiting shipment and, next to it, the berth of the pleasure steamers which sail round the Firth of Clyde in the tracks of the old puffers which once congregated at the up-river quays disappearing into the distance and framed by the Kingston Bridge. It is difficult, in the midst of silence and decay, to recall that a decade ago the docks were crowded, and that almost every foot of quay, from their entrances to George V Bridge in the centre of the city, was occupied by ships both large and small.

On a much smaller scale the harbours (apart from the earliest East India Harbour) and one impounded dock (James Watt Dock, 1878) at Greenock are still more or less intact, though the principal traffic now flows through the Container Terminal at the western end of the dock estate and the harbours are chiefly used by tugs. The most distinguished feature of the port is undoubtedly the very fine Custom House dating from 1818, next to the East India Harbour of 1809.

Hull is exceptional among the ports discussed above in retaining some visible evidence of its medieval and early modern condition. Bristol shares this retention of early features, largely for the same reason: the river berths were unsuitable for modern shipping but admirable for coastal vessels, so the latter remained to justify the river quays while the former were accommodated in docks elsewhere. At Bristol the Frome Basin survives in part, though modern buildings line its banks. The Floating Harbour on the Redcliffe and Welsh Backs boasts a number of distinctive 'Bristol style' warehouses, as does the Bathurst Basin (now closed at New Cut end). The earliest 'modern' development, Merchants' Dock, is filled in, and the most important feature, the Cumberland Basin which impounded the Floating Harbour, is now partially obscured by a major road which crosses it by the Plimsoll Swing Bridge. The bridge in fact swings over the port's most notable relic, namely Isambard Brunel's entrance lock (1848) with its eccentric shape to accommodate a single caisson gate and crossed by an unusual tubular-girder swing bridge, also designed by Brunel. The remains of the original lock are immediately adjacent to this lock.

Outside the chief commercial ports the degree of decay resulting from changing patterns of trade varies considerably from place to place. Worst hit are usually those ports created for a specific purpose—usually mineral shipment—and not subsequently adapted for other wider purposes. Despite their decay, the fact that they were not 'improved' does at least mean that surviving features illustrate a period of port history before the devastating rebuilding schemes of the post-1945 era. Gloucester, for example, was created as a canal port more than anything else, and its docks and very extensive range of warehouses for the corn and provision trades still survive almost intact. Hidden away behind the warehouses, Gloucester has its original seamen's Bethel. In most ports they seem to have gone, or at least to have been replaced by more modern or modest buildings.

Unfortunately most of the places involved in the mineral traffic have had all the associated works and railways removed, chiefly for their scrap value. In consequence they give the totally false impression that ports were a collection of holes full of water in the middle of cinder deserts. These cinders, now supporting grass and rosebay-willowherb, are often the best clue to the position of the old railway yards, where coal waggons waited their turn for the hoists or cranes. At the top end of the scale, in Cardiff, not a single coal hoist remains and the Taff Vale Railway no longer enters the dock estate, which is being 'redeveloped'. For all that matters of its trading history, Cardiff is dead. Similarly Methil, the great Scottish coal port on the Forth, is largely derelict, its equipment removed, its newest dock (No. 3, 1913) partially filled and deserted, and its oldest docks (No. 1 and No. 2) used only by the occasional small vessels. It is, however, still distinguished by the unique entrance to No. 3 Dock, now sheltering fishing boats.

By contrast the neighbouring smaller coal port of Burntisland retains many of its original features, together with a number of listed railway buildings around its entrance. Its coaling machinery has gone (though some inclines and the stone bases of hoists remain), and its survival in working order as a small 'museum' of a port is largely owing to the importation of bauxite for the nearby aluminium works. Although the port is too shallow to admit bulk carriers, they anchor in the Forth and transfer their cargo to vast barges which bring it to the East Dock (1901).

On the west coast of Scotland the situation is similar. The almost deserted railway port at Troon is an excellent example of a coal harbour, retaining its shape if nothing

Decay. Troon 1982 (above), the quay of the outer harbour now derelict. Scrap metal and old tyres remain on the opposite side.

Charlestown, Cornwall, (left) built in the 1790s has only recently ceased to ship china clay from the chutes on the right of the dock, fed in the last stages from a china-clay drying works (1907–70) whose chimney is visible behind the houses.

else. Neighbouring Ayr has also lost the bulk of its railway equipment, but its harbour and small dock are intact and it shares with Burntisland the distinction of still exporting some coal, though nowadays it is loaded by mobile conveyor and the ubiquitous motor cranes that have replaced the railed variety in almost every small port and some of the big ones. Further along the coast Ardrossan stands largely denuded of its mineral exports and imports (and Old Dock is filled in), but is still a flourishing port on the basis of its oil traffic and ferry services, one of which has its Ro/Ro ramp in what used to be the entrance to Old Dock.

Many coal ports relied on high-level staithes to deliver waggons to the ship. Partly because these were made of wood, they have almost entirely disappeared. The best surviving staithe is probably that at Blyth, while a fascinating example of a complete coal port may still be seen at Seaham, the most spectacular of the north-eastern harbours. On the north-west coast the great harbour of Whitehaven is still intact, and the channel down which coal was delivered to the staithes is clearly visible on the southern cliff face, by the side of the shaft of Haigh Pit. Maryport stands almost as it was when deserted, with harbour, docks and railway inclines giving a fine impression of what the port must have been like in life: iron rings still remain to tie up the ships which will never come. And, as one of the curiosities of the place, there remains a section of the

unusual wooden piers that Daniell drew when he visited here in the early nineteenth century. A few stumps of a similar pier can be seen at Harrington, but the harbour there is much altered with modern concrete, though the cut-away quays for low-level coal delivery shutes are visible to the south of the blocked up entrance. (A similar shute can be seen still working in the dock at Whitehaven.)

Of the ports concerned with other minerals, chiefly in Cornwall, little remains, and technically most of them were not ports at all since they dealt only in coastal traffic in materials not attracting the attention of the Customs. Most of them have returned to a state of nature, with stone piers and ruined buildings the only evidence that they once bustled with activity. Charlestown is one of the best examples, chiefly because its shipments of china clay ceased only very recently and the harbour is very well preserved. For most places the surviving remnants of piers that litter this tourist coast are those built in the eighteenth or early nineteenth centuries and recorded above.

If it is at all possible to recapture the atmosphere of early ports, it is best sought in those which did not enjoy substantial expansion during the Industrial Revolution or in those where expansion encouraged dock building outside the original trading area. Many of the fishing harbours fall into the former category. Their business did not, on the whole, increase with industrialisation (despite the great herring boom), and harbours built for inshore fishing boats remain little changed today, apart from the tendency to replace worn stone with concrete. There are more of them in Scotland and the West Country than elsewhere; places such as Arbroath and Fraserburgh, with their small harbours and integrated cottages and curing houses, being typical of the medium sized fishing ports. Peterhead, though still a fishing port, has begun a second life as a depot for the North Sea oil industry. Oil platforms are now fitted out in the huge southern harbour, built as a harbour of refuge by prisoners from Peterhead gaol who constructed a wall across the bay in the middle of last century. Many of the most primitive harbours in the country are to be found towards the north of Scotland, where simple piers following the line of natural rock formations sheltered a few poor boats for crofters eking out their living from the soil. They show what some of the Cornish harbours must have been like before they became resorts.

Indeed, in many places, especially on the south and south-west coasts, the features which rendered ports vulnerable to decay—isolation from industrial districts, hilly hinterland and rocky shore, shallow beaches and sand bars—also rendered them attractive for holidays or retirement. Poverty-stricken fishing villages and declining mineral outlets found that their inconvenient situation in coves and gorges was regarded as picturesque by those who did not have to make a living in them, especially in winter. There was, therefore, every incentive to maintain little harbours after their real trading purpose no longer justified it, and those places lacking an eighteenth–century stone pier built themselves a nineteenth-century cast-iron one. Thus Whitby, once a major shipowning centre, has hardly changed in general outline in the present century, but the harbour is more of a tourist attraction than a hub of commerce. The same is true of neighbouring Scarborough and Bridlington, turned by the railways into seaside resorts at the very moment when their port function was fading.

Some ports decayed so long ago that their early role is no longer very obvious. On the north Norfolk coast, for instance, Wells-next-the-Sea belies its name, though its 'harbour' still exists in the village. Nearby Blakeney and Cley also no longer have pretensions as ports, though Blakeney's fine mariners' cottages have been restored and refurbished by the local yachting community. In fact many little harbours around the coast are thriving far more than they ever did as commercial centres, through the interest of yachtsmen. The beautiful little harbour at Crinan was

never so busy while puffers held sway, and the congestion in the inner harbour of the semi-derelict port of Troon has to be seen to be believed. But these are still recognisably ports. Others, especially in the south-east, have only a historical memory, brought out by George Goldsmith Carter in his atmospheric *Forgotten Ports of England* (1951). Deal, Sandwich, Rye, Winchelsea and others retain ancient reminders that they were once on the route to France, strongholds for defence as much as agents of trade, a dual role that is nowhere more apparent than in Dover, whose magnificent harbour is overlooked by an equally magnificent castle which deserves to be more widely known if only for its more modern sections: Dover is without doubt the best example in the country of a defended port.

Few of the 'forgotten' ports offer any real impression of what medieval or early modern ports were like. Individual merchant houses or warehouses remain, but one is tempted to suggest that the best impression of an early port is gained from those places which retained their port function without obliterating their past. The ports of the Wash are probably the best in this regard. The great church at Boston, built from the proceeds of the wool trade, dominates a town centre which adheres to the medieval port plan, and river quays fronted by old warehouses, including the gaudy 'Van Smirren' warehouse which must be the most attractive, and smallest, tall warehouse in the country. In fact the river has been 'restored' in living memory with the ubiquitous sheet piling that is spreading through the ports, and the timber quays are largely swept away; and the warehouses are not medieval, though they are good examples of the eighteenth and nineteenth century types to be found in many ports until post-war demolition drove them out. Despite this the general shape of the port remains, and if one moves down-river to the modern quays and the little dock, one sees a reasonable cross-section of port history. There is the added attraction that the port has been thoroughly investigated and described by the Industrial Archaeological Group of the Lincolnshire Local History Society.[15]

King's Lynn is a far more substantial relic of the old days (and a far more substantial modern port). Many medieval lanes run between the river frontage (though the new South Quay has altered it somewhat) and the continuous line of King, Queen and Nelson Streets. Several of them have medieval and early modern mercantile buildings in them. The oldest, now called Hampton Court, stands

Custom House, King's Lynn, standing on the ancient mud creek Purfleet, is still surrounded by mercantile property of the C18th.

at the corner of the Nelson Street and St. Margaret's Lane, which also boasts the Hanseatic Warehouse, the frontage of which dates from 1428. The oldest part of the town lies between the two mud docks of Millfleet and Purfleet, the latter containing one of the most beautiful—and most photographed—Custom Houses in Britain, built in 1682 to the design of Henry Bell. North of Purfleet the houses in King Street are predominantly Georgian, with passages running through to the quays at the back as they did in Hull. (King's Lynn shares with Boston the benefit of having had its oldest buildings explored and described in detail.[16])

Important as the riverside buildings may be for creating the atmosphere of an early modern port, the most distinguished feature of the port is undoubtedly the Guildhall of St. George (King Street) and the Guildhall of the Holy Trinity (Queen Street), both dating from the early fifteenth century and bearing witness to the wealth and splendour of Lynn's mercantile élite at its peak. But they

should be viewed in the context of the port as a whole, for expensive buildings, whether Guildhall at King's Lynn or Port of London Authority Headquarters in London, are the product of trade carried on at countless staithes and warehouses of less pretentious appearance and therefore less enduring structure.

King's Lynn is now one of the most flourishing small ports, by virtue of the easy link with nearby Europe, and consequently it is possible within the space of a few hundred yards to see everything (for public roads cross the docks) from medieval warehouse to modern container traffic. The chief gap, so far as a cross-section of port history is concerned, results from the almost complete removal of the railway system and coaling equipment: but that is a problem in every port.

By 1980 the ports had gone full circle. Many had started in medieval times as trans-shipment places for great inland marts: towns of mariners and labourers and no great wealth. Gradually they had assumed the role of intermediary, their own rising merchants and shipowners developing old trades and pushing new ones, taking their cut of everything. Port-based industries added to the general prosperity. Employment opportunities were great, and growing, no matter how irregular and low-paid some port work might be. The ports were proud of themselves on the eve of the Great War. Massive investment, stupendous engineering and marvellous shipping had brought them to a peak of trade, in tonnage and value, unknown in the history of the world. When Glasgow claimed to be the 'Second City' of the empire, it was an empire—or an international economy—which was founded on trade and shipping and the work of ports as well as on industrial might: an empire that Glasgow had helped to found. The inter-war period came as a sharp reminder that prosperity and employment were fragile, but the depression was, after all, nation-wide, and post-war activity brought the ports, except for those previously engaged in the coal trade, to yet another high point in their history.

Now, despite the vast volume of trade still passing through them, large ships and bulk handling have almost ruined the ports. Large ships have encouraged the removal of deep-water docks or wharves away from port centres, and though the most modern docks are all of large size, they are nevertheless small in total area compared with the acreage of docks required to accommodate the nation's trade in 1970. Except in the smaller ports along the east coast, the old docks have almost everywhere shut down, and with them have gone employment for the docker and profit for the merchant. Furthermore, neither the merchant nor the shipowner is resident in the 'port', if by 'port' we mean the area surrounding the docks. Once again ports are trans-shipment centres for inland towns, and inland merchants and manufacturers. Vast areas of warehouses have been rendered useless as motor lorries and containers slip through ports in a matter of hours or minutes. Apart from the grain and timber trades, the ports appear to have slipped back to a position they held in the early Middle Ages.

Sources: *Annual Abstract of Statistics* and *Digest of Port Statistics.*

The Changing position of the major ports, 1913–1973
Value of Trade as a percentage of total National Trade*

	1913	1920	1921–25	1926–30	1931–33	1971–73†
Bristol	1·5	2·1	1·9	1·8	1·9	1·6
Cardiff	1·7	1·7	1·6	1·2	1·3	0·7
Dover**	2·5	1·8	2·1	1·8	1·6	5·2
Goole	1·4	1·4	1·4	1·3	1·2	0·7
Grimsby	2·7	1·7	1·7	1·7	1·8	2·9
Harwich‡	2·5	1·4	1·9	2·4	2·8	9·8
Hull	6·1	5·0	5·3	5·3	5·7	4·4
Liverpool	26·8	31·7	27·0	23·6	20·7	10·9
London	29·8	29·2	31·6	35·0	37·6	20·2
Manchester	4·1	6·0	5·0	4·8	4·3	2·3
Newcastle	1·8	2·0	2·2	1·9	2·1	0·7
Newhaven	1·5	0·7	0·9	0·7	0·7	0·6
Southampton	3·9	2·6	3·8	4·6	4·7	7·0
Glasgow	4·0	4·6	4·3	4·1	3·6	2·2
Leith	1·7	1·3	1·3	1·3	1·3	0·5
Others	8·1	6·9	7·9	8·4	8·8	30·3

*excluding Ireland   **includes Folkestone
†includes N. Ireland   ‡includes Felixstowe

Tonnage of Foreign-going Shipping in Cargo and Ballast arriving in Selected Ports, 1913–1970

('000 tons net, annual averages)

	1913	1920	1921–25	1926–30	1931–33	1968–70
COMMERCIAL PORTS						
Barrow	269	347	281	272	131	–
Bristol	1531	1436	2057	2445	2344	3015
Goole	760	312	664	665	554	–
Grimsby	2499	994	2189	1903	1827	5906
Hull	4507	3065	4910	5047	4768	5373
Liverpool	12054	9277	12098	14156	13259	16043
London	13725	11777	16051	21461	20947	35773
Manchester	1878	1737	2540	3518	3178	5571
Middlesbro	2375	1739	2087	2296	1533	6758
Port Talbot	824	625	751	717	772	1104
Dundee	429	331	489	614	557	–
Glasgow	3574	2637	3650	4162	3777	3624
Grangemouth	1089	622	1004	1137	937	1931
Greenock	1178	352	883	2001	2124	4084
Leith	1608	849	1416	1449	1249	798
COAL PORTS						
Blyth	1501	465	1177	899	804	159
Cardiff	7617	4448	6127	5417	3947	1892
Hartlepool	1136	711	821	796	668	–
Newcastle	7219	4518	6486	6174	5263	2817
Newport	2229	1587	2045	1905	1265	1607
Sunderland	1608	599	1272	1182	1035	–
Swansea	2120	1305	2266	2550	2592	1876
Methil	912	158	691	435	406	–
RAPID TRANSIT PORTS						
Cowes	16	19	496	1991	3810	–
Dartmouth	1117	1280	667	707	521	–
Dover	2417	1325	1611	1863	2178	12587
Falmouth	706	544	795	917	919	–
Folkestone	778	594	759	910	1057	1207
Harwich	967	709	1229	2282	2718	10914
Newhaven	491	271	496	633	665	1065
Plymouth	3809	2477	4227	6355	6288	394
Southampton	6701	3863	7678	10487	10029	19566
Weymouth	1117	893	587	735	676	–

Tonnage of Coastal Shipping in Cargo and Ballast arriving in Selected Ports, 1913–1970

('000 tons net, annual averages)

	1913	1920	1921–25	1926–30	1931–33	1968–70
COMMERCIAL PORTS						
Barrow	283	113	195	189	128	–
Bristol	1202	1292	1060	939	934	1732
Goole	661	138	330	408	519	–
Grimsby	558	100	364	379	486	1977
Hull	1200	488	774	821	828	1011
Liverpool	3521	3502	2568	2352	2544	5548
London	6363	4743	4778	5874	6700	7957
Manchester	807	543	502	547	364	275
Middlesbro	1042	691	728	810	873	1576
Port Talbot	560	485	358	317	358	–
Dundee	339	126	212	239	259	–
Glasgow	2528	1897	1891	1893	1533	1575
Grangemouth	483	247	351	387	368	–
Greenock	680	511	500	557	1025	1581
Leith	736	337	642	688	818	–
COAL PORTS						
Blyth	963	788	797	1225	1607	–
Cardiff	4986	5184	3256	2748	3031	1045
Hartlepool	526	521	353	542	757	–
Newcastle	4483	3874	3183	3398	3583	3042
Newport	1402	1545	1201	1241	1007	–
Sunderland	1681	1292	1485	1709	1946	1082
Swansea	1255	913	1114	1169	1071	2381
Methil	503	377	447	695	749	–
RAPID TRANSIT PORTS						
Cowes	1935	1285	1571	2107	2491	5399
Dartmouth	212	273	233	352	209	–
Dover	189	97	104	145	197	–
Falmouth	352	274	620	335	1079	–
Folkestone	76	14	57	76	86	–
Harwich	244	49	51	55	65	–
Newhaven	224	78	103	138	152	–
Plymouth	908	498	476	497	575	–
Southampton	1568	1032	1136	1419	1656	6271
Weymouth	215	125	105	238	236	–

FOOTNOTES

CHAPTER ONE

1. B. C. Short, *Poole, the Romance of its Early History* (Poole, 1932), pp. 24–44, passim.
2. G. C. Carter, *Forgotten Ports of England* (1951), pp.178–183; E. Gillett, *A History of Grimsby* (1970), p.13.
3. R. Jarvis, 'The Appointment of Ports', in *Economic History Review*, vol. XI, (1959), p.461.
4.. Contained in J. Thirsk (ed.), *Seventeenth Century Economic Documents* (1972), p.330.
5. D. Defoe, *A Tour Through England and Wales* (Everyman edition, 1928), vol. I, p.54.
6. Thirsk, pp.373–4.
7. R. H. Tawney and E. Power (eds.), *Tudor Economic Documents* (1924), vol. II, pp.49–50.
8. ibid., p.127.
9. ibid., pp.125–6.
10. ibid., p.131.
11. G. D. Ramsey, *English Overseas Trade during the Centuries of Emergence* (1957), pp.97n., 106.
12. A. P. Usher, 'Spanish Ships and Shipping in the Sixteenth and Seventeenth Centuries', in *Facts and Factors in Economic History: Essays Presented to E. F. Gay* (Cambridge, Mass., 1932), p.192.
13. *The Advocate* (1651), quoted in R. Davis, *The Rise of the English Shipping Industry* (1962), p.50.
14. L. A. Harper, *The English Navigation Laws* (New York, 1939), pp.281–3.
15. Davis, p.12.
16. Quoted in C. M. Andrews, *The Colonial Period of American History*, vol. IV: *England's Commercial and Colonial Policy* (1964 ed.), p.56.
17. Statistics from Davis, p.200, and his articles 'English Foreign Trade, 1660–1700', in *Economic History Review*, vol. VII, and 'English Foreign Trade, 1700–1774', in *Ec. Hist. Rev*, vol. XV.
18. The words are those of the earl of Danby, 1675, quoted in Andrews, p.121.
19. Harper, pp.304–6.
20. J. U. Nef, *The Rise of the British Coal Industry* (1932), Appendix D.
21. *c*.1580; Tawney and Power, vol. II, p.125.
22. Thirsk, p.806.
23. B. Supple, *Commercial Crisis and Change in England, 1600–42* (1970), p.102.
24. Harper, pp.283–4.
25. Defoe, vol. I, p.43.
26. R. W. K. Hinton, *The Eastland Trade and the Common Weal* (1959), p.57.
27. Thirsk, p.73.
28. John Keymer, *Observations Touching Trade and Commerce* (1620), in Thirsk, p.470.
29. T. M. Devine, *The Tobacco Lords* (1975), passim.
30. Davis, p.51.
31. ibid., p.27.
32. C. Smout, *Scottish Trade on the Eve of the Union, 1660–1707* (Edinburgh, 1963) is the best survey.

CHAPTER TWO

1. Statistics of trade and shipping are preserved in Public Record Office, Customs 17, from which much of the detail of this chapter has been taken.
2. G. Jackson, 'Scottish Shipping, 1775–1805', in P. L. Cottrell and D. H. Aldcroft, *Shipping, Trade and Commerce* (Leicester, 1981), pp.125, 134.
3. J. Guthrie, *The River Tyne, Its History and Resources* (Newcastle, 1880), p.62.
4. See, for example, T. S. Willan, *River Navigation in England, 1600–1750* (1936), chapter V.
5. Defoe, vol. I, p.17.
6. Willan, p.74.
7. ibid., pp.42, 75.
8. ibid., p.83.
9. S. Lewis, *Topographical Dictionary* (1845), vol. II, p.196; C. Hadfield, *Canals of Southern England* (1955), pp.33–4.
10. M. J. T. Lewis and N. R. Wright, *Boston as a Port* (Lincoln, Lincolnshire Local History Society, 1973), pp.9–10, 27–8; W. J. Wren, *The Ports of the Eastern Counties* (Lavenham, 1976), pp.64–65.
11. Lewis, *Topographical Dictionary*, vol. IV, pp.212–13.
12. For Ipswich, see *Minutes of Proceedings of the Institution of Civil Engineers*, vol. XX.
13. Wren, pp.45–6.
14. M. Gray, *The Fishing Industries of Scotland, 1790–1914* (1978), p.15. The vast number of fishing 'settlements' are marked on 7 maps in this extremely thorough survey.
15. Cornish ports are covered in F. Hitchens and S. Drew, *The History of Cornwall* (Helston, 1824). For Porthleven, see D. M. Trethowan, 'Porthleven Harbour', in H. E. S. Fisher (ed.), *Ports and Shipping in the South West* (Exeter, 1970).
16. Lewis, vol. IV, p.42.
17. J. Rennie, *The Theory, Formation and Construction of British and Foreign Harbours* (1854), vol. II, p.225.
18. ibid.
19. PRO, Customs 17/12.
20. *Reports of the Late John Smeaton* (1837), vol. II, pp.254–8.
21. R. Ayton, *A Voyage Round Great Britain* (8 vols, 1814ff.), vol. II, p.166.
22. *Reports of . . . Smeaton*, vol. II, pp.190, 193.
23. Rennie, vol. I, p.97.
24. Smeaton, vol. II, p.203.
25. ibid., p.187.
26. Rennie, vol. I, p.105.
27. Defoe, vol. I, p.122.
28. Wren, pp.79–80.
29. G. Collins, *Great Britain's Coasting Pilot* (1693, reprinted 1753), pp. 14–15.
30. J. Murray, 'An Account of the Progressive Improvement of Sunderland Harbour and the River Wear', *Minutes of the Proceedings of the Institution of Civil Engineers*, vol. VI (1847), p.274.
31. ibid., p.262.

CHAPTER THREE

1. Defoe, vol. I, p.41.
2. See, for instance, J. Bird, *The Major Seaports of the United Kingdom* (1963), p.281.
3. D. Swann, 'The Engineers of English Port Improvements, 1660–1830', in *Transport History*, vol. I, (1968), p.157. See also J. G.

Broodbank, *History of the Port of London* (1921), vol. II, pp.67–70.

4. Rennie, vol. II, p.216. The use of locks on navigable rivers is discussed in Willan, *River Navigations*, pp. 83–90.

5. Broodbank, vol. II, p.64.

6. G. Jackson, *The British Whaling Trade* (1978), pp.40–7.

7. G. E. Farr, 'Note on Seamills Dock', *Mariners' Mirror*, vol. XXV (1939), pp.349–50. Farr was mistaken in thinking this a commercial dock.

8. Defoe, vol. II, p.258.

9. J. A. Picton, *Selections from the Municipal Archives and Records* (Liverpool, 1883), vol. I, p.308.

10. F. E. Hyde, *Liverpool and the Mersey* (1971), p.8.

11. Collins, p.8.

12. Picton, vol. I, p.309.

13. Edward Moore, *Liverpool in King Charles II's Time*, edited by W. F. Irvine (Liverpool, 1899), p.104.

14. Hyde, p.14.

15. Minutes of the Town Council, 11 January 1737, quoted in Hyde, p.73.

16. Swann, 'Engineers', p.163.

17. G. Jackson, *Hull in the Eighteenth Century* (1972), p.238.

18. ibid., pp.241–3.

19. The problems associated with the building of the Haven are discussed in G. Jackson, *Grimsby and the Haven Company, 1795–1846* (Grimsby, 1971), chapter 2.

20. ibid., p.21.

21. Quoted in A. F. Williams, 'Bristol Port Plans and Improvement Schemes of the Eighteenth Century', in *Transactions of the Bristol and Gloucestershire Archaeological Society*, vol. LXXXI (1962), p.169.

22. Swann, pp.261, 272.

23. Bristol Chamber of Commerce, quoted in P. Tuttiett, 'The Port of Bristol and its Trade, 1650–1850', (BA Honours Dissertation, University of Strathclyde, 1980), p.45.

24. Problems facing Leith are discussed in B. Lenman, *From Esk to Tweed* (1975), from which much of the information in this section is drawn.

25. P. Colquhoun, *Treatise on the Police of the Metropolis* (1797), p.57.

26. Quoted in C. Capper, *The Port and Trade of London* (1862), pp.146–7.

27. *Report from the Committee Appointed to Enquire into the Best Mode of Providing Sufficient Accommodation for the Increased Trade and Shipping of the Port of London* (May, 1796).

28. Broodbank, vol. I, chap. 7; R. D. Brown, *The Port of London* (Lavenham, 1978), chap. 4; J. Pudney, *London's Docks* (1975), chap. 3.

29. Capper, p.156.

30. Broodbank, vol. I, p.155.

31. Capper, p.160.

32. J. D. Porteous, *Canal Ports* (1977), p.74.

33. B. Duckham, *The Yorkshire Ouse* (1967), pp.72–7.

34. ibid., p.88.

35. E. Parsons, *The Tourist's Companion* (1835), p.173.

36. Lenman, pp.45–6.

37. J. D. Marwick, *The River Clyde and the Clyde Burghs* (Glasgow, 1909), p.108.

38. J. F. Riddell, *Clyde Navigation: A Survey of the Development and Deepening of the River Clyde* (Edinburgh, 1979), chaps 4 & 10.

39. Minutes of the Worcester and Birmingham Canal Company, quoted in C. Hadfield, *The Canals of South and South-East England* (1969), p.348.

CHAPTER FOUR

1. *Evidence and Proceedings in the Committee of the House of Commons in Regard to the Aberdeen Harbour Bill, March–April 1839*, speech of Sergeant Merewether, pp.lxxv–vi, and speech of Mr Talbot, pp.307–8.

2. *House of Commons Committee on the Kingston-upon-Hull Dock Bill, 15 June 1840*, evidence of James Walker and John Agars; Hull Shipping Registers, Custom House, Hull.

3. *Hse of Comms Comm., 1840*, evidence of James Walker.

4. G. G. Macturk, *A History of the Hull Railways* (1879), p.54.

5. Capper, *London*, pp.450–1, 469. As late as 1860 only 30% of London's coal came by rail.

6. J. D. Porteous, *Canal Ports* (1977), pp.150–1.

7. Hyde, *Liverpool*, pp.237–9.

8. Picton, quoted in Hyde, p.81.

9. J. Rennie, *Theory of Harbours*, vol. II, p.218.

10. Capper, p.159.

11. Broodbank, vol. II, p.194.

12. Capper, p.161.

13. ibid., p.163.

14. J. Lovell, *Stevedores and Dockers* (1969), p.19.

15. Broodbank, vol. II, p.199.

16. Quoted in W. W. Tomlinson, *North Eastern Railway* (1915), p.221. Tomlinson is still the major source for the general history of the north-eastern ports.

17. C. Sharp, *History of Hartlepool* (Hartlepool, 1851), pp.42–3, 65.

18. Quoted in Tomlinson, p.210.

19. ibid., pp.329–30.

20. The present port of Blyth dates from the 1880s.

21. Guthrie, *Tyne*, pp.112–13.

22. Tomlinson, p.580; Guthrie, p.114.

23. Guthrie, p.114.

24. ibid., pp.122–3.

25. ibid., p.153.

26. This account is based on W. R. Smith, 'The Carlisle and Silloth Bay Railway and Dock Company', (BA Honours Dissertation, University of Strathclyde, 1973).

27. J. Marshall and J. K. Walton, *The Lakeland Counties* (Manchester, 1981), pp.34–5.

28. M. J. Daunton, *Coal Metropolis: Cardiff, 1870–1914* (Leicester, 1977), p.4.

29. ibid., p.21.

30. Jackson, *Grimsby and the Haven Company*, p.52.

31. Quoted in B. Lincoln, *History of Grimsby* (1913), vol. I, p.230.

32. The early history of Birkenhead is discussed in Hyde, *Liverpool*, pp. 83–8, and S. Mountfield, *Western Gateway* (Liverpool, 1965), passim.

33. C. Neate, 'Description of the Coffer Dam at Great Grimsby', *Minutes of the Proceedings of the Institution of Civil Engineers*, vol. IX (1849), pp. 1–23. The works at Grimsby were described in detail in E. H. Clark, 'Description of the Great Grimsby (Royal) Docks', ibid., vol. XXIV (1865), pp.38–61.

34. W. White, *Directory of Lincolnshire*

(1856), p.574.

35. Quoted in B. Lincoln, *History of Grimsby* (1913), vol. I, p.356.
36. Lewis, *Dictionary*, vol. II, p.244.
37. D. W. Gibbs, 'The Rise of the Port of Newhaven, 1850–1914', in *Transport History*, vol. III (1970), p.263.
38. W. C. Russell, *English Channel Ports* (1884), pp.104, 107.
39. Wren, pp.154–8.
40. P. Bagwell, 'The Post Office Steam Packets, 1821–36, and the Development of Shipping on the Irish Sea', in *Maritime History*, vol. I, pp.19–25.
41. ibid., p.16.
42. *Report of Select Committee on Tidal Harbours*, quoted in I. Donnachie, *The Industrial Archaeology of Galloway* (Newton Abbot, 1971), p.183.
43. D. J. Rowe, 'Southampton and the "Railway Mania", 1844–7', in *Transport History*, vol. IV (1969); A. Temple Patterson, *A History of Southampton, 1700–1914* (Southampton, 1975), vol. III, chapters 1, 6.
44. J. Glynn, *A Rudimentary Treatise on the Construction of Cranes* (1854), p.58.
45. This section is based principally on I. McNeil, *Hydraulic Power* (1972), passim. The pros and cons of hydraulic power were discussed at a meeting of the Institution of Civil Engineers and recorded in *Minutes of the Proceedings of the Institution of Civil Engineers*, vol. XXI (1861–2), pp.337ff.
46. G. Head, *A Home Tour through the Manufacturing Districts* (1835), p.395.
47. ibid. pp.347–8.
48. Tomlinson, p.437.
49. Head, p.301.
50. D. Ross Johnson, *Modern Dock Operation* (1929), pp.11–12.
51. Ayton, *Voyage*, vol. II, p.81.
52. J. Rennie, *Theory*, vol. I, p.136. Early dredging methods are described in Riddell, *Clyde Navigation*, chapter 5.
53. Hull Dock Company Papers, 'Huffam's Book', pp.35, 167–9.
54. Riddell, chapters 14–15.

55. Guthrie, *River Tyne*, p.247.
56. ibid., p.140.

CHAPTER FIVE
1. The figures quoted in this chapter are taken from *Annual Statements of Trade and Navigation*.
2. F. E. Hyde, *Far Eastern Trade, 1860–1914* (1973) and *Blue Funnel: a History of Alfred Holt and Co., 1865–1914* (1956); S. Marriner & F. E. Hyde, *The Senior: John Samuel Swire, 1825–98* (1967); P. N. Davies, *The Trade Makers: Elder Dempster in West Africa* (1973); D. A. Farnie, *East and West of Suez* (1969).
3. *Annual Statement of Trade and Navigation, 1910*, Parliamentary Papers 1911 (5840) LXXIX, p.253.
4. A. G. Kenwood, 'Port Investment in England and Wales, 1851–1913', in *Yorkshire Bulletin*, vol. XVII (1965), p.157.
5. An excellent description of the coal trade within the port context is contained in H. E. C. Newham, *Hull as a Coal Port* (1913).
6. ibid., p.35.
7. P. J. Perry, 'The Development of Cross Channel Trade at Weymouth', *Transport History*, vol. II, p.250.
8. *Report of the Select Committee on Humber Commercial Railway and Dock Bill, March 1904*. Q.321, evidence of J. W. Barry.
9. ibid., Q.2171, evidence of S. Fay.
10. J. F. Riddell, *Clyde Navigation: a History of the Development and Deepening of the River Clyde* (Edinburgh, 1979).
11. W. B. Forwood, quoted in Mountfield, p.42.
12. Hyde, pp.116–17.
13. Broodbank, vol. II. p.226.
14. ibid., p.264.
15. B. J. H. Brown, 'Bristol's Second Outport: Portishead in the Nineteenth Century', *Transport History*, vol. IV (1974), p. 84.
16. *Parliamentary Committee on the Hull and Barnsley Railway and Dock Bill, 1880*, Q.2802.
17. *Hull as a Coal Port*, pp. 16–17. The working of the dock and railway is described in detail in K. Hoole (ed.), *The Hull & Barnsley Railway*

(Newton Abbot, 1972).
18. Daunton, *Cardiff*, p.32.
19. Marwick, *River Clyde*, p.228; Riddell, p.234.
20. This section is based on D. Farnie, *The Manchester Ship Canal and the Rise of the Port of Manchester, 1894–1975* (Manchester, 1980).
21. Wren, passim.
22. The attempt of one of them to set up in Preston is recounted in P. N. Davies, *Henry Tyrer* (1979), passim.
23. Lenman, *Esk to Tweed*, passim; W. French, *The Scottish Ports* (1938), passim.

CHAPTER SIX
1. Details from *Annual Statements of Trade and Navigation*.
2. B. R. Mitchell and P. Deane, *Abstract of British Historical Statistics* (Cambridge, 1962), p.227.
3. F. M. Du-Plat-Taylor, *The Design, Construction and Maintenance of Docks, Wharves and Piers* (3rd edition, 1949), p.43; A. W. Kirkaldy, *British Shipping* (1913), p.112.
4. Du-Plat-Taylor, p.51.
5. Farnie, p.145.
6. C. Ellson, 'Dover Train Ferry Dock', *Journal of the Institution of Civil Engineers*, vol. II (1937), pp.223–60.
7. T. Stevenson, *Design and Construction of Harbours* (1874), pp.201–2.
8. Liberal Industrial Inquiry, *Britain's Industrial Future* (1928), pp.314–15.
9. Du-Plat-Taylor, p.28.
10. ibid., p.27.
11. ibid., p.46.
12. One of the best sources for recent developments in handling methods is the PLA's journal *Port of London*.
13. J. Pudney, *London's Docks*, p.183–4.
14. A. Ellis, *Three Hundred Years on London River: The Hay's Wharf Story* (1952) surveys the history of perhaps the most important of these wharves.
15. Lewis and Wright, *Boston as a Port*.
16. V. Parker, *The Making of King's Lynn* (1971).

BIBLIOGRAPHY

NOTE: The most important source for details of practically every harbour and dock work in Britain is the *Minutes of the Proceedings of the Institution of Civil Engineers*. The very first paper read to the Institution was an account of dock building in Hull, and engineers regularly described their works to their peers in later volumes. Only a small selection of these papers are contained in the following list.

GENERAL

R. Ayton, *A Voyage Round Great Britain* (8 vols, 1814ff.)

J. Bird, *The Major Seaports of the United Kingdom* (1963)

C. T. G. Boucher, *John Rennie* (1963)

G. Collins, *Great Britain's Coasting Pilot* (1693, reprinted 1753)

C. Crutwell, *Tour Thro' the Whole Island* (5 volumes, 1801)

P. N. Davies, *The Trade Makers: Elder Dempster in West Africa* (1973)

R. Davis, *The Rise of the English Shipping Industry* (1962)
   'English Foreign Trade, 1660–1700', in *Economic History Review*, vol. VII.
   'English Foreign Trade, 1700–1774', *Ec. Hist. Rev*, vol. XV.

D. Defoe, *A Tour Through England and Wales* (Everyman edition, 1928)

T. M. Devine, *The Tobacco Lords* (1975)

F. M. Du-Plat-Taylor, *The Design, Construction and Maintenance of Docks, Wharves and Piers* (3rd edition, 1949)

D. A. Farnie, *East and West of Suez* (1969)

J. Glynn, *A Rudimentary Treatise on the Construction of Cranes* (1854)

M. Gray, *The Fishing Industries of Scotland, 1790–1914* (1978)

B. Greenhill and A. Giffard, *Victorian and Edwardian Sailing Ships from Old Photographs* (1976)

C. Hadfield, *Canals of Southern England* (1955)

L. F. V. Harcourt, *Harbours and Docks* (2 volumes, 1885)

G. Head, *A Home Tour through the Manufacturing Districts* (1835)

F. E. Hyde, *Far Eastern Trade, 1860–1914* (1973)

Blue Funnel: a History of Alfred Hold and Co., 1865–1914 (1956)

G. Jackson, *The British Whaling Trade* (1978)

G. Jackson, 'Scottish Shipping, 1775–1805', in P. L. Cottrell and D. H. Aldcroft, *Shipping, Trade and Commerce* (Leicester, 1981)

R. Jarvis, 'The Appointment of Ports', in *Economic History Review*, vol. xi. (1959)

A. G. Kenwood, 'Port Investment in England and Wales, 1851–1913', in *Yorkshire Bulletin*, vol. XVII (1965)

A. W. Kirkaldy, *British Shipping* (1913)

S. Lewis, *Topographical Dictionary* (4 vols., 1845)

I. McNeil, *Hydraulic Power* (1972)

S. Marriner & F. E. Hyde, *The Senior: John Samuel Swire, 1825–98* (1967)

E. Parsons, *The Tourist's Companion* (1835)

J. D. Porteous, *Canal Ports* (1977)

G. D. Ramsey, *English Overseas Trade during the Centuries of Emergence* (1957)

J. Rennie, *The Theory, Formation and Construction of British and Foreign Harbours* (1854)

Reports of the Late John Smeaton (1837)

D. Ross Johnson, *Modern Dock Operation* (1929)

T. C. Smout, *Scottish Trade on the Eve of the Union 1660–1707* (Edinburgh, 1963)

T. Stevenson, *Design and Construction of Harbours* (1874)

B. Supple, *Commercial Crisis and Change in England, 1600–42* (1970)

D. Swann, 'The Engineers of English Port Improvements, 1660–1830', in *Transport History*, vol. I, (1968)

R. H. Tawney and E. Power (eds.), *Tudor Economic Documents* (1924)

J. Thirsk (ed.), *Seventeenth Century Economic Documents* (1972)

T. S. Willan, *English Coasting Trade, 1600–1750* (1938)

T. S. Willan, *River Navigation in England, 1600–1750* (1936)

THE EAST COAST

D. Akenhead and Sons, *The Picture of Newcastle upon Tyne* (Newcastle, 1807)

K. J. Allison, *A History of the County of York: East Riding, vol. 1: The City of Kingston upon Hull* (1969)

I. S. Beckwith, 'The River Trade of Gainsborough, 1500–1850', in *Lincolnshire History and Archaeology*, vol. 2 (1967)

E. H. Clark, 'Description of the Great Grimsby (Royal) Docks', *Minutes of the Proceedings of the Institution of Civil Engineers*, vol. XXIV (1865)

R. Davis, *The Trade and Shipping of Hull, 1500–1700* (East Yorks. Local History Society, 1964)

G. Dow, *Great Central* (2 vols, 1959)

B. Duckham, 'Selby and the Aire and Calder Navigation, 1774–1826', *Journal of Transport History*, vol. VII (1965)

B. Duckham, *The Yorkshire Ouse* (1967) (For Goole, Selby and York)

E. Gillett, *A History of Grimsby* (1970)

E. Gillett and K. Macmahon, *History of Hull* (1980)

J. Guthrie, *The River Tyne, Its History and Resources* (Newcastle, 1880)

K. Hoole (ed.), *The Hull & Barnsley Railway* (Newton Abbot, 1972)

E. Hughes, *North Country Life in the Eighteenth Century: vol. 1, The North Country* (1952)

G. Jackson, *Grimsby and the Haven Company, 1795–1846* (Grimsby, 1971)

G. Jackson, *Hull in the Eighteenth Century* (1972)

G. Jackson, 'The Struggle for the First Hull Dock', *Transport History*, vol. 1 (1968)

M. J. T. Lewis and N. R. Wright, *Boston as a Port* (Lincoln, Lincolnshire Local History Society, 1973)

B. Lincoln, *History of Grimsby* (1913)

G. G. Macturk, *A History of the Hull Railways* (1879)

J. Murray, 'An Account of the Progressive Improvement of Sunderland Harbour and the River Wear', *Minutes of the Proceedings of the Institution of Civil Engineers*, vol. VI (1847)

C. Neate, 'Description of the Coffer Dam at Great Grimsby', *Minutes of the Proceedings of the Institution of Civil Engineers*, vol. IX (1849)

H. E. C. Newham, *Hull as a Coal Port* (1913)

C. Sharp, *History of Hartlepool* (Hartlepool, 1851)

A. Stark, *History of Gainsborough* (1843)
W. W. Tomlinson, *North Eastern Railway* (1915)
R. Weatherill, *The Ancient Port of Whitby and its Shipping* (1908)
W. J. Wren, *The Ports of the Eastern Counties* (Lavenham, 1976)
W. Wright, 'The Hull Docks', *Minutes of the Proceedings of the Institution of Civil Engineers*, vol. XLI (1875)
G. Young, *A History of Whitby* (2 vols, Whitby, 1817)

LONDON
J. Bird, *The Geography of the Port of London* (1957)
J. G. Broodbank, *History of the Port of London* (2 vols., 1921)
R. D. Brown, *The Port of London* (Lavenham, 1978)
C. Capper, *The Port and Trade of London* (1862)
P. Colquhoun, *Treatise on the Police of the Metropolis* (1797)
G. Doré & B. Jerrold, *London* (1872)
A. Ellis, *Three Hundred Years on London River: The Hay's Wharf Story* (1952)
J. Lovell, *Stevedores and Dockers* (1969)
Report from the Committee Appointed to Enquire into the Best Mode of Providing Sufficient Accommodation for the Increased Trade and Shipping of the Port of London (May, 1796)
Port of London (Journal of the Port of London Authority)
J. Pudney, *London's Docks* (1975)
W. M. Stern, 'The Porters of London', *Economic History Review*, vol. XIII

THE SOUTH COAST
G. C. Carter, *Forgotten Ports of England* (1951)
C. Ellson, 'Dover Train Ferry Dock', *Journal of the Institution of Civil Engineers*, vol. II (1937)
D. W. Gibbs, 'The Rise of the Port of Newhaven, 1850–1914', in *Transport History*, vol. III (1970)
C. Hadfield, *The Canals of South and South-East England* (1969)
B. Knowles, *Southampton, the English Gateway* (1951)
A. Temple Patterson, *A History of Southampton, 1700–1914* (3 vols, Southampton, 1975)
P. J. Perry, 'The Development of Cross Channel Trade at Weymouth, 1794–1914', *Transport History*, vol. II (1969)

D. J. Rowe, 'Southampton and the "Railway Mania". 1844–7', in *Transport History*, vol. II (1969)
W. C. Russell, *English Channel Ports* (1884)
B. C. Short, *Poole, the Romance of its Early History* (Poole, 1932)

THE SOUTH WEST
R. A. Buchanan & N. Cossons, *Bristol* (Newton Abbot, 1970)
T. Fairclough & E. Shepherd, *Mineral Railways of the West Country* (Truro, 1975)
G. E. Farr, 'Note on Seamills Dock', *Mariners' Mirror*, vol. XXV (1939).
H. E. S. Fisher, *Ports and Shipping in the South West* (Exeter, 1971)
F. Hitchens and S. Drew, *The History of Cornwall* (Helston, 1824)
W. G. Hoskins, *Industry, Trade and People in Exeter, 1688–1800* (Manchester, 1935)
C. M. Macinnes, *Bristol, a Gateway of Empire* (1939, reprinted 1968)
R. Pearse, *Ports and Harbours of Cornwall* (1963)
H. Symons, 'Bridport Harbour through Seven Centuries', *Dorset Natural History and Antiquarian Field Club*, vol 33 (1912)
D. M. Trethowan, 'Porthleven Harbour', in H. E. S. Fisher (ed.), *Ports and Shipping in the South West* (Exeter, 1970)
P. Tuttiett, 'The Port of Bristol and its Trade, 1650–1850', (BA Honours Dissertation, University of Strathclyde, 1980)
C. Wells, *A Short History of the Port of Bristol* (Bristol, 1909)
A. F. Williams, 'Bristol Port Plans and Improvement Schemes of the Eighteenth Century', in *Transactions of the Bristol and Gloucestershire Archaeological Society*, vol. LXXXI (1962)

THE WEST COAST
P. Bagwell, 'The Post Office Steam Packets, 1821–36, and the Development of Shipping on the Irish Sea', in *Maritime History*, vol. I (1970)
T. C. Barker, 'Lancashire Coal, Cheshire Salt and the Rise of Liverpool', *Transactions of the Historic Society of Lancashire and Cheshire*, vol. CIII (1951)

J. V. Beckett, *Coal and Tobacco: The Lowthers and the Economic Development of West Cumberland, 1660–1760* (Cambridge, 1981)
P. G. E. Clemens, 'The Rise of Liverpool, 1665–1750', *Economic History Review*, vol. XXIX (1976)
M. J. Daunton, *Coal Metropolis: Cardiff, 1870–1914* (Leicester, 1977)
D. Farnie, *The Manchester Ship Canal and the Rise of the Port of Manchester, 1894–1975* (Manchester, 1980)
S. A. Harris, 'Henry Berry (1720–1812): Liverpool's Second Dock Engineer', *Transactions of the Historic Society of Lancashire and Cheshire*, vols LXXXIX and XC (1937–8)
F. E. Hyde, *Liverpool and the Mersey* (1971)
J. Marshall and J. K. Walton, *The Lakeland Counties* (Manchester, 1981)
Edward Moore, *Liverpool in King Charles II's Time*, edited by W. F. Irvine (Liverpool, 1899)
S. Mountfield, *Western Gateway* (Liverpool, 1965)
H. Peet, 'Thomas Steers, the Engineer of Liverpool's First Dock', *Transactions of the Historic Society of Lancashire and Cheshire*, vol. LXXXII (1930–32)
J. A. Picton, *Selections from the Municipal Archives and Records* (Liverpool, 1883)
S. Pollard, 'Barrow-in-Furness and the Seventh Duke of Devonshire', *Economic History Review*, vol. VIII (1956)
W. R. Smith, 'The Carlisle and Silloth Bay Railway and Dock Company', (BA Honours Dissertation, University of Strathclyde, 1973)

SCOTLAND
A. R. Buchan, *The Port of Peterhead* (Peterhead, 1980)
I. Donnachie, *The Industrial Archaeology of Galloway* (Newton Abbot, 1971)
J. R. Hume, *The Industrial Archaeology of Scotland* (2 vols, 1976/7)
B. Lenman, *From Esk to Tweed* (1975)
J. D. Marwick, *The River Clyde and the Clyde Burghs* (Glasgow, 1909)
J. F. Riddell, *Clyde Navigation: a History of the Development and Deepening of the River Clyde* (Edinburgh, 1979)